LOVE THE JOURNEY

Homeschooling:
Principles to Practices

Lampstand Press, Ltd.
Kingsport, TN

LOVE THE JOURNEY

HOMESCHOOLING:

PRINCIPLES

TO PRACTICES

MARCIA SOMERVILLE

LAMPSTAND PRESS
KINGSPORT, TN

Love the Journey: Homeschooling Principles to Practices

Published by Lampstand Press
1135 N. Eastman Road, Kingsport, TN 37664

Cover design & photo: David Somerville

First printing, 2014
Printed in the United States of America

ISBN 9780991571802

This book is dedicated to the mothers
and fathers who choose the road less traveled
because they love their Lord and their children.

May it be a blessing to you, chiefly by
helping you to love the journey itself.

Contents

Some Words of Thanks

Like so many of my other writing projects over the last twenty years or so, this one began at someone else's request. In this case, it was my son, Mike, who wanted me to write a book to young homeschooling mothers who were just starting their homeschool journeys. It was conceived as a companion component to his new program for Kindergarten-aged children entitled *Tapestry Primer.*

Also like so many of my other writing projects, I was surprised where the Lord took it. I was amazed to see how much He had worked in my life over the years through homeschooling, and (consequently) how long the book grew to be!

Another parallel circumstance with previous projects was the humbling nature of writing. One feels quite vulnerable when expressing personal insights or opinions, revelations that have worked for oneself, and teachings that have arrested one's attention. An author becomes so aware that she is going out on a limb when expressing these things, and she has no real assurance that her words will help others. Writing this book has been more of a leap of faith (if anything) than writing curriculum. At the end of the day, my prayer is that you will take to yourself whatever is helpful, and think charitably of me for whatever doesn't seem to ring true.

Finally, this project is like all previous ones in that it never would have gotten done without the help and support of others. Besides Mike and his wife, Jessica, who got me started with pleas and then encouragement, I would like to thank my daughter Christy, who spent weeks reading and minutely smoothing many awkward lines and questioning (or improving) theologically informed constructs. I'm also grateful for my son David for his brilliant cover design. It has been such a blessing over the years to work as a family on our various projects, and this one felt a bit like getting the band back together!

I also need to thank the staff at Lampstand Press for bringing their skills to bear so that this book could come to completion. It would simply not be here without you all; though the readers (and beneficiaries) of this book may not know of your efforts, the Lord knows their worth, and so do I!

Introduction

"Oh, this is nice!" said Jill. "Just walking along like this. I wish there could be more of this sort of adventure. It's a pity there's always so much happening in Narnia."

Jill, in The Last Battle

People have used many metaphors for the process of educating and discipling children that we have come to call "homeschooling." My favorite one by far is that homeschooling is a journey. And by "journey," I mean a long, extended trip full of adventures, sights to see, and unexpected delights—as well as the inevitable frustrating or hairy trials, the delays, and the trudging.

Somewhere out there on the horizon, one believes that there is a destination point where the journey will end. While we hope it will end well, and that we'll all make it to the end alive, a long journey is not mostly about getting to our destination. Or, if it is, we will sure miss a lot!

This book is written to women who are disciples of Jesus Christ and are new to homeschooling. It is not a "how to teach your kids from soup to nuts" manual. Nor is it a theoretical book: my husband, my six children, and I have actually made this journey, and we have enjoyed fellowship with many others who have as well! My experience has been that the homeschooling journey is worth the effort, and I'd like to do what I can to help you to start yours well!

What this book is, or is trying to be, is a book that helps you to find (and define in your own words) the principles behind wise homeschooling practices. It's a book about ways to be intentional, purposeful, and Christ-centered as you sit in your house, and as you walk by the way, as you lie down, and as you rise to serve your family, day after day. As you read it, picture yourself sitting across from me in some delicious setting, where I have all the time in the world to share encouragement, wisdom, and exhortation with you as an older woman who has been down this road.

It wasn't my idea to write this book. My now-adult kids alternately bugged and sweet-talked me into it. As the publication deadline loomed nearer, I have dragged my feet more and more. I know that not everything that I've learned on my particular journey translates to every other woman reading this book. So, I pray that if parts of this book don't help or speak to you, please just let my words fall to the ground. At the end of the day, I am just one beggar telling another beggar where I found bread.

As I got further into this project, I did feel that as an older woman I bore a responsibility to share how, in the context of homeschooling, younger women can better love husbands and children, become more self-controlled and pure, take greater delight in working at home, become more kind, and grow in heartfelt submission to husbands, and generally walk worthy of the gospel of Jesus Christ, that the word of God may not be reviled (1 Timothy 2). These goals define the heart of what I learned during my homeschooling journey, and I offer my insights and experiences for your prayerful consideration.

You might ask, "But what about practical stuff, like, about education and teaching?" Yep. That's here, too. I've learned many good things about managing a houseful of kids while teaching academics, choosing the right curricula for my kids, planning lessons and then implementing those plans, etc. They are all a part of the homeschooling journey, and I'm willing to share! Let me briefly explain the way that I've organized the book, so you can find your way around.

You may be contemplating homeschooling for a host of reasons, and in Section 1, we'll get into some of the most common motives that newcomers have. The chapters in this section are all aimed at helping you to identify and refine your reasons for and vision of your journey. Since God created all families unique, there is no one right way to homeschool, but with the bewildering array of choices that a new homeschooler faces, it can be really helpful to know which direction you're headed. That's what Section 1 is all about: helping you define your direction.

In Section 2 (Mountaintop Views) I am far less technical. This section offers some of the "big picture" principles that I hold most dear. You'll find broad theological, parenting, and educational concepts are shared here that inform one's whole journey from start to finish. As the quotation that opens this section suggests, these are some of the deeper principles (or fruit-producing processes) that can be invisible to those who are just taking to the homeschooling road. I hope that knowing about them serves you as you journey.

The titles of Sections 3, 4, and 5 are all taken from the passage of Scripture that many homeschoolers consider our proof text for the decision to homeschool: Deuteronomy 6:4-9 (ESV).

> *Hear, O Israel: The LORD our God, the LORD is one. You shall love the LORD your God with all your heart and with all your soul and with all your might. And these words that I command you today shall be on your heart. You shall teach them diligently to your children, and shall talk of them* ***when you sit in your house, and when you walk by the way, and when you lie down, and when you rise****. You shall bind them as a sign on your hand, and they shall be as frontlets between your eyes. You shall write them on the doorposts of your house and on your gates.*

These sections contain the bulk of the practical tips of this book; the chapters are loosely grouped, and they really may be read in any order. Indeed, to some degree, this whole book is a bit of a potpourri of my life experiences, things I've been taught along the way, and gleanings from the Word of God. But enough about me: let's get back to you!

Somewhere in the mix, I suspect that you're interested in the homeschooling journey primarily for either the sake of your children's characters or educational well being (or, for some, both). I hope that you also have a sense that God is calling you to homeschooling. Without His accompanying presence, you could find it a long, weary, and lonely road ahead!

But, let's suppose you have come to believe that our loving, Heavenly Father is saying to you, "Come this way, Daughter. I have an adventure for you!" What many younger moms really don't see coming until they're down the road a piece is that God will use the homeschooling journey to shape you fully as much as He'll use it to shape your kids. Homeschooling is a sanctifying experience—and broadening, just like travel!

You may not really like adventures much; they can be scary, exhausting, discouraging, and uncomfortable in places. Like Jill, in C.S. Lewis' *The Last Battle*, you may wish that you could just amble along with your family and friends, enjoying sunny days and some pretty spectacular scenery. There will be moments like that on the homeschooling journey: good days where laughter, learning, and peace are in perfect balance.

But on many other days, there will seem to be too much going on to really enjoy the journey. Then again, though, rest and relaxation are not the purpose for which God has called you to homeschooling. Not primarily, anyway. If you pursue your own soul's development while discipling your children, you'll find that, by the journey's end, you are more Christlike, more dependent on God, and wiser. I promise!

And that, Best Beloved, is the goal. Keeping that goal in the forefront of our minds is hard, but it is what enables us to embrace sanctifying grace and press on for a prize that will never tarnish or fade. It is what enables us to truly *love* the journey!

Romans 8:28-29 (ESV) is a sure promise that you carry with you as you go:

> *And we know that for those who love God all things work together for good, for those who are called according to his purpose. For those whom he foreknew he also predestined to be conformed to the image of his Son.*

Conformity to Jesus, dependence on God, and faith-forged trust are the fruits that you can savor as you follow God's leading to homeschool. We may define what would be "good" for us as an easier relationship with a child or being transformed into a superwoman who has no limitations (and no need to depend on God) but that is not how God defines our good. He defines it as something infinitely more precious than even the most flawless environment, relationships, and personal abilities. Did you catch it? God defines our good as us becoming more and more like His Son, our Savior.

For many of us, if we are brutally honest, that's not an exciting prospect (at first). But think for a moment about Christ: think of all His personal excellences and beauties, His strength and creativity, His sense of humor and kindness and sympathy and ... well... it's a long list! He is simply the most attractive person in the universe, and as you are attracted to Him, it is God's good pleasure you make you to be actually *like Him*. The reality is that God's plans for us are so much grander than our dreams for ourselves.

I'm praying as I write this that what I have included in this book will help you see evidences of God's sustaining grace, lovingkindness, and good work in you, so that you truly can *love* your homeschooling journey!

SECTION ONE

Your Homeschool is YOUR Homeschool!

Maria, this is your trunk. These are your gowns! You may arrange them in any way you wish. Lady Catherine will never know!

Elizabeth Bennet, Pride & Prejudice
(1995: screenplay by Andrew Davies)

In this opening section, my goal is to help you get better acquainted with yourself. While some parents make the decision to homeschool after careful thought, many start homeschooling for circumstantial or vague reasons. There's nothing inherently wrong with that, of course. Many times, God uses surprising means to get us to where He wants us to be. As with courtship, there's no "one right way" to become a homeschooler. God is the Author of variety and has His ways of getting us where He wants us to go! But, to extend this metaphor, just as there are wise (and less than wise) ways to go through a courtship, there are wise (and also less than wise) ways to go about beginning to homeschool. Being wise can minimize heartache and maximize fruitfulness; gaining biblical wisdom involves self examination for the purposes of establishing personal convictions.

Did you happen to notice the subtitle of this book? It is "Homeschooling: Principles to Practices." All the way through, this is the paradigm from which I am writing: I want to encourage you to start with the *why* of each topic before you move on to the *how* of it. This section is designed to help you identify your own, unique "why."

Here's another way to say the same thing. What gives us moral courage to say "no" to temptations to sin? Is it not our convictions (our beliefs, or principles)? If, for example, we truly believe that lying is wrong, we will not say that we *love* our friend's new dress, even if we know that she'll be disappointed by our lack of enthusiasm. Such a principle about right and wrong gives us the power to choose, and be confident and steadfast in our choices, even in the face of social discomfort; conversely, the lack of bedrock beliefs can get us into trouble.

Everyone who starts in any new field immediately runs into a slew of new terms, a variety of leaders, and a host of contradictory opinions on "how it should be done." I'm not going to start this book by telling you how I think you should run your homeschool.

Like Elizabeth in advising Maria, I want you to arrange your homeschool as you wish, and I will never know if you take my advice or not! However, I do really hope that you are eager to solidify core principles that will help and guide you as you start to make choices about practical things, like which Math program to buy, or whether or not to join a local co-op.

In point of fact, the chapters of this section are truly practical, but you might not realize it at first glance. This is because they are only practical if you take the time to work through the suggested exercises with your husband in order to establish the bedrock foundation of your individual homeschool. So, are you ready? Let's get principled *and* practical!

1.

Clarity of mind means clarity of passion, too; this is why a great and clear mind loves ardently and sees distinctly what he loves.

Blaise Pascal

Why Do YOU Homeschool?

I once conducted a very informal poll on my Facebook page where I asked homeschooling moms to answer three questions:

1. Why did you start homeschooling (what were the circumstances or what was the motivation)?
2. How long have you been homeschooling?
3. Why do you still do it today (in other words, what's your motivation now)?

I got a long list of responses, which interested me. Among them were clear patterns. Let me summarize what they said. As you read, maybe you will find some of your own motives listed among them.

First Question: Why Did You Start to Homeschool?

The first question received the most varied replies. About a third of respondents started homeschooling because they felt called by God to do so. Many added to this the sentiment that they wanted to be (or thought that they should be) the primary influence in their children's lives. Sending their kids to school, they believed, would be a loss, or even wrong.

Another very common motive for beginning to homeschool was that parents didn't feel the public school system in their area would do an adequate job. A variation on this theme was that some parents began to homeschool after pulling children out of school settings where they believed their children were being hurt, abused, or otherwise wronged by the system or the teacher.

Also common among these women's responses was the general idea that their husband was strongly for homeschooling—more so than were they, initially. A few were moved to start because of the example of neighbors, friends, or family who were successfully homeschooling. And the last common scenario was that the family was moving a lot—typically a military or missionary setting—and parents wanted to either stabilize their kids' school settings or avoid sending them to a boarding school.

Last Question: What Motivates You Today?

The respondents had been homeschooling for between seven and twenty years, and what interested me was the uniformity of their answers to the last question: "What motivates you today?"

In virtually every case, these women felt more convinced, confident, and assured that they were doing what was right for their kids and good in God's sight *after* years of experience that they had when they began. Here are just a few quotes from the pool:

> *Our core motives for homeschooling haven't changed. We believe even more strongly today that God has told us to homeschool. (Some days it's the only thing that keeps me going.)*

Today, we still feel called to homeschool. We feel that is where God would have us and our children. Not only are they growing academically, but they are growing spiritually and relationally. I think our convictions with regard to our choices have become firmer over time.

Why do I do it today? Because I am convinced it is necessary to do in order to be faithful to God's calling.

I guess my primary motivation today is that I have seen the fruit that homeschooling has produced in my two older, graduated children and that keeps me motivated! God, by His grace, also keeps me able to homeschool.

The motivation now is I love seeing them learn and be able to tailor the curricula to how they learn. They love being home (and have said many times, when we discuss public school, that don't want to go back to school). I love teaching them, and as long as they want to stay at home and learn, I will be there to teach them!

I am called, and still have a passion to remain a primary influence as long as we have been entrusted with our children. I love having closer relationship and fun learning together. We have the time to learn from living together the most important things they and I need to learn, character issues.

As the years have gone by our motivation [has become] wanting to train them ourselves, according to our values, and wanting to be with them, also we love the friendships they have developed with each other.

An Exercise for You

I promised that I'd get practical from time to time. Now I'm going to invite you to grab a piece of notebook paper (or a journal) and your favorite writing implement. Quiet your heart (and the clamoring details about what, when, where, and how you'll homeschool) and consider before the Lord this core question: "Why do I want to homeschool?" *Please write down what comes to mind.*

Got your initial answers written down? Good!

Now, ask it again in different ways, emphasizing different words, and gain even more depth of insight. Again, jot down notes of your answers on that piece of paper:

- Why do *I* want to homeschool?
- WHY do I want to homeschool?
- Why do I want to HOMESCHOOL?

You don't have to write a dissertation here, but if it spills onto the back of the page, that's fine.

Try to be honest with the paper. You aren't going to show this to anyone except your husband, and you don't need to try to appear more spiritual than you are. If your reasons are pragmatic, say so. If your reasons are lackluster in your own view, that's okay! What you want to capture here are your core *reasons* for homeschooling. A lot of this book is about self-discovery; that's part of sanctification and of the journey as a whole!

Have you written anything yet? If not, please put the book down and do the writing before reading on. Now, if possible.

* * * * *

Done writing? Good!

One immediate benefit of doing this little exercise is that it can bring some clarity. Did you notice (in the quotations on previous pages) how sometimes motives changed over years of homeschooling, and how sometimes initial convictions seemed only to deepen? Typically, those who start homeschooling for circumstantial reasons (bad school nearby, moving a lot, husband wishes it, etc.) only find their core beliefs about homeschooling after years have passed.

This book begins with several chapters designed to help you to identify bedrock reasons that constitute your foundations for a decision to homeschool. Homeschooling is a movement made up of many individuals who pluck up their courage to leave the main roads behind and set out for new territory. Though there is an extensive network of homeschoolers now, and the world at large will not think you as absolutely crazy as they did people like me when we first started, there are outspoken leaders, friends, and factions within the movement, whose conflicting opinions you will have to learn to sift for nuggets that apply to *your* unique homeschool.

Homeschoolers have no central authority or validating entity; there is no lock-step guidance with homeschooling. We are free to choose our own paths, and while that is terrific if you've found a great path to walk, it can be super scary to stand at the beginning of the journey and take those first steps.

Fear can reverberate deep in our hearts as we take our first steps. If I had to put it into words, it usually boils down to, "What if we choose *wrong*? What if my wrong choices *harm* my *children*? What if I *fail* them?"

I think you would be abnormal if you did not have this anxiety, at least at first. Why? Because the journey is long, and there are real perils along the way. It's the road less traveled, and success (as we tend to define it from our limited and human vantage points) is not guaranteed. But, God has great answers to these fear-filled questions, and some chapters of this book may be part of them!

What if we choose ***wrong?*** *What if my wrong choices* ***harm*** *my* ***children?*** *What if I* ***fail*** *them?*

First and foremost, of course, if you are a Christian, let's remember together that the ultimate responsibility for your children's welfare and sanctification doesn't rest on your shoulders. Not really. Your kids are God's creations. If He is calling you to this journey, His plans and purposes for you are all loving and kind. He is the one in control, ultimately, of all circumstances, choices, and events of the trip.

Remember Romans 8:28-29. God is in the business of working all things together for your good and His glory, which are both summed up in the greatest gift of the gospel: that you and your children who believe will be changed through His choices for your sojourns into the very image of the Beloved Son of God, so that you can one day be with Him and enjoy His glory forever and ever.

I think that the reason why older homeschoolers' convictions become more settled and steady over time is that they've passed down the road a ways. They've met with adversity, discouragement, doubts, difficulties, and yes, even disasters, and they've lived to see God be faithful and kind through it all.

We older homeschooling moms look back to you younger ones and say, "It's really doable! There is a good land, flowing with milk and honey! God is here; He is present to guide, sustain, and grow you as you look to Him to guide you in the paths you should walk, and to supply the company you should keep along the way. You have joy and fruit ahead of you that is sweeter than you can imagine, though the path to it might look scary and difficult." Take to yourself the words of the prophet Isaiah 43:1-3 (ESV):

> *"But now thus says the LORD, he who created you… "Fear not, for I have redeemed you; I have called you by name, you are mine. When you pass through the waters, I will be with you; and through the rivers, they shall not overwhelm you; when you walk through fire you shall not be burned, and the flame shall not consume you. For I am the LORD your God, the Holy One of Israel, your Savior…"*

Left to our own devices, we would perish, and our children with us. But, really, this is true in all of our parenting, whether we homeschool or not! When beginning the homeschooling journey, we have so much to learn about what to pack, how to prepare, and where to go. We can be pulled in many directions by the abundance of our opportunities and the strong advice of others around us. And, as women, we often are prey to the lies of the Enemy and the fear of what others will think. This is especially common when starting homeschooling, but for many, it continues for far too long.

With so many great ideas for homeschool implementation, and so little time to get them done, the stakes seem high—and they are! But God is with us. And in relationship with Him and our husbands, as unique women with families that are in many ways unlike any others, we would be wise to develop some guiding motives and directions for our schooling journey so that we don't become ineffective or distracted from our central goals for our family. Identifying these is what Chapter 2 is all about!

2.

And God said, "Let there be lights in the expanse of the heavens to separate the day from the night. And let them be for signs and for seasons, and for days and years, and let them be lights in the expanse of the heavens to give light upon the earth." And it was so.

GENESIS 1:14-15 (ESV)

Do You Have a Guiding Star?

If you are new to homeschooling and have done any Internet surfing or talking with women in your area, you have already found that there are a myriad of choices and voices. As with any new vocation, you must learn a new vocabulary, involving such words as "modalities" and "fine motor skills" and "Unit Study approach." It's a steep learning curve about a really important topic—your child's education! So, it can be both bewildering and stressful!

Many different vendors of curricula, leading authors, and well-meaning friends (or relations) may tell you that one program is "the best" or that one educational element is "the only" or "the essential" ingredient to successful home teaching and/or parenting. These mentors all sincerely believe what they say, or they wouldn't be teaching others to do as they do. But the truth is that there are a variety of different, valid methods by which you can achieve the general goal of successful homeschooling.

Because many of us did not grow up homeschooling or seeing it done, we can be like the early explorers or merchants who launched out by sea and land to seek a vaguely conceived treasure with only the most rudimentary navigational aids. For centuries, adventurers steered by the stars. So, to extend the metaphor, have you found your "guiding star" for the homeschool journey?

As I demonstrated in Chapter 1, parents start homeschooling for a wide variety of reasons. God has all kinds of ways (some full of humor) of drawing us to paths that He's marked out for us. I won't say it's bait and switch, but it sure feels like that some days! To review:

- Some start the journey as a reaction to life circumstances (from "my child's Kindergarten teacher was intolerable" to "we are a military family and move a lot").
- Some moms start homeschooling because they support someone else's vision (like "my husband grew up homeschooling and really wants me to, so I am going to give it a try").
- Some see homeschooling as a "get ahead" measure: they plan to homeschool only until their child is reading well, and then put them into a school. For them, it's a "head start" tactic.
- And then there are the ideologues: parents who homeschool because of certain principles, most typically related to educational goals, perceived parental responsibilities to their children, religion, and/or building family relationships.

These last types of parents have typically found early on what I'm calling their "guiding star" for the journey. My biggest concern for many young couples who are attracted to homeschooling for the more practical (vs. principled) reasons (whether corralled by circumstances or cajoled by others' opinions), is that they have not yet crystallized their vision. They can lack a clear sense of why they are homeschooling, nor do they have a definition of what success would even look like. When such parents are confronted with the vast array of early schooling choices, they may have no star to steer by and become lost.

You may be in this position now, or you may know young couples who are at this overwhelming starting point. Given the long-distance nature of the journey and the rigorous efforts that will be needed along the way, the more a newcomer peers out at the horizon, the harder it can get to begin. Without a star to follow, you might wonder if it's even going to be worth it—whatever "it" is!

Parents in their first years of homeschooling need motivation, need frameworks for making decisions, need trustworthy mentors, and need resources by which they can choose the first guiding stars that they can steer by. To borrow from a career book title by David Campbell, *If You Don't Know Where You're Going, You'll Probably End Up Somewhere Else.* The learning curve is straight up, and all choices of direction and voices calling you to them can seem equally valid.

> *My biggest concern for young couples is that many haven't yet crystallized their vision.*

I would like to argue that in this, as in most areas of life, couples need to take time to ponder their direction, not just the means that they will adopt to get to their destination. My husband and I have spent hours and hours and hours over the years (mostly on long car trips) talking around and through what we want to achieve in our parenting.

We have found we do best when we start with the destination first—answering questions like these:

- What are we trying to achieve?
- Where do we want to end up?
- What would wild success look like?

When we can answer questions like these about our destination in any way whatsoever, we can then begin to figure out our routes. These answers (determined by our values and goals) then serve as our guiding stars, no matter where the roads of the journey take us. Through rough and smooth, it is convictions (as opposed to preferences) that keep us going the right way.

For instance, we are Christians. This gives us vital information! It means that our homeschool will be Christ-centered, and that our Bible will have ultimate authority in all the situations that we encounter. As with all of our lives here on earth, the Bible doesn't tell us *everything* we should legitimately value (though it definitely tells us Whom to value most).

Since God is creative in the way He makes people, there are a number of individual values which are good but not universal—one of them might exist in one family but not in another. For instance, a love for books and ideas is a good value. So is a love for the athletic excellence, involving gracious winning, cheerful losing, and fair play found in the best participants of any given sport. Both are good values, but one typically needs to be prioritized because we only have so much time.

As an example, for my husband Scott and me, books are more important than sports, and teaching our children the principles or ideas of things are more important than rote memorization of trivia. Fair enough: these are some of our guiding stars. They might not be the same for your family!

Whatever they are, determining what your unique guiding stars—your values and convictions—are is essential. So, for homeschooling, let me ask you to discuss the following questions as a couple, ideally with paper and pencil in hand:

- What kinds of values do we see as major influences on our schooling choices?
- Are there any circumstances that God has placed in our lives that will affect our homeschooling decisions?
- Can we define what education is? Or, said differently, what would we say is the end game of education?
- How long do we think it will take to get there?
- What would "wild success" in homeschooling look like?

Before those questions overwhelm you, take a deep breath. Remember, you don't need to know the whole journey from day one. As you progress, the stars that you choose to guide you will change with the seasons, as do the constellations of our night sky, because changing seasons will bring different answers to the questions you've asked above. The stars that you follow during your grammar-school years may not serve you as well in the teen years.

As God grows you and your capacity to love and serve, you may find that your guiding stars are quite different at the start, in three years, and in ten years. But the great benefit of picking a star to follow early on is that such a choice helps you to make a host of other, smaller choices with some confidence. You can thus gain some early headway, instead of being paralyzed by anxieties or feeling sure that you're wandering around in circles!

You don't have to know each bend and turn in the road ahead. God's guidance is usually more like headlights on a car, illuminating only the path immediately ahead of us, than like a MapQuest printout that lays out the whole journey at a glance. That's where faith and trust in God get built, by relying on Him day by day for each leg of the journey.

But we do need to start our trip. And, to start, we need to pick a direction that we think is a good way to head. Only then can we begin to say "yes" to some choices and "no" to others! To see how that might look, read about practical approaches to answering some of these questions and finding an initial direction in Chapter 3.

3.

When you are a Bear of Very Little Brain, and you Think of Things, you find sometimes that a Thing which seemed very Thingish inside you is quite different when it gets out into the open and has other people looking at it.

WINNIE-THE-POOH, *BY A.A. MILNE*

Clarifying the Ends We Have in Mind

In the previous chapter, I wrote about the confusion that most newcomers feel when first confronted with the "night sky" of the homeschooling world. The night sky has its beauty, its darkness, its bright stars, its moving comets and its constellations (and the occasional passing plane soaring overhead, just to confuse things). In this chapter, I hope to help you to make sense of what now may seem like a bewildering multiplicity of choices.

Like any new star gazer, you must learn to see the patterns of the stars in the sky above if you hope to make sense of the night sky and receive useful guidance on your journey. There are two broad ways to pattern choices between homeschooling resources. One can group them by educational philosophy or by methodological approach. Let me define these simply.

Educational philosophy expresses the "why" or the "to what end" of education. It asks: "Why do we teach?" and "Where are we trying to end up?" It is focused on the meaning and goals of the educational journey.

Educational methods (or approaches) are the means that we adopt to get to the philosophical ends that we've defined. When considering methods, we ask questions like, "How do people learn? What content do we teach? What vehicles do we choose for information delivery? What do we use to measure success (as defined by our educational philosophy)?"

All homeschooling resources are based on some guiding educational philosophy. Some vendors are clear about theirs and explain them to the buyer. With others, it's either assumed (doesn't everybody already know that this is the goal?) or it's so underlying that it's virtually invisible to the newbie.

Many newcomers get caught up in the details of the methodology as a first step, but I'd direct you to consider the "why" of homeschooling before even beginning to look at the "how." All resources have a goal for education—the direction that they're heading and a place where they want to wind up. So, I posit that job #1 for the newcomer is to figure out *your* educational philosophy for *your* unique family. Start by identifying your destination and then your direction; then, choose a star in a constellation that will help you head there steadfastly.

Let's remember that we said that we're on a long journey here, so our educational goals (and often our methods) will change its differing stages. Say you were taking a trip from east to west across America in the pioneer days. Your first, short-term goal would be getting across the Appalachians on foot (needing light loads and some warm clothing). Next, you'd need to make it across the flat lands to the Mississippi (via horseback, or by stage coaches, or even by boat—and it could be turning quite warm). Then you'd need to cross the prairies to get to the Rocky Mountains (time for a covered wagon full of supplies for this phase). Finally, you'd need to get over or around those imposing Rocky Mountains. (Mules are good for this, but winter might catch you if you don't hurry!) At long last, you'd arrive at that destination so long anticipated, and paddle your toes in the Pacific Ocean while enjoying the sunset.

Each stage of the journey would have shorter-term goals (just to the other side of this one mountain, that's all) and equipment specific to that phase of the journey. You might even decide to stop along the way. You might settle down just after crossing the Mississippi, for instance, because you find that, hey, you like the flat lands of the Mid-West after all! Or, you might temporarily veer north to Canada following game or south to Texas while outrunning hostile Indians, but then get back on course and make it to California in the end.

While change and in-course corrections are always possible, the identification of long-term goals helps you make decisions about each leg of the journey such that each one will get you further down the road towards your overall goal (such as reaching the west coast).

We're on a journey here, so our educational goals will change with its differing stages.

With education, we likewise have short- and long-term goals and must try to start with the end in mind. But again: Where are we headed? Why are we going there? Once we know, we can pick a guiding star to steer in that direction and get started with packing our knapsacks and laying in provisions for the trip.

It's pencil and paper time again! I believe that you will best find your educational star if you sit down with your husband and ask a series of questions, some of which have little to do with education, but everything to do with direction. Here are some to get you going:

- What are we, as a couple and as individuals, most passionate about doing to glorify God and advance His Kingdom?
- What are immovable constraints that will shape our family— such things as vocational choices, regional conditions, and money issues?
- What is most important to us as parents? Finish this sentence: "My parenting would be a success if ______________."
- What things do we value in life that we most want to pass on to our kids?
- How big a family do we plan (or hope) to have? And then: How does that number of kids limit our time, energy, and financial resources?
- Who will primarily do the teaching in our home, and what kinds of gifts,

talents, passions, and weaknesses does this person bring to the endeavor?

- Where are we today? (How old are our kids, what jobs do we work, where do we live, etc.?) These form our boundaries and "givens" at the present time, but some things might be changeable.
- Where do we think we might be in 5 years? 10 years? 25 years? (Chart this one on paper, noting ages of kids, career possibilities, geographical location, etc.)
- What gifts, talents, and drives do we already notice in each of our children? (Allow one piece of paper per child: profile them academically, spiritually, and socially as they now are.[1])
- Which of the above gifts, talents, and drives do we think God wants us to steward and promote?
- What weaknesses have we identified, and how do we want to help strengthen each child over time, with God's help?
- If we had to boil our hopes and dreams for ourselves and our children down into a couple or three theologically-informed sentences, what might they be?

Let me help you out here! These are big questions, and it can be hard to get our arms around them at first. I've made up four, totally fictitious couples in order to show you how you can use the questions above to arrive at a sense of direction. While each is different, each has equal validity.

Example #1: Bill was an Olympic athlete who won a silver medal while a young adult, and Judy was, before she had babies, a triathlon competitor, ranking first in her state. As this couple talks and prays, they realize that glorifying God in the public arena through stewarding carefully the gifts and talents of each family member is most important to them as a family value.

Given this focus, a small family is planned so that there will be enough time, financial resources, and mobility to carefully steward the development of each child to his or her fullest potential.

Now we start with longest-term goals and work down to today:

- One supportive, educational, long-term goal that matches this family's val-

1 If your children are quite young, this won't be as helpful as if you are coming to homeschooling with older children. Do what makes sense, and don't worry if there's not much to put down for this point.

ues would be to work towards winning a sports scholarship to a university, for the purposes of making the most of gifts and talents that their five-year-old has demonstrated early as a gymnast.

- To this end, this talented first child will need a flexible academic program that leaves plenty of room for practices and meets throughout the junior and senior high school years. Since gymnastics is an individual sport, he doesn't need a school setting in order to further his goals, and homeschooling gives his parents the flexibility to control his schedule and provide Christ-centered tutoring.
- However, we all know that injuries happen, and there is life after sports, so Bill and Judy also want to prepare their child to serve God in other sports-related industries, such as becoming a sports therapist, or sports journalist.
- Since their eldest child is now five (but showing clear talent in gymnastics even at this tender age) they want to choose curricula that will serve God's purposes as they now understand them by allowing them to build a solid foundation in the 3 R's while still giving time for abundant gymnastics lessons and practices.

Please note that, so far in this process, no curriculum decision has been made. What has been established is clarity about the "why" (or direction) of the couple's homeschool journey. The curriculum that they'll choose won't take the child all day to accomplish, because he'll need significant time built into his homeschool schedule for practices and lessons. This kind of guiding star enables this couple to pick a point and begin to move towards it. (And please note that this example equally applies to any single-focus goal, such as with children talented in music, visual arts, or the performing arts.)

I chose this as my first example because of the obvious, perhaps over-simplistic, clear direction that this fictitious couple has. Not all couples have a single, clear-cut goal like this in mind when beginning to homeschool!

Also notice that such sports-oriented plans are sometimes more subject to change because of injuries or lack of enough talent to make the cut. So, these wise parents have a two-part approach: they plan to give their children Christian values and a solid academic education that back up a possible failure of the ambitious desire to have their student excel in the sports world to the glory of God.

Example #2: Bob and Sue both grew up in the same Midwestern farming country. Bob's dad owned the regional tractor dealership and farmed. Bob had seven siblings; five still live close by. Sue grew up in the town near Bob's farm, but she was an only child. As they talk, Bob and Sue realize that their central focus is family unity and generational discipleship.

Bob and Sue both envision having a large family and being involved long term with both sides of a multi-generational family that lives nearby and comes from a strong Christian background. Their long- and short-term goals look like this:

- As they talk and pray, the defining, long-term goal for this couple becomes the hard work of developing a family business so that Bob can be a hands-on dad. He can be much more available than other men in many other vocational contexts.
- A secondary benefit they see is that family involvement in a business can both train their children in valuable skills and bring generations together as they work in unity to the glory of God.
- To this end, the general academic direction of the children will include not only basic academic subjects, but a strong emphasis for each one on some aspect of the family business, determined by their emerging God-given gifts and talents.
- They see that there will need to be some time left in each day for Sue and the kids to assist in the business, especially during its early years of development.
- As they talk, they realize that between business demands and the number of planned children, their curriculum will need to be pretty simple to execute: open, point, and shoot. Rigorous academics that require a lot of time for Sue or the kids are not their focus in this season. Homeschooling is more a means to the greater end of family unity and business success at this time.
- Since their eldest child is now five, with a three-year-old brother and one-year-old sister, and Sue plans to be pregnant next year again, the curriculum and methodology they choose for early education will be very basic and easily accomplished in short lessons.

Example #3: John has chosen a military career to the glory of God, and is a gifted leader. He and Martha have chosen to homeschool, knowing that frequent moves would disrupt their children's education if they chose traditional school settings.

As they talk about their future, they realize that Martha is going to have to be the prime mover in homeschooling and discipleship of the children, since John is going to be deployed overseas, sometimes for a year or more.

- There will definitely be some times when this family will enjoy sweet fellowship and support on military bases, but also the couple can anticipate periods where Martha will be isolated from real-life spousal support. One long-term goal that they identify is to make computer technologies and long-distance communications a budget priority from the get-go.
- The curriculum and other family rhythms are going to need to be comfortable for Martha, who will function as a single parent for significant portions of the children's upbringing. But, they are looking hard at ways that John can actively lead his family from a distance, and help and support his wife and growing children as the years unfold.
- Besides academic lessons, this couple is going to want to determine how their kids' social needs are going to be met. Will the curriculum, the Internet, the social media outlets, or local church attendance be means of grace or avenues of sin to such kids? For instance, do they want to promote Internet relationships between the kids and their friends so that moves don't disrupt them, or limit these in favor of a series of short-term, local friendships whose longevity are seen as determined by a loving God's sovereign plan—and thus His shaping of each of their kids' lives?
- The vocational choice here doesn't really dictate curricula choices clearly. Martha's personal learning style, degree of personal discipline, strengths and weaknesses academically, and personal passions have much more influence for the choices that this couple makes.
- As they look at their eldest, a five-year-old daughter, they plan to be at their current duty station for another three years, with John home for at least the next two years. Having identified these parameters and values, the couple can now go on to learn about the diverse array of homeschooling resources available. What they now see more clearly from this analysis is that Martha will be the "lead duck" in choosing the curricula she is happiest with as they start out.

Example #4: Paul and Sarah grew up in different areas of East-Coast affluent suburbia and are comfortable in that lifestyle. Paul has a good job as a white-collar administrator for a large, stable accounting firm, and Sarah enjoys cooking, homemaking, crafts, and a close-knit circle of girlfriends. Since they met at college and decided to settle in the same area, their parents don't live close. Both are Christians and go regularly to a Bible-believing church, but active service of Christ and His Kingdom is not the conscious center of their world. Neither of them have discovered driving passions to help them define unique long-term goals, since their lives have fallen neatly into relatively easy, predictable paths.

Not all couples have a single, clear cut goal in mind when beginning to homeschool!

But, all of a sudden, new circumstances have forced them to recognize two things: their son's Kindergarten teacher is unacceptably harsh, and neither of them received a very strong education. In fact, they've never really thought about education much at all. They were both comfortable and popular in the public school system. They've always assumed that their children would be likewise, and so haven't looked into alternatives or tried to understand what their local schools are teaching these days. Now, this curve ball in their otherwise placid life has them scrambling.

The motive for this couple to homeschool is circumstantial and sudden: they cannot in good conscience leave their son in his current educational setting, and it is mid-year, which is the wrong time to attempt entry into a Christian private school. They are seeking a quick answer to the burning questions of implementation: "How do I homeschool? Where do I start? What do I buy to use to teach? Can I even do this?"

Paul and Sarah have advantages in this crisis that some other families lack. They have money and Sarah has availability. Their eldest child is not very far into his school years. There is time for them to learn all that they need to know.

What they lack is an overall understanding of their choices and the places that their choices can lead them. Given the tight time constraints, the best single thing that they can do is to look around their church family or friends for a mentor who knows the homeschooling world well. (Actually, even if their kids were much older, this would be the wisest course for someone who had a sudden need to homeschool, for whatever reason!)

Paul and Sarah can take their mentor's curriculum recommendation and purchase a program that will finish out the school year. With that mentor's help, Sarah can begin to set up her daily rhythms and begin to learn to teach their son. They should, however, realize that just because they have begun at the short-term end of the stick doesn't mean that they won't need to set those long-range goals if they are to succeed in homeschooling (and I would add: in life!).

After the crisis is resolved, Paul and Sarah can begin to pray and talk about their long-range and short-term goals.

- Shorter-range questions are like these: Should they continue to homeschool after this year? If so, why will they be doing it? (There are options! Christian private school is one; secular private school is another, or they could continue to homeschool.)
- The bigger, more far-reaching question awaiting this couple is, "Where are you headed?" To answer that, they will need to work through that starter list of probing questions from Chapter 2 and earlier in this chapter.
- The good news is that the present crisis will have clarified certain boundaries, and the catapult into homeschooling will have at least acquainted them with a mentor and some homeschooling jargon. God is at the helm of this couple's ship, and He will make clear to them where they are to head as they seek Him with fresh desperation!

Before finishing this chapter, let me flesh out for you what I mean in that last starting question that I gave you in the beginning of this chapter: "If we had to boil our hopes and dreams for ourselves and our children down into a couple or three theologically-informed sentences, what might they be?"

I've actually given you examples of possible answers in the profiles above. Did you catch them? (Go back and look, and even take a few minutes to jot them down as an exercise that might help you to do likewise with your own goals.)

- Bill and Judy's crystallized vision for their family might be stated as: "We want to glorify God in the public arena through stewarding carefully the gifts and talents of each family member."

- Bob and Sue might say, "Our vision is to build family unity and generational discipleship, expressed through the means of a successful family business, run on Christian principles, to impact our community and serve our neighbors to the glory of God."
- John and Martha believe that God has called John to the military. They would say, "We believe that serving and supporting John as he serves his country to the glory of God is the primary calling for our family. Secondarily, we believe that God provides grace and help for those in need. As the father of this family, I (John) believe that I should diligently seek God's will in supporting and loving my wife, and children, even when my vocation takes me away from home."

Paul and Sarah have never seriously sought God for a family mission statement or over-arching sense of direction. But lately, their loving Heavenly Father is orchestrating the events of their lives so that the desire to do so is awakened! Below are some other family mission statements that I have heard (and loved) over the years:

> *Our family is an outpost of the Kingdom of God. We want to build a loving, warm, stable family into which the world may come when invited, on our terms, so that our children may learn to recognize evil, minister to the hurting people of this world with compassion, and be equipped to answer the enemies of God in the gate of the city when they become adults.*
>
> *Our family lives in the inner city because we feel a call from God to minister to broken people. We live conscious of the fact that not a single sparrow falls to earth without God's permission, and so we trust Him for provision, for protection, and for the souls of our children as we function as His ambassadors here.*
>
> *Our family is called to be overseas missionaries. As such, we homeschool so that we may instruct our children academically [while] fulfilling our call to minister on the front lines of God's ongoing battle for the souls of men and women in this place, where Christian witness is practically non-existent.*

Inspiring, aren't they? What is God calling your family to? What's your guiding star? What is the end that you have in mind as you begin your homeschool journey? A central goal of this book is to help you figure out, as a couple, your unique answers to these questions.

Take time to talk with your spouse about this in an unhurried, exploratory way, or to commit to paper those goals that you have identified in the past, and then set times to review them quarterly as you continue your homeschool journey!

4.

ped·a·go·gy [ped-uh-goh-jee, -goj-ee]
noun, plural ped·a·go·gies
1. the function or work of a teacher; teaching.
2. the art or science of teaching; education; instructional methods.[1]

Developing Your Pedagogy

You may have read the title of this chapter and asked, "My what-a-gogy?" Join the club! My college-aged Education-major daughter taught me this term only a few years ago, so you're not alone. This is "eduspeak" for "your approach to education, specifically, your teaching philosophies and methods."

This chapter is not meant to be exhaustive on this topic; in fact, it may be a little over your head as a beginning homeschooler. It's located here because it offers a set of categories that can help you to sort through the myriad of educational resources that you'll encounter as you begin to dive into the details of how and what to teach. You

1 "pedagogy." Dictionary.com Unabridged. Random House, Inc. Accessed 21 January 2014. <Dictionary.com http://dictionary.reference.com/browse/pedagogy>.

may find that skimming this chapter for content, and then going on to the rest of the book, and then returning to this chapter afterwards will serve you best. As always, the choice is yours! I place this here mostly because I suspect that many of my readers find themselves at the point of choosing programs, and I want to help.

When professional teachers take education classes in college, "Pedagogy 101" is typically the title of one of them. In such classes, students are given categories for analyzing and discussing various educational approaches. I wish I had had them earlier, when beginning to homeschool, because they can help us develop our own convictions (philosophy of education) and methods (choosing/developing our own curriculum/lesson plans), as I've been discussing in earlier chapters.

In my daughter's pedagogy classes, she studied landmark educational philosophers and analyzed their approaches to education using a grid of five questions. After the students had thoroughly assessed everyone from Confucius to Erasmus to Rousseau to Dewey to Thoreau to Charlotte Mason (to name a few), the class culminated in an assignment for students to use these same five questions as a framework within which to express their own, personal philosophy of education—one that had developed as they studied the pedagogical constructs of these famous thinkers.

You may not have the luxury of studying and analyzing these great thinkers, but you need to develop your own philosophy of education. Consider this a crash course! These questions can help you both analyze the approaches of published programs currently available to homeschoolers and develop your own unique philosophy of education in real time. Here they are:

1. What is the epistemology (assumption/belief about how human beings come to know things) of the program?
2. In this program or philosophy, what is the role of the teacher?
3. Then, what is the role of the student?
4. Next, what is the role of the curriculum?
5. And finally, what is the highest good: what values are uppermost in the minds of the program creator(s)?

Let me expand on these questions to further define them for you.

Question 1: What is the epistemology of the program?

Epistemology can be defined as "a branch of philosophy that investigates the origin, nature, methods, and limits of human knowledge." [1] Traditionally, there have been a number of ways of explaining how a human being gets knowledge. Some say that the dominant influence in how we come to know things is our nature—how we are wired genetically. Others say that it's nurture: the environmental influences and relational or other kinds of experiences shape our knowledge base.

If you get deep into this subject, you'll find various camps of serious scholars that go by such handles as Essentialism, Perennialism, Progressivism, Empiricism, Idealism, Rationalism, and Constructivism. We're not going to go into the details of these varying camps in this book. My purpose for mentioning them is to demonstrate that this question of how humans acquire knowledge isn't simple. The question of how human beings learn, and the definition of "knowledge" itself, have long been debated, so don't be discouraged if you have trouble finding a satisfying answer in your own first attempts to arrive at an understanding of epistemology.

On the other hand, don't let a realization of the depth of this topic stop you! You must begin somewhere, and the first four chapters of this book are an attempt to give you different hand holds as you start to scale the wall that is the question of how your children will best learn in your home. Also, applying this question of epistemology more narrowly will help.

For instance, say you narrow it to the question of teaching beginning mathematics to a first grader, and are looking for a published program to buy. Your awareness of the question about epistemology would teach you to look for the program that would best communicate basic mathematical concepts to your student.

While researching, you will soon discover one major division in epistemological approaches to teaching mathematics. Some say that math is best learned using lots of solid objects (called manipulatives) that model math concepts. Other programs are designed with the premise that the memorization of addition and subtraction facts by rote is best, together with simple problems based on that memorization.

Very well. Our category of epistemology (how the young child learns) helps you to examine both designs in light of your own understanding of how *your* child will best learn math concepts. Is it easier for him to understand and remember that 2 +

1 "epistemology." Dictionary.com Unabridged. Random House, Inc. Accessed 21 January 2014. <Dictionary.com http://dictionary.reference.com/browse/epistemology>.

2 = 4 if he simply memorizes that as a verbal phrase? Or is it easier if you push two pennies and two more pennies into one group on the table, thus modeling with solid manipulatives this simple math concept as you explain it?

Let's say that you think that he'll gain the specific knowledge of math concepts better through manipulatives than via memory work. You decide to explore first any math programs that include manipulatives, and head off to make a list of such programs. Bravo! You have just taken the first step towards making an epistemologically-informed curriculum-buying decision!

Thankfully, the next three questions that help you arrive at your pedagogy are far more straightforward. They center on roles. They ask, "in a given educational philosophy or program of study, what are the roles of the teacher, the student, and the curriculum?"

Question #2: What will your role be as a teacher?

The idea of "roles" can be broad or more practical and narrow. Broadly, one can see that a teacher's role in a given program could be to guide the student, by assigning independent work, or suggesting places to research information, for instance, but not instructing him directly. Or, a teacher's role could be to model an action for the student, and then allow him to try it on his own, such as with a dance move, for instance, or with writing a story. A teacher might function as a questioner, where the student learns a body of knowledge and then the teacher hones the student's understanding by asking leading questions, as with Socratic discussions. Most commonly in schools, and above a certain age level, the teacher's role is to impart information verbally and task students with independent work, then find out how much students remember via testing.

My goal in giving this example of an analysis of a fictitious math program is to help you see how to use these five questions.

Let's now return to our example of assessing the beginning math program and get more narrow. As you look over the program, you find that your role will primarily be to instruct. You will need to explain concepts to your student, and then demonstrate them using the manipulatives.

You're glad to see that there is a teacher's manual for you to use, since you've never taught math before, and that the manual directs you clearly as to what you'll need to say and do. You see that the program is designed for you to sit with your student for at least a half an hour a day, five days a week, in order to complete the course in one year's time.

Finally, you are encouraged to find that there is an answer key for you to use when you get to the point where you'll need to correct your student's work.

So, as you look at your role, you decide that you are comfortable with the over-arching role of instructor, and pleased that there is so much support for you as a new one! So far, so good.

Question #3: What is the role of the student?

Again, let's begin to aquaint ourselves with this question by seeing what kinds of generalized roles we might find. Some programs call for the student to do discovery on his own and then come to you with his questions. Other programs put the student in a passive mode: his job is to pay attention to input. A very few programs ask for the student to design his own course of delight-directed learning.

As you look over our fictitious math program, you now are thinking about your student. This program has him listening to your instruction attentively, then responding actively by using manipulatives and filling in related work pages. The student will need to sit for about 30 minutes per day and listen to you, and also watch what you do with the manipulatives, then mimic your actions.

The program will also require him to do follow-up seat work using a pencil to work problems in a student notebook, and work with the manipulatives on his own while doing this work, for approximately fifteen minutes per day.

For some students at a young age, this program would require a role that would be hard for them: both the sitting still and then pencil work would be challenging. For others, this would be a welcome approach. As a homeschooling parent, you get to take this into account when considering the purchase!

Question #4: What is the role of the curriculum?

This one may be harder to get your mind around at first. Let me ask it in other ways. Is the program itself the means by which the student learns directly? Do the printed pages impart information directly to the student (as in, for example, a textbook), or is the program primarily an assignment sheet, providing tasks that are followed up by the teacher or student? Does it present questions for the student to answer, and if so, are there answers for the teacher to use? How are the student's answers checked? Is the program a springboard for learning, or is it a means of teaching, or does it actually directly teach independently of the teacher (as with a textbook or video lessons, for instance)?

Back to our example: looking it over, you find that our fictitious math curriculum directs you strongly as the teacher and also directly teaches the child via follow-up work pages. While the teacher's manual, student notebook, and manipulatives are sold separately, they are all available and together form a complete program.

The curriculum is designed to be very directive. There is little to no creativity called for on the part of the teacher or student; this is not a springboard approach, nor is much independent exploration called for, apart from the student using manipulatives during follow-up work.

Very well, you mentally tally your exploration sheet, matching up your skills, time allotment for teaching math, and your student's abilities and preferences. Finally, you want to answer that last question about values.

Question #5: What are the major, driving values of this program's creators?

Here are other ways to restate this question: What do the program's creators feel is important? Where do they want these lessons to take the student? What outcomes does this program seek?

With our example math program, you find that the creators of this program feel that it should take a significant chunk of time daily to teach basic math concepts to a young child. They also believe that manipulatives are essential for cementing the foundational concepts of mathematics in young minds. They do not particularly value memory work, nor do they place a premium on pencil/paper learning, though there is a little of that in the follow-up work in the student notebook. There is no "canned" component: no video or audio taped segments that explain concepts to the child. The main vehicle is a one-on-one, daily, sustained personal tutorial delivered by a live teacher (you), using tactile (touching/doing) reinforcement of the lesson(s).

Your Responses

Now come your personal responses to the analysis. Here are questions you can now ask yourself:

1. Epistemology: Do you agree that the use of manipulatives and a significant chunk of time spent by you each day with your child, one-on-one, is the best way for him to come to know basic math skills?
2. Teacher's Role:
   - Do you want to directly instruct your student in the manner prescribed by the Teacher's Manual? Is that a role that you're comfortable with?
   - Practically speaking: will you have time and discipline to sit and teach this program to your student, given all your other values and responsibilities as a homeschooling mother?
3. Student's Role:
   - Will your student be willing to sit for the required instruction session and seatwork exercises each school day?
   - Will your student want a more exploratory or creative approach (such as playing a computer game that teaches math facts), or does she do well with verbal input followed by demonstrations with the manipulatives?
4. Curriculum's Role:
   - Do you want a heavily directive curriculum, or will you want to have the freedom to be more creative?
   - Do you welcome the clear plan of study that imparts information to the student through you and the seat work because it's simple for you and you have a weak background in math, or does the program seem heavy-handed and constricting because you love math and have all kinds of ideas as to how to make it more fun, and so a methodical approach would not be your style?
   - Do you want a more entertaining program—one that draws the student in by asking questions and helps the student discover concepts for himself through them?
5. Values that underlie the program:
   - Do your values line up with the program's? Do you agree with its cre-

ators about what's important in a math program?

- Do you feel that the overall approach upholds the values and will be effective in reaching them? In other words, will you prioritize this program enough to make it work as designed?

My goal in giving this example of an analysis of a fictitious math program was to help you to see how to use these five questions. As you clarify your overall goals and direction for your family, you'll also want to be honing your pedagogy. These questions can give you categories that become guiding stars as you think about how your children will best learn a variety of subjects and skills in your home, how you can best teach them, how your children can best function as students, how various curricular approaches will work in your homeschool, and what values will rise to the top as pole stars by which you set your homeschooling journey's course.

Resources for further development of a Pedagogy

- Bloom's Taxonomy (found in many places on the Internet via Google)
- *The Seven Laws of Teaching* by John M. Gregory

SECTION TWO

Mountaintop Views

Here on the mountain, I have spoken to you clearly: I will not often do so down in Narnia. Here on the mountain, the air is clear and your mind is clear; as you drop down into Narnia, the air will thicken. Take care that it does not confuse your mind.

The Silver Chair, *by C.S. Lewis*

One privilege (and joy) that I am called to as an older woman is to share encouragement and perspective with those traveling the road now behind me. Having completed the homeschool journey with six children who are now adults and have made me the grandmother of eight (so far as I know at this printing), I am able to look back on the homeschool journey with the benefit of hindsight.

Some things that we encounter as we travel seem big at the time, but prove to be minor events that we quickly forget later. Other things along the path seem small or insignificant in life's daily grind, but when you get to the end of the journey, they prove to have been some of the most important, and precious, parts of the trip! My goal in this section is to point out some of those smaller elements, since they can be hard to see when you're slogging along the path with only the hazy stars to guide you through the fog.

This a not a section on educational theory, nor is it exactly the practical "how to" section of the book, though there are many practical tips scattered through it. Rather, I'm trying to share core elements of the journey that I hardly glimpsed as I began homeschooling, but that have become luminously clear as the years have unfolded and I gained hindsight. Many such deeper insights can only be gained with time or, indeed, can only be learned by trial and error. But my hope is that, if I describe what I have gleaned, you can perhaps make them your own earlier in your journey than I did.

5.

The great thing, if one can, is to stop regarding all the unpleasant things as interruptions of one's "own," or "real" life. The truth is of course that what one calls the interruptions are precisely one's real life—the life God is sending one day by day: what one calls one's "real life" is a phantom of one's own imagination.

Letter to Arthur Greeves, 20 December 1943, by C.S. Lewis

You Share Who You Are

Permit me to start this chapter with a different analogy than the journey: one that expresses how I believe that all of life (including homeschooling discipleship) works. Imagine with me a virgin forest: the kind with lots of tall, deciduous trees and not much thorny underbrush.

Year after year, this forest is undisturbed by man. Year after year, spring leaves appear on the trees. The sun warms them; the rain waters them. They grow. Autumn comes; they wither and fall to the ground. Winds blow, the snow falls, the ground freezes; a pale sun shines down. In the spring, the ground again thaws, breezes stir, new leaves appear, and the cycle starts again. After about 70 years of such undisturbed cycles, what would you find on the forest floor? Usually, deep, rich humus:

fertile, dark soil that has naturally occurred.

But, each forest's soil is different from every other. What if, in one place, a forest fire ripped through these woods about ten years ago? The soil would have evidence of that event: ash would have both reduced and enriched it. Certain places where animals wintered would have soils enriched by animal wastes, but also compression from where they made their homes and laid down, night after night, to sleep. What if men with large, heavy equipment and cans of soda pop came through and did some logging? Their tire tracks, empty cans, and felled trees would have left their mark. Etc.

Now, you can't hurry the natural processes outlined above; nor can you hope to duplicate them exactly from place to place. Each spring, summer, winter, and fall contributed different characteristics to the overall quality and makeup of the soil thus formed. Some winters were brutally cold; others were mild. Falls were wet; some summers brought drought. Even within one forest, the orientation of hillsides to sun and wind will cause differences in soils that result.

The fertile soil took decades to form, yet one could say that it was formed by individual leaves, by sticks, by animals, by weather, and by the grand design of God's creation working silently, at His direction, year in and year out. Change any of these contributing elements or conditions, and the soil would have been different. Each of these had a shaping role, but you wouldn't say that any of them was determinative. The soil is what it is, at its broadest level, because God caused it to be that way.

I think that our lives are like that forest. Season by season, year by year, we have thoughts, we have interactions with people, we have experiences, we make efforts, we read books, we make decisions, and we hear persuasive words. Some memories are clearly etched in our minds; other things that happened to us—and shaped us—we do not remember at all. Yet, taken together, these influences, our unique genetic makeup and "natural" gifts, the spiritual gifts that God gives us at regeneration, and our reactions to life's ups and downs—all these form us, almost imperceptibly, year by year. They make up the "soil" into which the gospel seeds fall and flourish, or barely survive, or fail to thrive altogether.

Who can say what makes one soul's "soil" more fertile than another's? Well, there are, of course, basic elements. Loving environments during childhood (or not), educational opportunities (or lack thereof), mentorship of an expert in one's field, opportunities for (or impediments to) advancement, and the everyday people who alternately teach us, cheer us on, or trip us up—these all play a part, certainly.

Somewhere in there are also our own choices in reaction to life's trials and triumphs. And for Christians, God is orchestrating events for the enrichment of our souls, to His glory and for our good, which He defines as making us more like Christ (Romans 8:28-29).

Here's the question for parents, and especially for Christian, homeschooling parents, who shoulder so much of the influence that their children will have. Can any parent hope to control the complex set of factors that shape a human life?

Americans are "can do" people. We love self-help books, lists of steps to success, and the joy of individual achievement. When we moms start thinking about homeschooling, we naturally ask, "What must I do to be successful?" When looking into curricula, we ask, "Will this one make me a successful teacher, and my child a successful student?" And because we moms end up putting so much time into researching and implementing the academics, the outside lessons, the carpooling, the social networking, etc., we can think that these are the elements that really matter. These are how we'll control what shapes our kids into the happy, healthy, godly people that we want them to become.

Here's the thing that I want to say about how people learn: you were not formed by any one influence, and neither will your child be. What I see, both from looking back and by asking them directly, is that my children remember *so little* of the day to day, nitty-gritty of what we did in our homeschool.

I sweated the details of scheduling, purchasing, planning, teaching, correcting, and re-teaching academics and character lessons for years. That daily teaching and learning mattered: please do not misunderstand me to say that we can just sit back and expect our children to thrive academically. Sweat, toil, and tears are necessary elements to the construction of healthy souls and minds.

But, at the same time, my conscious and disciplined efforts to teach my kids were just a *few* of the factors that shaped my children and—in hindsight, seeing with 20/20 vision—they were much more of a minor factor than they seemed to me to be at the time! So many other little moments were almost as life-changing as were the academic pursuits, and often they were things I couldn't control or predict. Experiences like one emotionally painful encounter with neighbor kids, or becoming lost in a grocery store, or triumphing at a Little League game, or being caught cheating on math corrections by Dad—these kinds of moments in time created contexts for reactions and responses from us as parents and from our children as learners.

Because we were homeschoolers, my husband and I became the biggest single influence in our children's lives. We were surprised to realize that it was *who we were* as Christians and as unique people, and, thus, how we reacted to life's situations—great or small, happy or sad, challenging or easy—that influenced our children most. Our characters, passions, hopes, and dreams have translated, in various forms and in various degrees, to all of our six very different now-grown children. Things that we did not value, esteem, or promote have secondary places in their affections to this day.

Can any parent hope to control the complex set of factors that shape a human life?

For instance, our pastors emphasized serving in the local church to the glory of God. Scott and I wholeheartedly embraced this value, and for years we served alongside our children at our local church. Today, all six of our children are characterized by regular, active service of others for Jesus' sake. They look for ways to serve. They lay down their preferences for others. They work with joy in their local churches to strengthen their pastors, care group leaders, and fellow members.

As I've become less busy in recent years, I've had a chance to look around at other young adults. I see that this value for service is not universal among Christian young adults. Our children "caught" this from the way that Scott and I walked in the way, talked about serving, stayed up late and got up early in order to serve others.

Similar things could be written about how our children today love learning and education. These are things that Scott and I value highly, modeled consistently, and spoke about earnestly season after season. Scott loves to read aloud, and I love to read silently. In those years when we struggled through the fog of determining how to react to the opportunities and challenges presented in the 80's and 90's by the increasingly ubiquitous presence of technology—first cable TV, then video cameras and players, then personal computers, and then computer games—reading aloud remained one of the chief family joys and alternatives to digitally-based entertainment that we embraced. Scott read aloud almost nightly to us, and I designed a curriculum for my kids that included a ton of silent, independent reading.

Scott and I were also readers of Christian books and of the Bible. Our kids' bookshelves in their adult homes reflect that interest. We both love the Old Testament, and several of our children have a special love for it as well. One son chose to become an amateur expert on the story of 1-2 Samuel, for his own pleasure. Another daughter says she gets far more out of the New Testament because she has a rich understanding of the Old Testament (which she loves to read and re-read). Another son is passionate about helping both older children and adults go back to Old Testament stories that they may not have touched since Sunday School so that they can understand and apply its lessons about who God is.

The point is that our children saw all these values of ours on a daily, weekly, monthly, and yearly consistent basis *because it was who we were.* They were then (and remain today) shaped by what they saw modeled and what they experienced for themselves.

I could also write about the kinds of things that we did not particularly value: professional sports, for instance. Neither Scott nor I was a sports-minded person. There's nothing wrong with following a team and being a fan, but for Scott and me there just wasn't much attraction to it.

Nor were we devotees of fashionable clothing. For one thing, we didn't have the money for it, but for another, we just weren't attracted to keeping up with current trends and dressing to impress. Again, I don't think that Christians can't be fashion-conscious! I'm just saying that, for us, it wasn't a premium value.

Interestingly, my Aunt came to live down the street from us when my boys were young teens, and she loved professional sports. In a few short years, her example of delight in her teams influenced my two older sons to begin to follow pro teams, though I would have to say that this has never become a passion for any of them. Rather, it's a social pleasure: something to be shared with friends and enjoyed, but not a central ticker in their hearts. Yet, my aunt added that ingredient to their "soul soils." I suspect my grandchildren will carry trace elements of this "event" as well!

As for fashion, my sweet daughter-in-law loves it, and my own daughters have spent considerable time defining their own styles for themselves. They enjoy dressing up now, but I don't think that dressing for success is more of a value for them than it has been for Scott and me.

What's my main point here? People are more often caught than taught. As a parent, you cannot help but teach what you are. Though you may try to hide faults from your kids, and may try to lead them into what you consider right and true contrary to your own example, if you are not yourself modeling the things you are teaching, you may find yourself ineffective as a discipler.

So, as you begin to consider homeschooling academic subjects (evaluating things like curricula, outside classes, hobbies, and electives) consider yourself as well. To begin with, your soul's "soil" is still forming. God is not done with you yet. Embrace this fact, and put your growth moments on full display.

The best single thing you can do for your child is to grow yourself. Grow in godliness. Grow in humility. Grow in servanthood. Grow as a helpmeet to your husband. Grow in repentance and in forgiveness. Grow in kindness. Grow in dependence. Grow in trusting God. Certainly, grow in diligence as you learn to teach academic subjects. Of course, actively instruct your child as you rise up, and as you sit at home, and as you lie down.

Do make the effort to find the best fit for this season for academic curricula. But, I hope you can learn from my experience. Though I stressed most about choosing plans of study and my abilities (or lack thereof) as a teacher of academics, in looking back I see so clearly that it was how Scott and I grew in character, not the content of lessons from books written by others, that most shaped my homeschooled children.

One more thing, and this is especially important: as a disciple of Christ (and a homeschooling teacher), it is not required that you present a perfect picture of a Christian to your child, but you do want to present an authentic one: a passionate, pursuing, growing, changing, and ever-more-lovely (meaning, of course, more Christlike) one! If you are growing, believe me, your child will grow likewise! If you are stagnant, your instruction will lack that life-giving spark of authenticity that children need to be inspired to imitate you. "Do as I say, not as I do" has never produced good results as a pedagogical philosophy!

Before you get overwhelmed, let me just say this: God is already at work on this project! He has created you, your husband, and your children as unique beings, and given you to each other as the perfect influences for what He has planned. His plans are good, and He makes no mistakes!

God will use your experiences in this season of journeying with your children as part of the mix of your (and their) unique "soul soils." You aren't finished yet, and as He equips you to meet and greet the challenges of the homeschool journey, the hills, the vistas, and the valleys are all part of the process that He beautifully orchestrates to bring forth the varying expressions of Himself in you and in your children.

Like that forest soil forming, the journey is full of so many imperceptible moments and elements that no one but an omniscient, loving God could ever orchestrate. But we do have such a God, and He really is at work! He is the mover and shaper of your homeschool; you do not bear sole responsibility for outcomes! Be of good cheer, for, with Paul, I can say with certainty that "I am sure of this, that He who began a good work in you will bring it to completion at the day of Jesus Christ" Philippians 1:6 (ESV).

6.

Keep your heart with all vigilance, for from it flow the springs of life.

PROVERBS 4:23 (ESV)

Keep Your Heart

Why do many Christians decide to homeschool? Well, as we said in Section One, the presenting motives—those of which we are aware—can vary widely. Many parents become homeschoolers because of circumstances, rather than reasoned principles. But many start with a biblical conviction that impels them.

As I wrote in my introduction, those who look for Scriptural support in seeking a principled reason for the homeschooling journey most often quote Deuteronomy 6:5-9. I've bolded it in its context below.

> *You shall love the LORD your God with all your heart and with all your soul and with all your might. And these words that I command you today shall*

> *be on your heart.* ***You shall teach them diligently to your children, and shall talk of them when you sit in your house, and when you walk by the way, and when you lie down, and when you rise.*** *You shall bind them as a sign on your hand, and they shall be as frontlets between your eyes. You shall write them on the doorposts of your house and on your gates.*

It is argued that parents cannot fulfill God's mandate to diligently teach our children the ways of the Lord in this way that He commands if we send them off each day to spend most of their waking hours in another place. To those who cite this verse, it doesn't really matter what that other context might be—public, private, or Christian schools—because attendance at these places means that their children are not *with* them as they go about their everyday lives. And if they are not with them, how can they teach them in the way these verses portray: saturating their daily lives from morning until evening with the Word of God?

Since I have known many Christian parents who have managed to send their children to traditional school settings and effectively disciple, train, and parent them, I cannot agree that homeschooling is the *only way* to fulfill this command. However, homeschooling sure makes it easier in one way. We are indeed always with our kids! So, this verse has sustained me many a time, especially when I've wondered if I'm really serving them by homeschooling.

Here's the thing I want to point out, though, and it is connected to Chapter 5's insight about primarily giving your kids who you are. The passage has an underlying assumption about *what* you are teaching as you spend so much time with your children. Look again at the same passage; this time, I've emphasized a different portion.

> ***You shall love the LORD your God with all your heart and with all your soul and with all your might. And these words that I command you today shall be on your heart.*** *You shall teach them diligently to your children, and shall talk of them when you sit in your house, and when you walk by the way, and when you lie down, and when you rise. You shall bind them as a sign on your hand, and they shall be as frontlets between your eyes. You shall write them on the door posts of your house and on your gates.*

It seems to me that this passage is much more concerned with *what* is on your heart than about *where* you teach it! The exhortation to parents to teach their children diligently, day in and day out, assumes that you yourself are thinking about God's Word, living out God's Word, saturating yourself in God's Word, and being yourself transformed by God's Word. If you yourself aren't intimately acquainted with God as a person, knowing His nature and seeing His ways and relating to Him, how will you show Him to your children?

It is not primarily phonics, math, and handwriting that we are tasked to teach from morning until night. When we keep our children with us, they will become like us. As I said in Chapter 5, it is who we are (and are becoming) that will most imprint on our kids. If we lose sight of this and are content to teach primarily information or skills (even excellently), we may raise competent, contributing members of society, but there is less chance that we will raise Christians.

Parents who did not spend time with God could not successfully pass on what they themselves had no knowledge of.

The reason I am continuing this theme is not to bring condemnation—I promise! I'll say repeatedly in this book that mothering is a guilty business, and I'm sure not here to pile guilt on you. We live daily seeing the obvious ways that we fall short. We could always have prayed more, we could have been more patient, or more kind, or more diligent, or more organized, or… well, this is why mothering is a guilty business! It's all true. We could have been. I get that. But, that's not where I'm going.

The point of this chapter is to encourage you to tend the flame of your own passion for Christ. As moms, we have so many things tugging on us. This would be true even if we didn't homeschool. Women handle a lot of roles, typically, in our modern society, and most of us are also highly relational: we are daughters, wives, mothers, and friends. Sometimes, we are also bosses, employees, and co-workers. Each of those relationships brings a host of tasks, as well as opportunities to fall short. I know; I experience this every day!

But if you desire to transfer a love for God to your kids, you're going to need to carve out a spot in your daily schedule for regular times where you are one-on-one, talking to Him. You need to read your Bible. I also recommend that you be reading (or listening to) at least one spiritual book that enlarges your understanding of God or fires your passions for Him ongoing, as a regular practice. Scripture is crystal clear on this: we can't *make* disciples unless we first *are* disciples.

Let me make this point from Scripture. The speech that I have most often been asked to deliver by hosts of state homeschooling conventions is entitled "The Nearness of God is My Good." In this speech, I follow the thread of God's nearness to people as it is woven through the Old and New Testaments. God is very distant at first. He is practically unknown by His chosen people until the time of Moses, except by a handful of men. Through Moses, God reveals in a very short time much about His character. Central to this epoch of revelation is His holiness. Over and over, God reveals through displays of power that He dictates how He will and will not be approached.

A most memorable moment comes when all of Israel is gathered to hear from God at the foot of Mount Sinai. The very voice of God thunders the ten commandments, and the people are terrified. To be near to God is, for them, a fearful thing! Notice their response (Exodus 20:18-19, ESV):

> *"Now when all the people saw the thunder and the flashes of lightning and the sound of the trumpet and the mountain smoking, the people were afraid and trembled, and they stood far off and said to Moses, "You speak to us, and we will listen; but do not let God speak to us, lest we die."*

For the rest of their time wandering in the wilderness, Moses operated as a mediator, drawing near to God himself, but allowing the people to stand afar. It was Moses who spoke to God face to face on the Mountain and in the Tent of Meeting. Moses' face was radiant and his faith was firm as a result. But after he passed on to glory, and after Joshua had led the Israelites into the Promised Land and then passed away, the generation that followed those who had been taught in the wilderness fell away from God. We read in Judges 2:7-10 (ESV):

> *And the people served the LORD all the days of Joshua, and all the days of the elders who outlived Joshua, who had seen all the great work that*

> *the LORD had done for Israel. And Joshua the son of Nun, the servant of the LORD, died ... and all that generation also were gathered to their fathers. And there arose another generation after them* ***who did not know the LORD*** *or the work that he had done for Israel.*

Parents who did not spend time, one on one, with God could not successfully pass on what they themselves had no knowledge of: the glory, worth, and proven character of God Almighty. This is why we are to have God's Word—and a vibrant relationship with Him, purchased through the blood of Christ—on our hearts as we diligently homeschool our children. The generation who discipled those who became apostate after the death of Joshua were warned! Moses had written in Deuteronomy 4:9:

> *"Only take care, and keep your soul diligently, lest you forget the things that your eyes have seen, and lest they depart from your heart all the days of your life. Make them known to your children and your children's children..."*

This exhortation is echoed in that proof passage for homeschooling: we parents simply must find a way to keep our relationship with God, and passionate love for God, burning brightly if we wish to disciple our children. Unlike the Israelites of yore, God has purchased for us with the blood of His Son the ability to have Him actually indwelling us. Yes, He remains holy, but His lovingkindness as displayed by Christ in life and in death should beckon us to intimacy and dependence. Let us embrace the exhortation of Hebrews 4:15-16:

> *For we do not have a high priest who is unable to sympathize with our weaknesses, but one who in every respect has been tempted as we are, yet without sin. Let us then with confidence draw near to the throne of grace, that we may receive mercy and find grace to help in time of need.*

When Scott and I went on the road teaching about homeschooling and parenting as a couple, we felt that our best recommendation as speakers was the fruit of our years of homeschooling: our six godly children. Since they all had busy lives at home, they couldn't exactly come with us and speak to audiences all over the country to commend us as teachers, so we decided to do the next best thing. We produced a video that we entitled (from its inception) "What Do They Remember?"

The initial design for this video was simple and straightforward: I planned to plunk down each of our young adults in front of a camera and have them reminisce about the good and the bad of their homeschooling lives. I wanted them to relate the major influences and memories that had stuck with them. (At this time, they were aged 15 to 25.)

Discipleship is at the core of the homeschooling process, whether we realize it or not.

I had a stock list of about six questions that I asked each of them, and then I just let them talk, without any preparation or direction from me, in front of the camera. Their answers about the things they remembered changed my comprehension of what really matters in homeschooling forever!

While I vividly remember poring over curricula, going to conventions, reading books on homeschooling, and painstakingly, diligently planning hundreds of lessons that were taught, corrected, and retaught over my 22 years of homeschooling, they did not. Not one of them—even when prompted—wanted to talk about those things.

What they remembered (and wanted to talk about on video) were things like special foods—grilled cheese sandwiches with ketchup on Sundays, or the coffee cake that Dad made each week, or sundaes on Sundays. They remembered that we read aloud as a family each night, and that significant moments involving Scott's or my reactions and responses to key events crystallized for them who God was and who they were in Him.

For instance, my husband's tight, consistent focus on mirroring the character of God the Father to his children in different situations was remembered by several of them. My never playing favorites was cited by the daughter with whom I'd had the most struggles. Our then college-aged son talked about how the transfer from home to a liberal, secular college wasn't hard because he'd learned that his siblings and parents were sinners at home, so at school he didn't really get surprised by the presence of sin—though its increased volume among his peers saddened him greatly.

They remembered consistency, and humor, and servanthood… and as they each reminisced about how they came to Christ in answer to a question about how they were saved, each story was different. Not one of their salvation stories featured either Scott or myself actually praying the sinner's prayer with them. God had met each of them personally, profoundly, and at a time when we were not present.

However, all of them did say that, in the moment of the dawning light, they knew where they were in their story because they knew from our teachings about the Bible what was what. They knew the story of mankind. They knew that they and their parents were sinners, and that the wages of sin was death. And, they knew to Whom they could turn when all that became personally, unbearably painful to them.

One cried out for salvation as the result of a nightmare, another from the depths of a deep depression, and a third sought a way out of the trap of years of believing lies. One of them was converted when her Savior spoke to her through a peer at a youth retreat to say, "I love you." It shattered her heart in a single instant, and then He made her whole. Imperfect as we were, Scott and I tried to be consistent in our message of the gospel of grace. And God honored that, even though we did not get a front row seat at His work in our children's hearts sometimes.

In all of our parenting, and in all of our homeschooling, the truth is that discipleship is at the core of the process, whether we recognize it or not. What happens to so many of us women is that the busyness of mothering, housekeeping, serving in the church, tending to our husband's needs, and teaching lessons that match the check-off boxes to which we are legally beholden—all these and more crowd out the "most important thing": sitting at our Savior's feet and tending the flame of our passion for Him so that we can faithfully share Him with the next generation.

If you do nothing else right in your entire homeschool career, do this one thing: keep your heart diligently. It is the wellspring of your life, and the source of the most important difference you will ever make in your children's lives.

7.

The teaching of the wise is a fountain of life, that one may turn away from the snares of death.

Proverbs 13:14 (ESV)

Cross-Eyed Parenting

Homeschooling is parent-concentrate. One of the big ideas that I'm trying to convey in this section is that, because we are with our kids so much, who we are day to day really matters. As I've said in the previous two chapters, who you are will most impact your children, and keeping your heart passionate for the glory of God in Christ is the surest way to help them become faith-filled, Christian disciples.

I want to say it one more way by presenting one more analogy, followed by a couple of examples from my own family's life.

Here's the analogy: we parents are like the top bowl of a three-tiered fountain, as pictured on the following page. As you see, water first enters the topmost, smallest bowl from the fountain head, which is Christ by analogy. It then overflows that bowl, and cascades down into the second, larger one. Eventually, that bowl, too, overflows, and water pours into the third, largest bowl.

When Christians decide to homeschool, one of our fondest hopes is that our children will grow up to excel in godliness and influence for Christ in the world. We pray that the careful instruction and nurturing that we can give them in our homes will one day enable our children to go out into the world and lead God-glorifying, productive lives that influence those around them for good.

The fountain pictured above represents how life-giving godliness is produced in such a way that it affects the world. If the top bowl represents the parents of a family, then the larger, middle bowl represents the nuclear family: children and parents together (or, your homeschool). The third and largest bowl represents the general population—your neighborhood, broader community, and the world at large.

If our dreams for our children are to come true, we simply must make time for devotional lives. Christ is overflowing love, as well as the water of life, and only in daily concourse with Him, where we behold Him and interact with Him, will our bowls be filled to overflowing with a humble, gracious demeanor that pours out the love of Christ—with all its power, sacrifice, mercy, and grace.

Arguably, God's love for mankind was expressed most succinctly in the death of Christ on the cross (1 Peter 3:18). By keeping the cross of Jesus Christ firmly in our view daily, we become cross-eyed parents in two senses of the term:

1. We daily remember that we are flawed creatures. Sin has made our vision crippled, and our visage marred.
2. But keeping our eyes on His cross also heals and changes us to become Christ-centered parents who can raise world-changers to the glory of God.

To become cross-eyed (in the good sense), we need to daily preach the gospel—the good news—to ourselves. In doing so, morning by morning, we start our time with God with meditations on the three central elements of the Good News:

1. The holiness of God.
    - We consider that He is set apart, gloriously beautiful, and wholly differ-

ent in substance than we are (Isaiah 55:8-9).
- We can consider ways that He is perfect, powerful, and unapproachable by anyone who is less pure than He is (Hebrews 12:18-29).
- We can soak in the realization that God is a happy being who does not need us to serve Him (Acts 17:24-25).

2. The sinfulness of sin.
   - Here we want to meditate on specific sins that we ourselves have committed since just yesterday!
   - We want to open our eyes to our faults, trying to see them as our holy God does (Psalm 5:4-6). Our reason for doing so is to be healed (1 John 1:7-10). Rather than trying to hid our faults from God, ourselves, or others, we should seek to bring them into the light.
   - If possible, we want to look for underlying idols of the heart that tempt us to replace God as the object of our affections and the Lord of our lives (Jeremiah 2:13).
3. The amazing nature of grace.
   - God saw our need before we did, and sent His Son to die in our place, taking all the wrath that each of those sins we identified deserved (1 Peter 3:18; 1 John 3:1; 2 Corinthians 5:21). We could probably meditate all day on the perfections of Christ, and His sacrifice, but we move on.
   - We take our sins to Christ and confess them. We then receive the pardon He offers for them and are both humbled and grateful (Romans 5:11; John 1:16).
   - We are freshly amazed by God and filled with a love for Him that is renewed during this process (Romans 5:11; John 1:16).

We emerge from such a quiet time amazed, strengthened, and humbled. He loves us despite our fallen, broken, sinful natures. He extends mercy and grace to us daily, and turns all of our defeats to victories!

Having thus filled our own bowls, we can overflow to our children and fill our families with grace. In having remembered that we need forgiveness for actual sins committed so recently, we can remind ourselves that the sins that our children (and husbands) will commit this day have likewise been paid for by Jesus' death on the cross. Cross-eyed wives and mothers remember that the ground is level at the foot of that cross.

We do not stand on high moral ground with relation to our husbands or children. We need their forgiveness for our faults, and they need ours for theirs. None of us is perfect, but all of us are growing towards perfection because God has promised to take His children by the hand and lead them to that goal.

Though we are always imperfect, and will have good days and bad days, God promises that sanctified, unified, and growing people who delight in the grace of God and extend it willingly to others will overflow that middle fountain bowl to give love, refreshment, and the Good News to a sin-sick world. John 13:34-35 records this command and promise of Jesus:

> *A new commandment I give to you, that you love one another: just as I have loved you, you also are to love one another. By this all people will know that you are my disciples, if you have love for one another.*

One of the ways that we parent with our eyes on His cross is to present an authentic image of the Father to our children. My husband, Scott, was a master at keeping his eye out for opportunities to image God's character to our children. Here are just two stories that illustrate the opportunity that cross-eyed parents have of putting the gospel on full display. (They are, of course, told with our children's permission.)

Story #1: David and the Taz Flash

Our son, David (age 5-6), went over to his best friend, Lincoln's, house one day to play. While there, he saw and coveted an action figure: a bright, compelling Taz Flash®. By day's end, he had stolen Taz Flash from Lincoln's house. Then, he hid Taz in a sock under his pillow for a few days, taking it out to play with it from time to time.

Over the next few days, though David was eaten up by guilt, he was also afraid to confess his sin to his parents because he knew that he had broken several of the Ten Commandments in this matter. In our family, there were pretty severe physical consequences awaiting those who broke these commandments, as David well knew. However, by God's grace, David's tender conscience was stronger than his fear of his father, and finally, he approached Scott to confess his sins.

What happened next surprised David, and he has never forgotten it. Scott did not choose to punish David in the customary way after he confessed. Scott forgave him, and told him the reason why. Scott explained that while he was responsible to administer justice and train David through appropriate punishments, and while it would be just to punish David for his grievous sins of covetousness and theft, Scott wanted David to know that Father God's heart towards His children is a merciful One.

He shared that he, Scott, David's father, was an undeserving sinner. He, Scott, had been forgiven many grievous sins because of the death of Jesus, God's own Son. And now he, Scott, extended a father's forgiveness to his son, not because David deserved it, but as an object lesson in unlooked-for mercy, because the Bible teaches that, "If we confess our sins, he is faithful and just to forgive us our sins and to cleanse us from all unrighteousness" 1 John 1:9 (ESV). David was amazed by grace that day, and the image of Father God that was imprinted on his young soul was a lasting one!

Story #2: Mike and the Broken Window

In this case, it was a lack of wisdom rather than a moral failing. Seven-year-old Mike had a brand new slingshot, and he wanted to do some practicing. It was fall, and cold outside, but we had a long, skinny mudroom that separated our main house from our garage. It was 22' long and Mike thought it was a perfect place for target practice! He set up some boots as a base, and then perched some tin cans on those, right in front of the 4' X 8' Thermopane window. Yep, Mike's first shot missed and shattered the window. The repair cost $80.00.

To become cross-eyed, we need to daily preach the gospel—the good news—to ourselves.

In our family, we had a lot of kids, so money had to stretch. Our kids weren't given many treats beyond what they saved to buy out of their allowances. Mike had a weekly allowance of $1.00 that could be used to pay us back for the window he'd broken. We felt like our kids needed to learn about consequences for foolishness, so, for 12 weeks of that fall season, week after week, Scott would hand Mike his allowance, and Mike would hand it back to Scott in payment for his window debt. He did it manfully and cheerfully, but it did cost him. And 80 weeks was going to be a long time!

Then, Christmas morning came, and we were opening stockings. In Mike's stocking, there was an envelope. It was the bill for the window, which was stamped "Paid in Full," and pictured a cross below this stamp. Mike looked at his dad, astonished. Scott told him that he, Mike's father, had paid the debt, and he told him why.

He began by reminding Mike that this was Jesus' birthday. It was the day that we remember that Christ left Heaven for our sakes to take on human flesh, which was a huge act of sacrificial love for us.

He then said something like this: "Mike, I'm a sinner. I have never deserved any mercy. But God sent King Jesus to be born in a manger, and then to die on the cross, in order to pay the debt that I could never have paid. My debt was far greater than yours was, son. So, it cost God more than my payment of your debt has. But on this, Christ's birthday, be released from your debt and rejoice, Mike! And never forget what God has done for us sinners."

It was another of those moments: the imprinting on a young soul of who his father was, and what God the Father is like. It was Scott's overflowing fountain!

David never forgot that display of mercy. Mike never forgot that moment when his debt was cancelled. These weren't the only opportunities Scott took to communicate God's image to our children, but they stand out in our family culture as some of the richest. Both of these now-grown and married men are purposefully passing on the image of Father God to their children.

As a homeschooling mother of daughters, I had my share of chances to display mercy for chores left undone or forgotten, forgiveness for mistakes made, and loving corrections for unlovely behavior. What I have learned from the years of seeking first the face of Christ for my own sins, and then reaching out with gospel-motivated grace to my children, is that it's not hard to find common ground with my children at the foot of the cross of Christ.

As I grew in cross-eyed parenting skills over the years, whenever I had occasion to adjust my children, I learned to look first for a way that I, too, needed similar forgiveness. Did my son forget a chore? Well, when was the last time I forgot to do something that Scott asked of me? Or when was the last time that I failed to obey my Lord? Did my daughter speak rudely to her sister, and snatch her toy? Well, when was the last time that I spoke sharply and acted selfishly? For any given instance of shortcoming in my children or husband, I don't have to look far to find heart attitudes and unlovely actions mirrored in myself!

It was the regular review of the gospel message, applied to my real sins at the feet of my Lord on a daily basis, that kept my heart soft and humble enough to learn to identify with my children and become a cross-eyed parent. It was Scott's steadfast desire to display the character of God the Father to his children that helped him respond so winningly to the situations we faced as parents.

Of course, we did not do these things perfectly. My children could tell you many, many stories of moments when I became angry with them instead of considering my own offenses with God. There were plenty of times when I was not patient, or made hasty, uncharitable, self-righteous judgments. However, my children's testimony is that Scott and I presented an authentic (note: not a perfect) example of applying the gospel to our own lives, and that this had a transforming effect on them.

You may think that bringing your children into the inner room of your soul, to witness your own weakness and need to repent to God, would cause them to lose respect for you. We have found the opposite to be true. When we showed our children how it looks to humble yourself and repent to God, then rejoice in His forgiveness, they grew in respect for us and chose to imitate our example. They also saw from the beginning how to deal with their own sin, and how the gospel was powerful enough to transform their own little guilty miseries into redeemed gladness. Thanks be to God, whose strength really was displayed in our weakness!

And note: these family stories are still being told. In this book, they are now overflowing our own family's basin and going out to many. They are impacting readers like yourself, who then will seek grace for their own situations unique to their own families as God gives opportunities to be cross-eyed parents. Who would have known that one family's pursuit of God could overflow so widely and impact so many people?

8.

"All things are lawful," but not all things are helpful.
"All things are lawful," but not all things build up.

1 CORINTHIANS 10:23 (ESV)

Training in Liberty

One of the most fruitful parenting (and educational) paradigms that I ever learned came from Gregg Harris. (You may recognize Gregg's name, as he is the father of Brett and Alex Harris, co-authors of *Do Hard Things*.) Back in the 1980's Gregg criss-crossed the nation while presenting weekend seminars to help give parents a vision for homeschooling. I attended one of these seminars in 1985 and caught my vision for family renewal in the context of homeschooling there.

That weekend, Gregg told a little story to illustrate what he meant by a parenting principle that he called "training in liberty." He taught that parents need to be aware of how much freedom they are giving their children. As those who keep watch for the good of children's souls, we need to see to it that they can manage their liberties well (by which is meant "to the glory of God"). Our freedoms as Christians seem boundless (as the Corinthians whom Paul quoted in the passage on the previous page indicated), but as part of our discipling efforts, we are to teach our children how to choose wisely the things that "build up."

Since then, Scott and I have applied this paradigm to so many areas of parenting and homeschooling that I've long taken any possible opportunity of passing it along.

Here's Gregg's illustrative story that explains the general principle, as I received it years ago (from memory):

> *A boy was given a ball for his fifth birthday. It was a big, red, India rubber ball. Immediately after presents were all opened, the boy wanted to play with his ball. So, his mother helped him find his jacket and sent him out into the back yard of their suburban house with very specific instructions.*
>
> *"Joey," she said, "You can play with the ball all you want to in our yard. But, if the ball goes over the line into our neighbor's yard, I want you to please come and get me. I'll get the ball back for you."*
>
> *Mom went into the house, and Joey began to play with his ball. His back yard was a typical, small suburban one. It backed up to similar, small yards on two sides and in the back. There was nothing separating those yards, save for a few bushes here and there and a small difference in the height of the grass that had been more or less recently mowed. Certainly, there was no danger or harm presented to Joey if he crossed those boundaries.*
>
> *This is what he thought about after the ball went over one of those lines after about ten minutes' play. There it was... about ten feet over the line. He looked around. The house seemed far away. He would have to go into it, and find his mom, and then wait for her to come. It seemed like it would just be so much easier to go and get his own ball! So, he did.*
>
> *Mom knew his temptation. She was watching out the window to grab the teachable moment for training in liberty. As soon as Joey stepped across that line to retrieve his ball, Mom was out the door, and calling her errant*

son to herself.

"Joey, what did Mommy tell you?" she demanded in a stern voice.

"To come and get you if my ball went over the line?" asked Joey.

"Right. And did you?"

"No, Mom. I didn't." Joey mumbled, and felt ashamed.

His mom was firm, but kind. She reminded him of the rule, and said that he really must obey it, even if he did not see a good reason for it. Joey nodded, and ran off to resume playing. Mom went back into the house.

Ten minutes later, the ball had bounced in a different direction, and into another neighbor's yard. Joey sighed. He looked back at the house and could see Mom doing dishes at the kitchen window—and watching. He sighed again, and reluctantly walked back to get her. She came right out, got the ball, and praised him for a good choice.

Over the next week or two, Joey went out to play almost daily with his beloved ball. At first, it was a tussle to obey his mom's rule. But, after about a week, he realized that she meant it, and began to be really okay with going to get her, though he still didn't understand why.

After two weeks, he was cheerfully and reliably obeying the rule. An entire four days elapsed without one infraction, even when Mom was watching from windows where Joey couldn't see her.

At the end of that week, Mom called Joey to her, and said, "Well done, good and faithful son. You have obeyed me consistently and have called me to get your ball whenever it rolled over a line, though you did not understand why. Now, enter into the joy of your mother! You may now play in the front yard with your ball, where there is a busy street, and danger for you from cars. I know that, if your ball rolls out of the yard and into the street, you will come and get me so that I can safely retrieve your ball!"

There are several principles here that serve parents really well. One is the emphasis that it places on the responsibility of parents to set the amount of liberty that a child exercises. This is our job! And if we do not do it well, the child is given too much liberty and will not be able to manage it. Imagine a child who is told that he can set his own limits for watching TV, or playing with video games? Or that he can entirely manage his own academic lessons from the tender age of five? Or that your young children can all decide when it's time for bed?

It is the responsibility of parents to set the amount of liberty that a child exercises.

Scott and I got into a situation more than once as parents where we had given a child too much liberty, and they were either overwhelmed, frightened, or sinning regularly as a result. One example of this was the season when Scott was busy with work and told one of our sons to regularly check his math assignments, and then rework those he got wrong, and then bring to his father the ones that he still did not understand. Scott would work with him then. It was three months later that Scott found out that this son had done his homework daily, but never checked it. The work was riddled with errors, and the child was getting into a deep hole of confusion about math concepts as a result.

Or, there was the time when our daughter developed a selfish and arrogant attitude about those who did not, like her, own and love horses. We discovered that she was being rude and dismissive towards all girls in our new church who did not share her passion for riding. After trying to correct her in less drastic ways, we decided that her liberties needed serious adjustment, and determined that we would sell her horse and take her out of riding altogether. It was one of the toughest decisions we ever made as parents, but it was done in love and in light of this principle!

In situations like this, we found that it was sweet to go to a child who was erring and say, "Son (or Daughter), I am sorry. It is my fault. It is my job to control the amount of liberty you can have so that you can successfully grow into skillful living. In this case, I have given you too much liberty. We need to dial back the amount of freedom you have until you can manage it well!"

You can use this principle of training in liberty in a hundred different ways as you go through your homeschooling journey. When they are little, for instance, you can use it to help your kids learn to keep toys and other belongings in order.

Let's say that you struggle daily with toys being strewn all over your floors. Start with an analysis: maybe it's your fault, really. For instance, are there too many toys for them to keep neat because storage is lacking? If so, you need to establish a place for everything, so that everything may be put into its place.

But, now let's say that there are good places on a shelf for toys, but your daughter owns twenty, and none of them actually make it back to that shelf, day after day. What you do according to the principle of training in liberty is this: you get a big box, label it "Susie's Toys," and come to her with your apology about having allowed her too much liberty. With her agreement, you have her choose the five toys that she'll keep out on the shelf in the upcoming month. You and she put the remaining fifteen toys and dolls into the box and store it.

Over the next month, you train Susie on keeping her five toys neatly on the shelf. Like that mom in Gregg's story, you have to put in some energy here! You must faithfully teach, correct, and train Susie to keep the five toys in good order. You must define clearly what "good order" means. Is she allowed to leave the toys out when you call her for lunch? Or are you going to require her to put each toy back on the shelf each and every time she is done playing with it? (In our house, we settled on doing a morning and evening pick-up of all toys and school supplies, but you might choose a different standard.)

If she does well during the first part of the monthly training, great. If she does poorly, warn her that she may still have too much liberty, and she'll have fewer toys to keep track of at the end of the month. If this discipline tempts her to rebel, you'll need to deal with her heart attitudes towards her authority as a separate issue.

At the end of a month's time, retrieve the box with Susie's toys in it. If she's done well, allow her to exchange any five toys out and to increase her liberty by choosing an additional two toys to take charge of (and play with). If she's done poorly, reduce the number of toys that she'll have access to, but allow her to change out and keep out any three toys she chooses.

In all this, you must remain kind, gentle, and encouraging. Putting aside bad attitudes about your authority for now, and focusing attention on the actual skill of keeping belongings in order, your restrictions on her liberty are not to be a punishment for Susie's lack of skill. You are training her by giving her only as much liberty as she can handle. This is very key to this principle: it is not punitive! Posture yourself as being in her corner, ready to help, and *eager* to give her ever *more* liberty.

You can easily see how to use the same principle on a host of life skills that you'll need to train your children in as the years unfold. Such things as time spent with friends (or, actually, doing any desired activity, like playing video games or attending sports events) while balancing other responsibilities, like chores and schoolwork, leap to mind. In that case, you'll be limiting the enjoyable activities according to the way your child handles responsibilities.

As your child gets older, issues arise about the kinds of friends teens hang with. If their liberty (choosing their own friends) begins to adversely affect them, then you (the parent) can apologize for giving them too much liberty, and (hopefully with their agreement) scale back the time that they are spending with poorly chosen friends.

This idea applies to choosing music, clothing, or TV programs—if your child isn't able to choose well and wisely for herself, then you have erred in giving her too much liberty. She has not yet developed enough discernment or self-discipline to handle her liberties well and you, as responsible parents, must scale them back (gently, in the fear of God, and hopefully with the child's full understanding of this principle and agreement).

Driving or other privileges—visiting friends, babysitting, any kind of job during high school—all these can be governed by the same principle of training in handling liberties: we don't want to give our kids more than they can responsibly manage! The things that they must do must come first; the things that they wish to do are privileges given to responsible young people.

In all of this, remember: the beauty is that you get to sit far more often in their cheering section than in their critics' corner! You can (and should) verbally express time and again how eager you are for your children to demonstrate competence in an area so that you can responsibly trust them with more liberty in that area. They need to know that you are *for* them. Tell them so, and demonstrate it by celebrations of key milestones along the way!

One final word: it's certainly easier to begin training in liberty—and putting this approach into both practice and your family's culture—when children are small. But, young or old, we humans don't like our wills crossed! And, we tend to doubt that our authority figures are really for us when they are telling us "no."

Let's think together about those times when taking away liberties will initially spark anger and/or resentment. You need to be okay with this, in terms of *your* choices. You stand before God, first and last, as the gatekeeper of your child's soul, so you'll need to take some heat sometimes. What helps is to realize that rebellious children are really fighting with God, not you, as long as you're truly acting on God's behalf. (Passages like Exodus 16:8, 1 Samuel 8:7, Luke 10:16, and Romans 13:2 clearly demonstrate this truth. You might need to gently remind them of that sometimes.)

Narrowing down liberties often becomes a relief to your overburdened child!

Try not to personalize what isn't personal when your children respond badly to reasonable restrictions. Since they are tussling with the Almighty, be with them in that tussle—not with them against God, but with them in the sense that you are sympathetic to the pain of being a sinful human being who is wrongly beating his tiny fists against the loving lordship of the Master of the universe. As they sense your compassion, love, and identification with their situation, they'll usually turn to you in their misery after a bit of fussing, as long as you don't give in.

When we took away our daughter's horse, she remained angry with us for three years. Her idolatry of horses was deeply entrenched by the time we addressed it. But, over time and especially after she became a Christian, she came to see that we really had acted out of love. Since then, she has often thanked us for what we did, and told us that it was the right choice; she actually told us that we had acted well—she had been in a bad place, and we had rescued her.

It may surprise you to find (especially with children who have been taught this over the years, or are still young) that narrowing down liberties actually becomes a relief to your overburdened child! Our daughter is not the only one who has come back to thank us for having stepped in and saved her from the pain and/or the embarrassment of being in too deep to handle her liberties. What a joy it is when that is the reaction, and how God must feel the same when we turn to him in a similar way!

Parenting in the fear of God involves training our children to faithfully handle both their responsibilities and their leisure time. Keeping those in balance in our modern society is a skill that takes years to master. I hope that this one principle will aid you in your quest to do the very best job that an imperfect sinner can do of helping your child to grow in both liberty and responsibility!

Remember, though, that without God's help, no parenting principles are worth much. Please do ask the Father to help you to see how you can use this tool in joyful submission to and dependence on Him.

9.

In one of my favorite movies, Sabrina, *the plot revolves around an extremely wealthy family, whose eldest son, Linus, is falling in love with the chauffeur's daughter, Sabrina. In one scene, they are on Nantucket, and she is taking pictures of a house that he wants to sell.*
She asks, looking out the window, "Which views do you want?"
He waves a hand, "All of them."
She stops, tilts her head, smiles, and says, "More isn't always better, Linus. Sometimes, it's just more."
Handing him the camera, she says, "Pick one."
He looks through the camera viewer, looking for something to focus on, and as a result gains a whole new insight because the camera focuses his attention on a lighthouse keeper.

More Isn't Always Better

I hear this dialogue in my head so often when talking with beginning homeschooling moms. There are so many options for us these days, and so many different competing homeschooling programs! And, naturally, the people who create homeschooling products have done so because they think that they offer value and merit. Thus, they typically market their work using such words as "very important" or "a key feature of any curriculum" or "the answer to your problem."

There isn't enough time in one's year to make use of all the good programs out there. And once you choose one that fits you well, there is still some tailoring to be done so that it will perfectly fit your unique students. One skill that we must develop as homeschoolers is the ability to choose among good options, and then rest—at least for a time—in those choices. (I say "for a time" because seasons do change, and children do grow through phases. Within families, what may work great for your first child may really not work for your second or fourth one. So, yearly reassessment is necessary.)

Part of this choosing is made easier when we identify goals for the season we are in, as discussed in the early chapters of this book. For instance, if we have decided that sports practices and competitions are highly valued, then we won't be enrolling our children in the chess club or debate society of our local co-op group. If our child is musically inclined, we may choose not to give him computer science courses, even if others say strongly that this is "important for life." As discussed in earlier chapters, if you can distill a central mission statement for your family each year, then assess at the beginning, middle, and end of your school year how well you feel you are tracking with those goals, you'll save a lot of self-doubt and guilty feelings.

New homeschoolers often become anxious because they feel uncertain about making key choices.

Women who are new to homeschooling often express the anxiety that, because of their inexperience, they don't know how to make key choices. You are not alone! We moms care so much about doing the right thing by our kids (or we wouldn't be homeschooling in the first place). For many, our perplexity arises from the fact that we never were homeschooled ourselves, so we have no internal compass that will help us sense if we're on the right path. This tempts us to answer our concerns with, "Well, I'll just do it *all* so I don't miss *anything*!"

Added to this dynamic is the fact that new homeschoolers are at the start of their homeschooling career and there are no mistakes in it—yet. We really want to do well! Whether we feel like we lack key information or have misgivings about the advice we've received doesn't matter. We don't want to make mistakes—even understandable ones—and become bad teachers. So, the tendency for beginning homeschoolers is to try to do too much, and then wonder how it is that anyone continues to homeschool for twenty weeks, let alone twenty years!

Part of the answer to this dynamic is more fully fleshed out in Chapter 29, entitled "It's About Commitment." There I dwell on the idea that your homeschooling efforts are—like all other Kingdom works—from start to finish, in the Lord God's hands. He knows your frame; He knows your skill set; He knows your marriage, your finances, and your kids. In fact, He sovereignly chose you for them and them for you!

God is at work in your homeschool; it is His role to be the provider, enabler, and sustainer of your efforts. He ultimately directs both the process and the product of your homeschool. As you go along and gain experience, you may begin to feel more confident in your choice, which will comfort you.

But life has a way of throwing us curve balls, and I've come to believe that one of God's purposes for taking us on the homeschooling journey is to school us in happy dependence. From its earliest days, American culture has valued independence (and later, the self-made man). We are a can-do society, whose booksellers stock thousands of how-to titles. So this may be a new thought to you: did you know that you were created to be *happily* dependent on God?

Before the Fall, God created Adam and Eve as dependent creatures, with Himself as provider and sustainer. When Eve chose the fruit, she chose self-dependence (which is the same as independence from God). When we get into parenting and homeschooling, we often encounter tasks and problems that are too big for us to handle. We struggle to juggle priorities, we labor to get everything done and fail, we seek to make wise choices but make mistakes instead. Children get sick, or can't do their work through learning disabilities, or bewilder us with their bad attitudes and stubborn wills.

All of these trials and obstacles to the "happy homeschool" are tools in our Father's hands. They send us to Him, which is right where we belong! He is so eager to give us what we need, and to bring solutions that we would never think of on our own. God is the giver; we were created to receive with joy and gratitude.

The more we embrace happy dependence on Him, the easier the journey becomes, and the more we can love it. Instead of dreading the next bend in the road, we can begin to look with expectation. As new obstacles appear, we can think, "Huh. Look at this problem. I can't solve it. I wonder how God is going to provide what I need for this one!" Then we can walk on, looking to Him for His certain provision.

Your husband is a great resource for you on your journey, and again, there's a whole chapter in this book[1] about making him your bulwark against the doubts and guilt that our enemies—the world, the flesh, and the devil—typically throw at us as we travel the homeschool roads and make choices.

Whether through our own thoughts or through the words of others (well-meaning or not), after we've made our choices we will be confronted with the reality that it is always true that we could do *more*: pray longer, work harder, be neater, choose more wisely, etc. This is part and parcel of being limited, mortal, fallen human beings. It is a result of this fallen world that we have to work for the blessings that were warped by the curse when Adam and Eve chose to walk independently from their God.

Resting in our creatureliness and trusting in God's ability to get through to us with His will for our kids and their lessons is a tremendous skill! Such trust becomes a place of refuge from the driving, prideful, or guilty urges to do more and more. Part of tapping into God's sustaining grace for homeschooling involves our ability to recognize our real limitations and to be willing to leave well enough alone. I believe that the best way to do that is to pray and talk with your husband about which programs to use for a year or so (and which to leave for another time) and then to stick with that choice for the appropriate season by resting in God's unfailing love and grace.

Psalm 127:1-5 (ESV) contains much wisdom in this area. Note the connection between building our "house" (directly representing building our families, here) and resting in God's grace for both the process and the outcome.

> *Unless the LORD builds the house, those who build it labor in vain. Unless the LORD watches over the city, the watchman stays awake in vain. It is in vain that you rise up early and go late to rest, eating the bread of anxious toil; for he gives to his beloved sleep. Behold, children are a heritage from the LORD, the fruit of the womb a reward. Like arrows in the hand of a warrior are the children of one's youth. Blessed is the man who fills his quiver with them! He shall not be put to shame when he speaks with his enemies in the gate.*

Sabrina has it right. Though we Americans are wealthy in the number of opportunities we have when making educational choices for ourselves and our kids, "More isn't always better. Sometimes, it's just more."

1 See Chapter 11: The Husband Suitable for You.

10.

Oil and perfume make the heart glad, and the sweetness of a friend comes from his earnest counsel.

PROVERBS 27:9 (ESV)

But as it is, God arranged the members in the body, each one of them, as he chose.

1 CORINTHIANS 12:18 (ESV)

Who Are Your Best Friends?

I was talking with a fellow homeschooling mom, Yvonne, one day about the frequency of our co-op meetings, and she casually said, in the context of our discussion, "Of course, we always want our husbands and children to be our best friends..."

I'm not sure quite what she said next, because this fragment went to straight to my heart and I stopped listening. I realized instantly that what she had said was not an "of course" to me. I really wasn't on the same page as she was. I didn't really have it firmly fixed in my heart that my husband and children *could* be my best friends.

If you had asked me, before Yvonne had spoken these words, whom I considered to be my best friends, my mind would have ranged through people like her: other homeschooling moms, or church ladies, or neighbors—women whom I knew and loved, some of whom now lived at a distance.

While Scott and I have had a great marriage and began as best friends, somehow by then I would not have thought of him first if someone had posed this question to me out of the blue. By this time we were deep into the family-building years, and we were more a team than "best friends." And even if Scott had made the list, I certainly didn't think of my kids as being candidates for "best friend" status!

What's even more interesting about my own story is that, when Yvonne said these words, I had long felt lost in the crowd of faces at my large and vibrant church. It made *no* sense that this should be so! I was in step with the central vision and theology of my church, involved in serving and the youth programs, and regularly attended the large support group of homeschoolers that our church sponsored. Weekly, 2,500 people or more attended there. One would have thought—and I certainly did—that it shouldn't be very hard to find a handful of kindred spirits with whom I could be best buddies. Yet, so it had proved!

I had been a member of my church for about five years when Yvonne uttered her statement. I had tried hard to make close friends, and I had many warm acquaintances, but for some reason that I could not explain, I had no "best friends." I consistently felt the lack of women in my life who sought me out, who invited me over on the spur of the moment, or who shared their confidences with me. I was pretty sure that there was nothing unusually wrong with me. Rather, I simply felt that I hadn't discovered many people with whom I "clicked." In the past, I'd enjoyed such close friendships, but not in this church, and not for five long years. It had often puzzled me, and I had felt lonely and sad about it more than once.

Friendship involves investment. One has to spend time with others in order to forge a bond. Friends have shared experiences, and best friends have lots of them. Friends have shared views of life and God, or know how to respect their differences when they don't. Friends love one another from their hearts, and care about the details of their lives. They are tuned in to the hopes, the disappointments, the desires, the triumphs, and, yes, even the sins, of those closest to them.

When Yvonne said, "Of course, we always want our husbands and children to be our best friends..." something clicked into place. I suddenly saw why God had not allowed my heart to be satisfied with close friendships with other women at church. He had already chosen my best friends for the next season of my life, and for me, He had decided that they were to be found inside my own home. He wanted me to press into my own family, and give them the time, lavish the care, and devote my full attention to winning them as my best friends.

You can only have so many best friends. The maintenance of a close friendship consumes a lot of time and emotions. I think this is especially true for women. We need to touch bases verbally, to ask and hear and tell how we are doing, what's new, and what we're thinking about. Guys often bond by doing stuff in groups; women tend to relate more intimately one-on-one, or in very small groups of trusted friends.

So, as Yvonne went on with our discussion about co-op that day, I missed what she said next. And, over the month or so that followed, I kept hearing her words repeated in my mind and questions came. Did I want to make my husband and children my friends? What would that even look like? Did it mean that I couldn't have women friends? Would my family love me back as friends? What did God's Word say about all this? These thoughts and a variety of emotions jostled in my heart.

Did I want to make my husband and children my friends?

After a season of prayer and mulling, though, I decided that I was with Yvonne, heart and soul. *Of course I wanted to make my husband and children my best friends!* Whom did I love more? With whom did I spend more time? In whom was I more heavily invested? Whose details of daily life, hopes, dreams, and sorrows did I care more about? If these were the substance of friendships—of human intimacy—then yes! It was a no-brainer! I wanted to make my husband and children my best friends for keeps. So in response, I actively changed my focus.

The first benefit that I felt from reorienting myself towards actively building *friendships* with the members of my family was that my new efforts dovetailed with my other daily pursuits. I didn't need to carve out time to get together with my family. They were already present! I didn't need to work hard at figuring out things that would delight them, or find enough time to listen to their thoughts, or seek ways to serve them better. It wasn't hard to pray for them, or to discover practical ways to serve them. I had worked along at all these means of building friendships with the ladies at church for years with very little intimacy resulting. Now, it seemed so easy and fruitful. All it took was effort, and I was glad to be making that for their sakes!

Another early benefit was that I enjoyed a renewed love for my home, my husband, and my children. Serving family as friends gave a new dimension to maintaining a pleasant, pretty, orderly environment. As conscious acts of friendship, I regularly and creatively served meals. Chores were done more to say, "I love you; have a nice day!" than to just check them off a "got to" list.

I also found that the simple pivot to treating my husband and children in some of the same ways as I would relative strangers meant that I worked harder to be careful about how I worded things and made requests. I found that I was quicker to ask rather than tell, to request rather than demand, to inquire before judging, and to seek to encourage them verbally. These are all things that I would regularly do for girlfriends; now I found myself freshly invigorated to do them for family.

Later on, after I had begun to enjoy the sweet fruits of a focus on making my family my best friends, another insight came. I suddenly realized one fine day that I was no longer lonely. It had been months since I had wondered to myself what was wrong with me, that I couldn't have (or make) intimate friends with ladies at my church. In pressing into my family friendships, I was loving and being loved in return! I realized afresh that relationships aren't primarily of our making, but are one of the good gifts of God. Psalm 68:6a, NIV, says "God sets the lonely in families..." While I had often heard this verse referenced for ministry or adoption, I realized that for me, in a very real way, it had become true. I had been lonely, and God had directed me to set my affections on my family. Now, I was no longer lonely.

Then, there was the fun of it all! Like most homeschooling families, ours developed a distinct subculture that featured in-jokes, idioms, and many moments of witty repartee. We were bookworms who enjoyed reading aloud, quoting movies and books in conversation as riddles for each other, and engaging in long theological discussions or biblically informed analyses of the issues of the day.

My husband is a punster, and would elicit frequent chuckles and groans from us, his captive audience. Scott also is full of wholesome mischief, and fully supported the children playing practical jokes on siblings or friends with parent involvement. The children would bring their ideas to us, and we would (most often) approve and improve them or, if there was good reason, we would veto them (after explaining why).

Over the years, the friendships we enjoyed became deep, rich, and lasting! Something I did not realize until much later was that I was not the only beneficiary of the intimacy I worked to create. As our children have left home, Scott and I are overjoyed to see that they still love each other and us, even though several are married with families of their own, which necessarily take the lion's share of their focused attention. Hardly a day goes by when I don't get a phone call from two or more of my adult children: they are either checking in, or seeing if they can come to visit (we do live on a farm, so it's a big draw for the city dwellers), or wanting to collaborate on some educationally-oriented project that we're working on, or asking for advice. I now believe that the investments Scott and I made will pay dividends to the third and fourth generations of our family to come!

When I realized that I had found everything I was looking for in the friendships God had enabled in my home but not in my church community, I began to think about God's church. Many verses express a variation on the theme of 1 Corinthians 12:18 (ESV): "But as it is, God arranged the members in the body, each one of them, as he chose." It has come clear to me that, as with everything, God is actively sovereign over all of our friendships. It is He who gives them, for specific purposes and specific seasons.

God Himself wanted me to press into my own family relationships, and I believe that it was His active involvement that ordained that I not be able to form intimate friends with ladies in my church during that season of my life because He had something else for me. I have come to see that one can do all the right things to be "in" with the people one desires to know, and be doing nothing wrong, and still not attain the goal one is seeking. It comes back to Psalm 139:1-6 (ESV):

> *O LORD, you have searched me and known me! You know when I sit down and when I rise up; you discern my thoughts from afar. You search out my path and my lying down are acquainted with all my ways. Even before a word is on my tongue, behold, you know it altogether. You hem me in behind and before, and lay you hand upon me. Such knowledge is too wonderful for me; it is high; I cannot attain it.*

We Americans don't typically think of being hemmed in behind and before as a good thing. We love our freedoms of choice and movement. But, it is a good thing to be hemmed in when God does it, since both His wisdom and His love are boundless towards His children. Because He prevented me from building intimacy with church friends, I felt lonely. He then kindly put Yvonne's words on my heart, and showed me a way that, for me, was to become more fruitful and joyous than the way I thought was best at the time. I can survey my relational landscape today and say wholeheartedly, with King David, "The LORD is my chosen portion and my cup; you hold my lot. The lines have fallen for me in pleasant places; indeed, I have a beautiful inheritance" (Psalm 16:5-6, ESV).

Now, does this mean that every woman will find her closest friends in her home? Not necessarily, I think. Notice the principle here is that God chose my friends and led me to them, not that the friends He chose were necessarily in one sphere or another. I don't know all of the reasons why God chose that, for me, my best friends would be people in my own home, but I can guess some.

Notice the principle here is that God chose my friends and led me to them.

Since the conversation with Yvonne that I described, God has led my husband and me to change towns and churches twice (both times in order to better reposition ourselves for service to the calling He gave us). Because my family members have become my best friends, I was able to "take them with me" through both of these moves, whereas otherwise I would have lost relationships. (God did allow me to keep Yvonne, since her son married my daughter Charity, so that now she too is a family member and we share grandchildren!)

In addition, though I had no idea of it at the time, God intended for us to begin the family business that became *Tapestry of Grace*, where our close family friendships would prove absolutely essential to our mission and our very survival as a company. Those friendships have been much tested over the years, and they have stood—in part, I believe, because God redirected my focus towards strengthening them before I ever had any notion of becoming a curriculum author.

These are ways in which I see God was both kind and strategic in directing my attention to my family members not only as my highest priority in love, faithfulness, and investment, but also as my best friends. To many wives and mothers, however, I know that He has given some rich and deep friendships with other women. These, far from detracting from their first priority of husband and children, help to make them better wives and mothers and friends to their family members. After all, it was my friend Yvonne whom God used to first put me in the way of thinking about making my husband and children my best friends! So while I firmly believe that all women are called to make our husbands and children our first priorities—as is clear from Scripture—and that this focus may wonderfully lead to family members to become our closest friends—I do not intend to suggest that they should or will *always* be our *best* friends.

That said, I do think that my experience extends to all women in that I would suggest we all consider how we might invest in our husbands and children as friends. I believe that such an outlook will bring a rich blessing to any woman, whether she has close women friends or not. Remember, the principle is that God chooses who will be our best friends, but the kinds of ingredients that go into making and maintaining friendships are essential for wives and mothers when interacting with their husbands and children. This is even more true when homeschooling, since our children's social interactions are more limited than those who attend traditional schools.

I can broaden the principle even further. God Almighty has chosen that you will walk the earth *now.* You aren't living 100 years ago, or 1000 years ago, nor 500 years in the future, but you are walking the earth now. And, as you do, there is a finite list of people that you will ever meet (or even affect).

To put it in slang: *these are your peeps!* The ones that you meet—from the waitress on your date night this coming week, to the mailman to whom you wave each day, to the neighbor whose dog digs up your prize flowers each spring—these are the people to whom God sends you as His ambassadors. And no one is more in your natural circle of influence—especially if you homeschool—than your husband and children. He sends you to love, serve, and befriend them in His name and for His glory. It's so easy to take them for granted, or worse, to grow casual about ways that our sinful habits effect them.

How will you choose to interact with those whom God has sovereignly chosen and placed in your family? Will you make them first in your life, lavishing all the best of your creativity, energy, care, and prayer on them—which may very likely be the groundwork of "best friendships" with them—or will you allow other people and priorities to fill your days? It's a question of long-term investment. Looking back, I'm glad that God showed me how to invest in my family as my friends, and then moved so that they became the best friends whom I didn't have to leave behind.

SECTION THREE

When You Sit at Home

"You shall therefore lay up these words of mine in your heart and in your soul... You shall teach them to your children, talking of them when you are sitting in your house..."

DEUTERONOMY 11:18A,19 (ESV)

Homeschooling is largely carried out when you sit at home. As a woman new to homeschooling, you will doubtless hear a variety of voices that proclaim that this or that activity outside the home is essential to the proper formation of your children. Much of what I have to say in this section will challenge those voices. The choice is, of course, up to you.

As you take up homeschooling, you may also find yourself wrestling with your own nature, especially after the novelty of home teaching wears off. Many women among us are goers and doers at heart. Some of us led fast-paced lives before we had children, and to us it can seem boring—even wasteful—to sit at home and do the daily tasks of nurturing, raising, and instructing our children. I've felt that way.

But, as an older woman, I see it differently now. Scripture gives me good guidance as I write this section of this book.

> *Older women ...are to teach what is good, and so train the young women to love their husbands and children, to be self-controlled, pure,* ***working at home****, kind, and submissive to their own husbands, that the word of God may not be reviled.*
>
> *Titus 2:3-5 (ESV)*

In the following chapters, I will argue for the value of submitting to one's husband, and also of scheduling your time in order to bring stability to your and your children's lives so that you and your family can reap the benefits of regular rhythms of learning, play, rest, nutrition, and recreation as the foundation for successful homeschooling, to the glory of God.

I'll also pass on some practical tips in the later chapters of this section. One chapter relates to ways that home teaching differs from traditional school settings. My hope in this one is to free you from the oppression that I felt in trying to make my home just like one of those classrooms. As part of this loose collection of principles and practices, I also write a bit about how to keep preschoolers occupied when you teach their older siblings, and then argue for the necessity of making time in your busy school day for those same little ones. Then, I'll share some different ways that I managed chores when I had a houseful of kids.

This section concludes with a helpful paradigm for responding to the attitudes and actions of your children that you might not appreciate. Days can get long when you sit at home, and mothers can easily jump to confusions by too quickly judging their children's heart attitudes. Paul's wise advice in 1 Thessalonians 5:14 helps us remember that things are not always as they first appear.

11.

Thus says the LORD: "Stand by the roads, and look, and ask for the ancient paths, where the good way is; and walk in it, and find rest for your souls."

Jeremiah 6:16 (ESV)

The Husband Suitable for You

The title of this chapter might have caused you to roll your eyes and grit your teeth because you're pretty sure of what I'm about to say. So, I'll say it. If you are married, God has given your family a leader—your husband—and cast you in a supportive role: as a helper to that leader. This role relationship isn't popular with modern Americans, and it is often both confusing as well as difficult. I think that's true for a good reason.

The tensions that arise as we struggle to obey God in this area result from our sinful condition as fallen creatures. God created men first, and made them rulers over His creation. Women were created as helpers to men. The curse did not remove males from the leadership role. And just as our first mother, Eve, chose independence from God while ignoring her husband's instructions, many of us struggle with submission to the leadership and instruction of our husbands. Indeed, many Bible scholars interpret Genesis 3:16 ("Your desire shall be for your husband, and he shall rule over you") to mean that marital strife would be part of God's curse because women would desire their husbands' place of authority.

Whether or not you read it that way, it's clear throughout Scripture that, no matter how much more capable, educated, or aware we women think we are of the dynamics of any given situation, our husbands are in authority. They are leaders, whether they like it or not (and many men do *not* like their role any more than many women like theirs)! Leadership is tough, especially when those who are supposed to fill a supporting role, or follow along behind, choose not to do so. If those being led really dig in their feet and refuse to budge, there's very little a leader can do. Generally, a leader fails at that point.

The Bible tells us that God created humankind "male and female." Both sexes are God's image-bearers. However, they reflect different aspects of His one character. In the excellent book *Recovering Biblical Manhood and Womanhood*, John Piper offers these general definitions of biblical, mature manhood and womanhood:

> *At the heart of mature masculinity is a sense of benevolent responsibility to lead, provide for and protect women in ways appropriate to a man's differing relationships.*
>
> *At the heart of mature femininity is a freeing disposition to affirm, receive and nurture strength and leadership from worthy men in ways appropriate to a woman's differing relationships.*[1]

Piper proceeds to unpack each word of each of these definitions carefully in this excellent chapter. I recommend the book to you if this area of biblical teaching confuses or offends you, but let me get on with what I wanted to say.

Both sexes need brains, courage, persistence, and faithfulness in order to fulfill

1 *Recovering Biblical Manhood and Womanhood*, by John Piper and Wayne Grudem. Wheaton, IL: Crossway Books, 1991, p. 29.

their God-given roles while raising a family. To both, the Creator has given biologically indwelling traits that help them accomplish God's purposes. Both sexes reflect God's nature; they "image forth" different aspects of His one character.

Men deal with thorns and the heat of the day as they labor to bring home their family's daily bread. That's their part of the curse issued at the Fall. It's tough for them out there, but God has designed them (as a sex) to be the ones who can labor out in the world and bear its frustrations with fortitude. He has given them what they need to fulfill that role. As a sex, men tend to be logical rather than emotional, forgiving of each other once battles are settled, and up front with their lusts, sins, and ambitions.

Personally, I'm glad to be a woman. I'd rather be tending a sick child or nurturing an elderly parent than leading a company through an economic jungle, or making life and death decisions as a military commander. (I know that, today, women do fill these latter roles, but I'm not sure they are reflecting God's created order in all its beauty as they do.)

Women are not angels, and our lots are not always easier. While men in traditional roles deal with thorns and thistles, women in traditional roles deal with messes, with pain in childbirth, and often with loneliness and isolation. As a sex we tend to be emotional under stress, can be easily discouraged or frightened, and often try to explain away (or justify to self or others) our sins and ambitions, which can give pride and self-righteousness great latitude.

Still, I like it that I'm female. I like being intuitive and verbal and in touch with my feelings. I love it that I get to nurture, help, and support others. I am grateful to be able to regularly show the love of God to those who are suffering. It's great work if you can get it! And, I'm grateful that God gave me my husband, Scott, to help me with my weaknesses as we journey through life together.

Obviously (since I'm writing this book, and have been a speaker at homeschooling conventions and am a businesswoman) God has led me to do things outside my home as well. In our modern world, decades of teaching and the host of labor-saving devices that level the playing field for women have blurred some of the distinctions between the sexes. Those pursuits that I have undertaken outside my home have been ones that Scott has felt called to himself, or has felt that I should do with his guidance and protection for the help, nurture, and support of other families—largely, for other women and children.

The thing that I most wanted to communicate in this chapter has to do not so much with submission *per se*, or even with obedience, but with the protection and guidance that we can receive if we embrace God's plan for men and women. Just as we were created as helpmeets for our husbands, they were created as protectors for us. I hope to show you why homeschooling moms need protection, and why we often don't see that God is providing just that through our husbands.

The Challenge for Women

When we women begin homeschooling, we are typically entering a career for which we have had no training. Many of us have not seen it done by our mothers, nor were we able to go to school for it. It's been quite awhile since we ourselves learned our 3-R's, so it's not like memories of our own school experiences can help us out either now that we're the teachers. So, to some degree, most newcomers to homeschooling are dependent on either their own research or the mentoring of others, whether one-on-one or in the context of a support group.

The Internet is a mixed blessing as one is getting started. Information abounds, but anyone can post it. How do you sort and sift it without anything like personal experience, a trusted recommendation, or some inner compass to guide you?

Personal opinions of more experienced moms you know can be just as confusing when you're starting. There are a lot of strong women in the homeschooling world, and many of them have different (and often conflicting) lists of "must do's" and "can do's" and "don't do's." We are a highly individualistic, yet strong minded, group of ladies! We all bring our own theological orientations, personal preferences, educational experiences and desires, and value judgements—along with our sinful cravings—to this party!

Now, before you really check out, remember that I've suggested one way to approach the sea of choices confronting you in the first three chapters of this book, and note that in those chapters, I frequently mentioned your husband! What I want to focus you on now is the very special role that your husband can play, and then discuss why I needed to write this chapter at all.

God's provision for women

God is our Father, and He knows that we need help. Most women are wired to be highly intuitive and are tuned in to the emotions that others project. It's a reason why we can nurture and tend children better than most men. It's also a reason why we tend to tie ourselves into pretzels when we know that others are mad at us, or when we feel like we've let others down, or done a bad job in general. Often in my life, I've become really upset when I've felt unjustly criticized. At such times, my husband will look at me mildly and say, "Why does it bother you so much? You know there's no truth in it."

He's right, of course, but he's also male and doesn't get it. I feel badly when someone else feels badly towards me. It's not a question of the justice of their criticism; it's a question of the emotions and relationship at risk. I feel badly when things are out of joint, and because I'm female, I tend to feel like *everything* is out of joint if one relationship is significantly unsettled. The more important the relationship is to me, the more upset I am, almost without respect to the substantive content of the rupture.

For instance, if I'm unjustly accused by a reader of this book whom I've never met, it will unsettle me. But if my mother-in-law voiced the same criticism, I'd tend to be unable to leave it alone, anxious, and voicing all kinds of self-doubt until things were resolved.

It is precisely because Scott doesn't feel knotted up by his emotions that he can help me sort out mine. It is because he tends to hang on to truth steadfastly and process it logically that he can help me remember things that I don't want to forget but that seem to be washed away by the ebb and flow of my reactions and responses to circumstances of life. While Scott may not see the intricacies in a situation like I do, that doesn't mean that God can't use him to protect and lead me!

Just as we were created as helpmeets for our husbands, they were created as protectors for us.

What God has revealed because we wouldn't know it otherwise

Enter Scripture, specifically the Apostle Paul writing to Timothy on how churches should be managed. These have to be some of the least-loved verses of the New Testament.

> *I do not permit a woman to teach or to exercise authority over a man; rather, she is to remain quiet. For Adam was formed first, then Eve; and Adam was not deceived, but the woman was deceived and became a transgressor.*
>
> *1 Timothy 2:12-14 (ESV)*

What is Paul saying? Adam ate the fruit, too, right? Do women have to sit down and hush up forever because Eve was deceived?

I think Paul is referring to the dynamic that I've been outlining above. Women are more easily ruled by their intuitive, emotional, relationship-oriented selves than are men. Think for a moment about the kinds of situations that your pastor hears about daily: everything from cheating spouses to accusations of child abuse in Sunday Schools to church splits over theological issues. In general terms, in the passage above, Paul is seeking to protect the infant church. First of all, men need to disciple men to be men; women can't do that, so they shouldn't teach men. But more importantly, again, God has gifted redeemed men to lead in ways that build the church.

Were women in authority over men in the churches, they would predictably be swayed by their swirling emotions in response to the highly relational and horrific aspects of the kinds of significant problems church elders face. By and large, women (as a sex) didn't receive the kind of temperaments that ride out such storms with steadfast patience, persistence, faith in a good God, and good cheer. Women tend to evaluate life's curves and bumps, as well as their own sense of right and wrong, more emotionally and holistically than logically. Don't think so?

Look at Eve's *reasons* for eating that forbidden fruit:

> *So when the woman saw that the tree was good for food, and that it was a delight to the eyes, and that the tree was to be desired to make one wise, she took of its fruit and ate, and she also gave some to her husband who was with her, and he ate.*
>
> *Genesis 3:6 (ESV)*

Note these features in this account: Eve *decided* that the fruit looked really good for food: healthy and appetizing (certainly organic, right?). She was *delighted* by its physical beauty—what's beautiful is good, right? She also *desired* it because she wanted to become more than God had made her to be: wiser than she was. I can just hear her arguing, "Isn't it good to want to be wiser? Duh!"

So, she took and ate. She had all these good "reasons" (amounting to leaning on her own understanding) for disobeying the clear command of God. She *felt* these things after first choosing to believe the whisperings of Satan, rather than remaining steadfast to God's Word. And rather than following the leadership of her husband, who had instructed her in that Word, she first ate without even giving him the courtesy of asking for his opinion, and then decided to give him some of the forbidden fruit as well.

And what about Adam? He, a male, looked at his wife, having eaten, and he looked at the fruit, and then he made a simple choice. His wife won. He knowingly and boldly chose to disobey God. The Bible doesn't record a long thought process for Adam as it does for Eve. Adam didn't do any research or take any polls. He just decided to sin.

One of my husband's observations about males and females (and in all this chapter, remember that we're painting with a broad brush) is that men generally choose to sin and plan to take the consequences on the chin, while women tend to want to justify their sinful choices, convincing themselves that they aren't really doing a bad thing. An example that Scott would give is that men on a diet will just *decide* to go ahead and get some ice cream, right in front of their wives. When challenged, they'll sit there, smile, enjoy the forbidden calories, and then take the fat (and criticism) that goes with them. Women will justify to themselves and to others why they transgress a diet. "I was so tired of not eating anything yummy" or "I'd lost ten pounds and it was time to reward myself." I think Scott's got something there. I, personally, see this dynamic in the passage quoted above from Genesis.

Back to the homeschooling context

Now, it's not a sin to feel confused and pulled by the strong and varied opinions that you'll find when you when you start to homeschool. Rather, I'm trying to point out that we women can become easily confused and overwhelmed, and that our emotions can do us more harm than good. As I've observed earlier in this book, the stakes are high, and all our mother-bear instincts come into play. Things don't get better as we get more experienced, because mothering is a guilty business, and there's always someone doing it better, or more creatively, or with better results. And we stand rightly accused by our Enemy and ourselves when we finish each day where we could have been more patient, or more diligent, or more wise. It's so easy to come to the point where we become discouraged enough that we just want to quit!

But we don't usually quit. We recover our balance, and decide to work harder, smarter, and faster. And, here's the trap: we tend to think we know more than we do, and are smarter and more capable than we are. Let me explain why.

Typically, women would rather stand on the shoulders of giants, while men want to see if they can find their own way. Women confront a problem and think that if someone else has something figured out, well, why do we have to go to the effort of figuring it out for ourselves? To invoke a cliché: why not ask for directions?

The male instinct is just the opposite: he thinks that it's his privilege and glory to seek out a matter. Why ask for directions and forfeit the challenge and credit of finding one's own way through the concrete jungle? Women think of men as being too proud to ask; men think that if we don't work things out for ourselves, we may lose the ability to find our own way when all the lights are out and there's no one to ask.

His decision-making paradigm includes factors that I don't even recognize.

Both sexes have valid approaches to problem solving. (Did you catch that? *Both* of our approaches have strengths, and they complement one another.) There are certainly times when it's wise to read consumer reviews, like when you are looking to buy a new DVD player. There are also many times when we have to figure out how to make the new DVD player work apart from directions: like, for the engagement party slide show in twenty minutes, even though the manufacturer left a key part out of the box! It's at such moments that the male approach comes into its own, since the owner's manual doesn't tell us how to hot wire the DVD player. Men and women were created to work together as complements. That's why God gave kids two parents.

Now, since women tend to be askers and researchers, and willing and eager to be led by others in order to get where they want to go, they can feel like they know a lot. Eve probably felt that she'd done a pretty thorough assessment before taking that fatal bite! Because our impulse is to take over the leadership role that God has delegated to our husbands (Genesis 3:16), and also because American culture values head knowledge so highly, we don't have to take many steps in order to cross the line into arrogance and contempt towards our husbands. Let me offer a common scenario from our home.

I might come to Scott after days of research and painstaking investigation of two competing math curricula for my 3rd grader, and in a fit of frustration say to him, "I just can't decide which is the best choice! Will you please help me?"

Wanting to help, Scott would listen to me explain in great detail the pros and cons of each program for about ten minutes, which would include testimonials of women friends as well as reviews by experts, and then give his opinion of a logical choice, based on what I've told him.

My typical reaction to his leadership would be something like this: "How can you choose so quickly? It's complicated! There are these considerations, and those concerns. I just can't figure out which way to go!" My assumption is that he can't *possibly* make a good decision by listening to my summary for all of ten minutes, when I've spent *days* wanting to be *right* about this.

Meanwhile, his decision-making paradigm includes factors that I don't even recognize. He reasons that the child I'm teaching is in 3rd grade (or was it 2nd?). No matter, the point is that he's young, with a lot of years of work in mathematics ahead. There is lots of time for us to do a good job teaching basic math, and I (his wife) am a smart, capable, diligent woman. From Scott's perspective, it pretty much doesn't matter which curriculum I choose at this time. He rightly believes that I will do well if I use tiddlywinks. Teaching 3rd grade math isn't rocket surgery; it's basic. Our son is young and has been doing well in grade school so far.

All this has crossed Scott's mind while he tried to also take in the important details that I summarized for him about what friends and experts have had to say about the features the two competing math curricula. He gives his opinion succinctly and frankly, with a real desire to help me.

In reaction, I then feel a host of reactionary emotions. I *feel* like Scott doesn't really *care* about our son's academics. I *judge* Scott, jumping to the conclusion that he doesn't *want* to really get down and dirty with the details. He's not *willing* to master the same material that I've been sweating over for weeks. He takes homeschooling casually, and doesn't see how *important* this all is! My growing feeling is one of contempt and uncertainty. Because I trust my own instincts, emotions, research approach, and intelligence, I am missing a vital truth that is clear in Scripture.

God graced men, with their genetically-wired temperaments, to be the leaders of families. You don't always have to master information in order to sense the proper direction to head through a thicket of confusing details. In this example, Scott's response was based far more on the big picture of how math is learned, where our son is in the process, and what kind of teacher I am. Given the basic truths that he's decided to pay attention to, either of these fine math programs will serve us well! He is above the fray and able to set direction for me, even without mastering details.

But what if he's wrong?

The whole concept of wifely submission to a husband's authority (and the protection we wives gain from it) is *not* based on the premise that men are always, or even mostly, right in their decisions—though, if we were better followers, helpmeets, and supports, they might be proven right more often. What submission is based upon is faith. Not blind faith, and not a vague "faith" that has no object, and not even faith in our husbands' ability to lead, but faith in Christ.

Every time that a wife submits herself to her husband's direction and leadership *as an act of faith in God's decree that husbands should lead*, she is worshipping God and declaring to the watching hosts of angels and demons that she trusts God's revealed Word above her own understanding. She is, in fact, reversing the curse and returning her household to Eden.

Exercising the God-given roles of headship and submission brings peace, order, and a picture of Christ and His church to a watching world. And no one is watching more closely than are your children. Ephesians 5:22-27 (ESV) gives us this picture clearly:

> *Wives, submit to your own husbands, as to the Lord. For the husband is the head of the wife even as Christ is the head of the church, his body, and is himself its Savior. Now as the church submits to Christ, so also wives should submit in everything to their husbands. Husbands, love your wives, as Christ loved the church and gave himself up for her, that he might sanctify her, having cleansed her by the washing of water with the word, so that he might present the church to himself in splendor, without spot or wrinkle or any such thing, that she might be holy and without blemish.*

There are many voices that lay claim to our allegiance as we start homeschooling. God has provided protection from error, from guilt, from confusion, and from emotional exhaustion for us. There is a way to enjoy the journey with your husband, and it's found by taking the ancient path of biblical submission. American culture teaches that being identical to men is the true definition of equality. Scripture presents a different picture, one in which man and woman stand equal in their humanity at the foot of the cross, but also take delight in playing out the different, complementary roles that God has provided, which are designed to display variety within unity, and proclaim the glory of Christ to a watching world.

The 3rd grade math curriculum choice was a test: would I trust God by seeing my husband's advice as a gracious word from God, given for my peace and comfort, or would I choose to treat my husband's opinions with contempt because he arrives as his opinion by looking at different criteria than I chose to esteem? You'll have similar choices to make in the future. Recognizing the battle for what it is makes it so much easier to fight Satan as a team, rather than letting him bring division and strife.

I'll leave this chapter with one more true story. When I was a mother of three preschoolers and a six-week-old infant in arms, we moved to a new town and church family. As a newcomer to a small church, I was eager to fit in and be accepted by other women. Among the members was an older woman who commanded great respect. She had several daughters in their late teens who were godly girls.

This woman was very strong in her conservative beliefs, and one of her strongest teachings was "you never put your baby down." For her, it was truly wrong to deny a child your arms and your breasts; babies *must* be held constantly and nursed on demand, and they *must* share your bed at nights. I'm sure that she sincerely believed that in teaching younger women in the church to follow these practices, she was doing them and their children only good!

My children were aged 5, 3, 18 months, and six weeks old. There was no way that I could hold my newest baby 24/7. I had not nursed his siblings on demand, but had scheduled them. In my heart, I did not agree with what this woman was teaching so strongly, but I tied myself in knots trying to comply with her views (even in the privacy of my home, when no one could see) in order to be one of her crowd and be accepted by the other women in my new church.

One day, I tearfully confessed to Scott my exhaustion, lack of peace, and fears of becoming a social outcast. He listened to me patiently for a bit. Then, when there was a lull in the storm, he asked, mildly, "Well, is it in the Bible?" (He meant, was this woman's teaching that this was the one right way to raise infants supported clearly in Holy Scripture?)

I blinked twice and sniffed as I mentally reviewed the passages I knew. "No," I finally answered.

"Then," he replied, "Don't do it if you don't want to."

My heart leapt at this simple slice through my tangled web of woe. He was right! I had bound myself to a practice—which I didn't even believe was needed—because I craved acceptance of the many, when God had so ordained it that I only needed to listen to one voice: my husband's, as informed by Scripture.

As I put my baby tenderly into his crib for a nap and pulled out a book to read to my three-year-old, my heart was light and joyful for the first time in weeks. I'll never forget how grateful I was for God's protection, as provided in my husband, from my own doubts and worries. And that was not the last time that I found peace, direction, and assurance when heeding Scott's words in faith that they were, for me, leadership provided by my Heavenly Father.

12.

Better is a dry morsel with quiet
than a house full of feasting with strife.

PROVERBS 17:1 (ESV)

Keeping a Quiet Home

It seems to me that raising children is one of the most challenging careers on the planet. If we are engaged in this endeavor, we should take it seriously and work at it diligently. It has been well said that "it is easier to train children than to repair men." I would respond that training children is only easier if one is giving one's full mind to the training and, even so, this work requires huge amounts of grace for both parents and children.

Giving one's full attention to raising children necessarily mandates that we say "no" to other pursuits. And when our call to train them includes homeschooling, we add to the nurturing tasks common to all mothers the added ones involved with giving academic lessons to our children. It is at this point that I believe that the idea of keeping a quiet home becomes almost a necessity. Let me define what I mean by a "quiet home" and then show you some scriptural support for my position as we get into details.

By a "quiet home," I mean a home that has a peaceful, orderly environment, in both its spiritual and physical aspects. This is a home where voices are modulated (though not to the exclusion of the occasional noisy romp, dance, or tickle session). Here, time is taken to do things well and in order, and living is consciously done to the glory of God a majority of the time. (Naturally, sinful behavior will exist; a Godward focus, though, means that repentance, forgiveness, and love will transform much sin to glory.) This home is clean and well maintained, because God is a God of order and beauty, and because clean environments are healthier and safer ones for children to grow and learn in than are messy or ill-maintained ones.

A quiet home is not an empty home, where no one really lives because its people are out all day doing other things. Nor is it a place where family members catch fragmented meals or sleep when midway between a myriad of appointments and obligations that scatter family members in a variety of different directions. By definition, a quiet home is a home that is lived in, loved in, and worked in. It is a place of safety for small children, and also an outpost of the Kingdom of God.

All of the chapters in this section are meant to fill in a picture of a quiet home. As you read, I encourage you to be asking God what He would have of you in your unique situation, and ask Him where change might be needed. I hope you may find rest in this assurance: if the Spirit nudges you to order your home differently, He will also empower and grace you to do it!

Having painted a word picture of this quiet home, I now want to turn to discussing the commonly experienced temptations that draw us away from occupying such a lovely spot.

Working at Commercial Business Pursuits

Many of us worked outside the home before marriage and liked it. Also, in hard economic times, we wives may need to help earn money. So for many of us, the urge to "do business" is often present, but I'm going to argue that it's probably not preferable to choose an outside job unless you and your husband feel that you are actively led into commercial enterprises by the Lord—and there are more reasons that I can list why this might be so.

Working on business pursuits will necessarily take time, creativity, and energy away from a focused attention on home management and child rearing. In the beginning, the desire for an outlet for these very things is a common motive for starting a job, especially with home businesses.

As new brides, and even young mothers, we can feel under-challenged at home with an easily-maintained house to tend and one small baby to mind. (This impulse may be strengthened by the transition to married life itself; many of us feel a strong desire to contribute money to the family budget.)

We can minimize what we do at home as "not enough" because we have been accustomed to working a job, or because American society does not recognize (except perhaps in magazines) the real value of a clean, orderly homes and well-regulated schedules for infants. To be honest, too, the daily tasks of caring for the home and infants really can be mind-numbingly boring, and our desires for escape can be a motivator for us to seek relief in some not-so-good places.

1 Timothy 6:6-11 (ESV) offers young women who feel this host of temptations some ageless, wise advice. Paul writes:

> *Now there is great gain in godliness with contentment... But those who desire to be rich fall into temptation, into a snare, into many senseless and harmful desires that plunge people into ruin and destruction... It is through this craving that some have wandered away from the faith and pierced themselves with many pangs. But as for you... flee these things. Pursue righteousness, godliness, faith, love, steadfastness, and gentleness.*

Developing a heart for your home and small children can be really challenging in our pleasure-oriented, entertainment-sodden society. My own choices included doing various home-based businesses both as a young mother of babies and later, while homeschooling. As a result, I really had to work hard to keep child rearing a priority. Though I was very organized and had a lot of support from my husband, I well remember consistently feeling like I was walking a tightrope high above ground and without a net.

In my heart, I felt certain that one fine day, something important was going to come crashing down. I felt that I lived in constant triage, always asking myself, "Okay: who will *die* if I don't get to them next?" So I'm speaking from real-life experiences when I talk on the subject of motherhood and working a job.

On the other hand, I can also honestly say that God worked in me through the stretching I'm describing. There was some good fruit in my life that God graciously brought from this tension. Looking back, I can see that it produced humility as I clung to Christ and struggled with condemnation. I often enlisted my children to help with mundane tasks like stuffing envelopes, and as they grew older, I made it a special thing to take one of them to my home party presentations as a special helper. I taught them to cook and clean and gave them practice in these areas partly because I needed time to do other things.

> *By a "quiet home," I mean one that has a peaceful, orderly environment, both in spiritual and physical aspects.*

God often showed me how to use these things in their lives for good. We had many great times stuffing envelopes, many special one-on-one times traveling to and from home parties, and my daughters particularly are grateful for their training in home management, now that they find themselves a little ahead of the curve in that area.

My children also learned that they were not the center of the universe, and to value serving others before themselves. But, as with most rough roads, it wasn't easy, and there were costs, as well as opportunities for sin. Though they were all "on board" with my role outside our home, some of my children were at times tempted with selfishness, bitterness, and self-pity. They had to learn how to deal with these sins. There was also for all of us the legitimate hurt of sacrifice, of losing one thing to gain another.

God met and taught and grew each of us through these things, and I do believe it was His plan for our family uniquely (remember, each family is uniquely called by God to glorify Him in the ways He has chosen for them), but still, I would not recommend that you *seek* to run a business, raise young children, and homeschool unless clearly led of the Lord (which can, of course, include acceding to your husband's requests that you work).

So, you might wonder, "Why is she going to argue for an at-home focus so earnestly if this was not her own example?" Or "Why should I forego the rewards of working a job and raising children and homeschooling if she saw so much good fruit from it?"

In John 15:2, we read these words of the Lord Jesus:

> *I am the true vine, and my Father is the vine dresser. Every branch of mine that* ***does not*** *bear fruit he takes away, and every branch that* ***does*** *bear fruit he* ***prunes****, that it may bear* ***more*** *fruit.*

Look closely at this passage. Jesus says that He prunes what is *good* in favor of what is *best*—or, most fruitful.

My life was what God intended it to be. I see the good fruit that God brought out of my sincere efforts to please Him and serve my family. But I am aware of ways that my choices did affect my children adversely, and made my home less quiet than it could have been. There were times when I was "too busy" to nurture well. There were moments missed and there were lessons untaught and there was damage to relationships that would not have occurred if my attention had been more focused on my home.

Again, I'm content with the "soil" of my life. God has shaped it; I believe that by faith. I believe that part of why it worked out well for us was that we were aware of the choices we were making. One can't do everything, and my work with writing *Tapestry*, for instance, cost my children some, but benefitted them more.

I think my goal in writing this chapter is simply to alert younger moms to the fact that choices do involve opportunity costs, as economists call them. Saying "yes" to a job means saying "no" to other things. It is a myth of our culture that we can successfully "do it all" in a sustainable way.

If pruning is a practice that Jesus follows, should we not, with our husbands, seek Him for wisdom concerning the choices that we make for our days? If we see that our pursuit of a job is from unwholesome or self-centered motives, should we not seek to cut away unfruitful avenues, and even to prune back (or limit) good ones, so that we can produce the greatest possible crop of godliness? We can tend to settle for "good" when God wants the best for us.

Hearing Voices

This idea of pruning the good in order to obtain the best also takes us to a second major area of distraction from keeping a quiet home: paying undue attention to the many and varied opinions of others. From friends, to neighbors, to parents, to our own consciences, women hear many voices. The Bible is clear that, as a sex, we are susceptible to undue influencing from them. I've talked about this at length in Chapter 11, but let me give a fresh example in this context, and then let's talk about pruning.

As was commonly known, when I was a young mother, "they say" that anyone who wants to be at all good at the violin needs to start lessons with a bona fide Suzuki instructor at the age of four. Your son, Chris, has decided that he'd like to play the violin, and you are eager to encourage this, since playing a musical instrument is high on your list of good skills for him to have. Chris is almost seven—way late! You live in rural New Hampshire, so violin teachers aren't plentiful. Indeed, the only good one you've heard of lives about half an hour away. When you call him, you find that his teaching slate is full except for one slot: the 11:30 AM lesson on Tuesdays, for a half an hour. So, you commit to a year's worth of lessons.

As the fall progresses and cold weather sets in, your family settles nicely into its homeschooling routines. Tuesdays are the only days that aren't working for you. It's because of the violin lesson, and you've come to dread it. Why?

Well, because you have four kids who need to all be bundled up in their winter coats, boots, and mittens and loaded into the car. You have to strap the babies into their car seats and, of course, it is a given that one of them will fall asleep as you drive the half-hour to the lesson. Naturally, you're not going to then drive home during the lesson. You've decided to pick up a few perishables from the nearby grocery store.

When you get home, everyone's hungry and cranky. You all pile into the kitchen, where all your kids drop their wet winter boots and coats, and (since they've been out in the cold) they start clamoring for hot chocolate. You dump the groceries next to the clothing. You manage to barely keep your temper while slapping together peanut butter sandwiches for a quick lunch for them, putting away the groceries and their clothing, and serving the hot chocolate. The toddler and the baby are both out of sorts from interrupted sleep cycles, and everyone is headed for a sugar crash.

Discouraged at the prospect of a long, unpleasant afternoon ahead, you give up on doing any more lessons for the day and announce that this is a video day. You guiltily park them all in front of a Disney movie while you escape to Facebook and your favorite home decor magazine for the bulk of the rest of the afternoon.

* * * * *

Now, let's go back. Why did you schedule this violin lesson when you did?

"Well," you respond, "*they say* that Chris is late getting started... he's six! And *they say* that you really need a Suzuki instructor, and this was the only Suzuki teacher's only slot... and I thought I could manage it because, as moms, we have to be able to do it all or our kids will suffer, and... um... that's why."

This kind of thing happens so often to homeschooling moms! You will encounter so many who have strong opinions, and who will insist that *their* way is best for *you*, too. Some will be well-meaning. They sincerely want you to be happier, or do a better job, and if you participate in their play group or Bible study group, or if your child has this or that instructor or opportunity, they are convinced you *will* be happier. But you can't do them all, and you will need to prune some good things so that you leave time—and plenty of it—for the important things, which are the things you and your husband agree that you've been called to do.

Jesus says that He prunes what is good in favor of what is best—or, most fruitful.

Sometimes, you will need to prune out the opinions of those who voice negative sentiments. Well-meaning friends and relations may question your motives or abilities in choosing to homeschool. They may project fearful future scenarios on the screen of your mind. They may seek to undermine your resolve to follow your husband and the Lord on this journey by predicting horrific ends.

Proverbs 29:25 says, "The fear of man lays a snare, but whoever trusts in the Lord is safe." We covered this in the previous chapter, but it bears repeating: one reason we women listen to the voices of others—either urging us to do more or trying to have us do less, to the point where we lose peace and joy in our God-given roles—is that we want so desperately to succeed. This is a natural desire, for sure, but as with the violin lesson, our motive can be more about winning the approval of others than the glory of God or the best for our kids. Pruning out the noisy voices in our heads and quieting our proud hearts take work!

Examining our ability to homeschool when others disagree with our choices can be both humble and wise. We know that we are not strong enough to succeed in homeschooling on our own, and at times we do need to adjust our course. But a right response to doubts and worries brought on by the voices of others would be to prune the weight you give them, if after prayer and discussion with your husband you find that you are not actually called to make changes based on what those voices advise.

By limiting your primary counselors to God's Word, your husband and then (with him) to a few well-chosen mentors, you access real helps. God provides us with only a few voices to whom we must really listen intently. We are to obey God's Word and His Spirit, and our husband. Those are, in essence, the only voices we *need* to really listen to when making decisions about homeschooling and parenting.

There is wisdom in consulting a variety of counselors when big decisions or serious adjustments are needed. The advice of friends, family, pastors, and homeschooling leaders can be valuable! But at the end of the day, Scripture only commands women to submit to the leadership of God and our husbands. This ancient way of pruning enables us to travel light on the journey. Pruning frees us from many heartaches if we take it seriously, and it enables us to give value and attention to the less obvious (or glamorous) requirements of a quiet home.

Self-Reliance and Self-Focus

Finally, there are the restless emotions of our own hearts and minds—those discouraging, escapist, or condemning thoughts that we speak to ourselves. These come from bumping up against our own sinful humanity, from being forced to face the very real limits that God has placed in our life, and from our Enemy whispering in our ears in an effort to destroy us. These, too, can keep us from joyful service in a quiet home.

In fact, one of the largest distractions from keeping a quiet home comes from too much reliance on our own thoughts, feelings, priorities, and plans. Like Eve, we so often choose to do what seems best to us, without stopping to ask God and our husbands for guidance. Again, this can be especially true for us if we've been used to a lot of social or ministry interactions before we were married, or have lots of ideas for going and doing outside the home once we have children. Self-reliance can lead us into heartache. Here's one of the scariest Scripture passages I know. It helps me to remember to not lean on my own understanding!

> *Behold, all you who kindle a fire, who equip yourselves with burning torches! Walk by the light of your fire, and by the torches that you have kindled! This you have from my hand: you shall lie down in torment.*
>
> *Isaiah 50:11 (ESV)*

From curriculum purchases to participation in learning groups to whether or not to take violin lessons to deciding to work an outside job—all of our choices affect our ability to keep a quiet home. If we rely on ourselves and our own understanding, we take on a tremendous burden—one that God never meant for His daughters to shoulder! In Genesis 3, we read that Eve sinned because she chose to follow her own inclinations, rather than submit herself to either the Word of God or her husband.

Bad results from bad choices

When we bow to the tyranny of others' voices or our own feelings and thoughts, we so often end up taking on more than we can handle in a quiet and orderly way. We find ourselves rushing, which makes it easy to give in to temptations to be rude and unkind to our children and husbands. In rushing them out the door, we go yelling through the house to hurry them up. While busy with other tasks, we rebuke with a sharp word or sudden swat, or because we are among outsiders, we grit our teeth and try to pretend that the two-year-old kicking and screaming on the department store floor isn't our baby! Because we are on a conference call from home for our job, we find that we can't take the time to correct our children's misbehaviors with grace and gospel.

In this bustle and sin, we open ourselves up to feelings of self-pity, condemnation, and discouragement that tempt us to either quit or escape. As we wobble off-center, we find ourselves failing to undertake things that would be straightforward if our pace was slower, or our life simpler. In pursuit of great opportunities that we've not previously planned for (or prayed about) we find that we are changing plans often, then skipping many of the daily disciplines associated with keeping a clean, orderly home. The mess piles up and becomes so daunting that we can't face it: we do more activities outside the home, and avoid (or justify) tasks at home left undone.

Because we are not sitting at home, we skip daily lessons that are essential to productive homeschooling. Our children begin to learn that our plans are not reliable, that they don't know what they can expect from us, that the deadlines we set aren't real ones, and that it's okay to blow off the mundane in search of the exciting or new things of life. If we're busy with other things, they tend to react by attention-gaining behaviors, such as tantrums, whining, sulking, or rebellion.

Better fruit from better choices

Quiet homes that result from wise choices to prune and submit as God and our husbands lead, by contrast, provide maximum opportunity for us and our children to flourish. The balance of work, rest, and nutrition conducted in a clean and well-ordered environment gives both the best possible foundation for the central goals of a homeschooling family: providing Christian discipleship through an authentic model (in you and your husband) and regular progress towards academic excellence.

It is much easier to train children using the gospel-centered teaching and correction with gracious tones when parents are well rested, well fed, prayed up, and not rushed. Discipleship involves not only setting our children examples of faithfulness in little things, and of Godward choices during many small moments in life, but of repentance (admitting our own faults) when needed. Discipleship also involves listening carefully to the questions and problems that our children have when they are perplexed or in trial. It is just hard—in general, though again there is grace for those of us who are called to undertake a full schedule—to do these things well while also doing life in a high-speed, high-pressured way.

Likewise, academic progress results from many small lessons faithfully completed. If you are well rested, unhurried, and at peace, you will find it easier to plan, teach, correct, and re-teach those lessons. If your children wake up each morning to a stable, predictable rhythm of life which includes rest, good nutrition, and periods of recreation and work, and where deadlines and expectations are clear and consistent, they will have the best possible platform for success in academics.

Giving your heart fully to the care of your home and your children is not commonly valued very highly in today's American society. You won't get many accolades for choosing the ancient paths of loving and serving your own husband and children with kindness and faithfulness, or for choosing to live at a lower income level rather than take on commercial pursuits. However, you are living your life for an audience of One, not for the audience of many. If this is the task He has given you to do, you can rest in that.

Also, if you believe the Bible, believe that the promises of heavenly crowns are true! In addition to our motivation of love and gratitude for Jesus (we love because He first loved us) God does not seem to consider it inappropriate to motivate us by rewards. Therefore, we run this race in part to hear Him say "well done, good and faithful servant. Enter into the joy of your master." While others may feel that you're bearing an unnecessary burden by adding academic teaching to parenting responsibilities, and missing "the good life" in the process, if keeping a quiet home is God's leading, you can rest assured that the pruning that goes with it—even of good things—will not fail to yield sweet and abundant fruit, as well as rich rewards, for God is faithful to His promises.

* * * * *

For the rest of Section Two we are going to get a bit more practical about ways to manage your homeschooling tasks and children as you are keeping your quiet home.

13.

The earth was without form and void, and darkness was over the face of the deep. And the Spirit of God was hovering over the face of the waters. And God said, "Let there be light," and there was light. And God saw that the light was good. And God separated the light from the darkness. God called the light Day, and the darkness he called Night. And there was evening and there was morning, the first day.

GENESIS 1:2-5 (ESV)

Schedules and Structure

Looking back on my homeschooling years, one of the key building blocks of success was a focus on *schedules* and *structure*.

By "schedules" I mean that I worked at actually writing out detailed schedules in order to make sure that all the commitments I had made, both to my own family (cooking, cleaning, and schooling) and those outside our home (music lesson teachers, friends, extended family, church members, etc.) really could fit into specific time slots in my week.

By "structure," I mean keeping a steady focus on the flow of our daily lives such that the children knew what would likely happen day by day, and knew with reasonable certainty how to fit themselves into that flow.

Let's take these one at a time, with a special focus on ways that they relate to how children in homeschool settings learn both character and academic lessons.

About schedules

In my experience, there are women who love to make (and have) schedules, and women who don't. Very few of us are in between the two extremes. Those of us who love them tend to be generally organized, are often neatnicks, tend towards being controlling in general, because we can have trouble with life situations where we just have to "go with the flow."

We are most often the ones that are called "Type A" personalities. We like to have all of our ducks in a row. We tend to buy curriculum for the next school year in March or April, if not sooner. We're planners and researchers, and we like to run a tight ship or, at the very least, serve on one! We know that sometimes we can trample on relationships, and we're sorry about that, but for us the importance of the mission usually trumps the feelings of others. We are the Marthas of the world, and while Jesus rebuked Martha for her focus on the tasks at hand, we point out that houses don't clean themselves, meals don't cook themselves, and someone has to give direction for the *work* that life demands!

Those of us who don't like schedules tend to be creative, passionate, and somewhat (okay, a lot) disorganized and messy. We usually don't want to take things too seriously, we value relationships above tasks, and we don't want to be hemmed in by either our own choices or the rules that others make. In fact, one thing that most attracts us about homeschooling is the freedom that we have to make our own decisions day to day so that our creativity, our Spirit-led ministries, and our joy in living and learning can be fully expressed!

The idea of planning our weeks seems like everything from busywork that is unnecessary (a waste of time, actually, given all the unexpected twists of our days) to a straitjacket that will stifle us if we are forced into it. We secretly feel that, if Martha had just remembered how Jesus miraculously fed the five thousand, she could have relaxed a bit about getting dinner on the table and spent some time listening to Him instead!

Now, I know I'm painting caricatures here, but I do believe that there really are such personality tendencies (to differing degrees, to be sure) among us homeschooling moms, and that these will influence us significantly as we get down and dirty with decisions about how we will teach and how our kids will learn. And remember, the learning we keep discussing in this book will be not only about the content of academic lessons, but also include our character as displayed in how we approach everyday life. These traits will then be reproduced in our children.

Here's the message of this chapter in a nutshell: God is at once the most orderly and the most creative Being in the universe. Order and creativity do not have to cancel each other out; they can complement one another.

For a Scriptural example of this, look at Genesis, chapters 1-2. Here we see God "bringing order out of chaos" as He makes an entire world in six days, yet in a way that was bursting with creative energy as well! Leland Ryken, style editor of the English Standard Version of the Bible, remarks on this in his book *Words of Delight*:

> *"In this story [of creation] the great opposites of human experience—rule and energy, order and impulse, restraint and abundance—complement each other. On the one hand, the process of creation is described as an instantaneous act of God's word and as an ordering process. . . . In this pattern, the verbs name acts of ordering [e.g., specific things being created on specific days], as God is said to have* separated, called, *and* set.
>
> *But [this description of an orderly creation] . . . is balanced by passages that describe creation as an act of biological generation. . . . The imagery is physical rather than abstract, and the language stresses energy and vitality rather than rule and order. We read about* plants yielding seed *and* fruit trees bearing fruit in which is their seed. . . . *The motif reaches its climax in God's command to creatures to* be fruitful and multiply and fill the waters in the seas, and let birds multiply on the earth *(v.22). Such images of overflowing generative energy complement the passages that describe creation as an ordering process brought about instantly by the word of God.*[1]

I believe that children learn best when order and creativity are in balance, and to that end, I'm going to try to describe the beauty of schedules by showing how they

1 *Words of Delight: A Literary Introduction to the Bible*, by Leland Ryken. 2nd ed. Grand Rapids, MI: Baker Book House, 1992, p. 94-95.

serve creativity, flexibility, and Spirit-led ministry, especially in the homeschooling context.

Let's think about God's world together. He created such order, and yet such variety. In the plants and animals of this world, in the bodies of people, and in the ways that people image Him in their daily lives, we see a vast symphony of creativity that is exquisitely orderly at the same time.

It was the sin of Eve, who listened to Satan's lie that she could disobey God and walk well through His world on her own (and the sin of her husband, who agreed with her) that brought sorrow, death, disorder, and mind-numbing sameness into God's perfect world. In seeking to accurately image my Creator to my children, I believe that I need to balance my desire for freedom in the moment with keeping our days full of orderly, steady patterns of work, rest, and the joy of discovery.

Humility would teach me that I need to use my time wisely because I am a mortal and fallen creature. Unlike my Creator, I am neither infallible nor inexhaustible. I need food, I need sleep, and I need rejuvenation. If I try to "do it all" as if I did not have limits, I lie to myself and I will eventually disappoint someone, or sin against someone, or burn out quickly.

As a woman who wears many hats, I have too many tasks and obligations to do all that I would like to do (or even ought to do). Making a schedule helps me to identify and quantify the bits and pieces of my life, to consider before God which are most important in the short and long terms, to prioritize accordingly, and then to see what I can and cannot accomplish within my limited time frames. They help me to number my days aright so that I may gain a heart of wisdom (Psalm 90:12).

Obviously, homeschooling adds another layer of complexity to the already-significant list of tasks associated with being a wife, bearing and raising children, keeping our house and possessions in order, caring for our aging parents, being a good friend and church member, etc.

Were it not for the leading of God and His sustaining grace, I do not think women would succeed in all that we are called to undertake! One of the features of homeschooling that helps us, though, is that it overlaps our other roles, rather than pulling us from them—and here is where the quiet home concept begins to make sense.

When we become pregnant with our first child, many of us must decide whether or not to keep working outside the home. Modern society enables and encourages women to work. Many young couples find that they need the extra income to make ends meet, while others find that they can either live frugally on one income, or are blessed with abundant income from the husband's job.

The decision to put small children into day care, or with family members to baby sit, is entirely between you and your Lord; I'm not going to preach here, for I have seen a great variety of choices made well in this area. Some parents I know worked, and some didn't; we're not all the same, and those choices made in faith will always have God's enabling grace to sustain them.

Order and creativity do not have to cancel each other out; they can complement one another.

One thing is clear, however. When women do work out of the home, their focus is split and their lives are more complex than their sisters who stay at home full time. After there are two or three children in the family, the economics for most of us make it at least an even shot as to whether it benefits the family more for the mom to be home full time or continuing to work.

For many Christians, the decision to homeschool adds worth, as it were, to the impulse that many of us have to focus our attention on our families, and to disciple and raise our own children rather than allowing others this privilege. If we choose to stop working a job and care for our husbands, children, and homes full time, our lives become centered primarily in our homes, and all our roles begin to overlap and contribute to one another. Thus, raising the younger children and early education of those just coming into the grade school years go naturally together, along with the tasks associated with helping to support our husband's career, keeping our homes neat and clean, and befriending those in our communities.

But even if all of our focus has now shifted to the home, because children grow and change so fast and because with homeschooling we are now adding new tasks into our daily lives, making a written schedule of the weekly tasks and events is a highly useful exercise, especially when we are beginning to actively teach academics. As with orderly physical environments, making a schedule helps us to find a place for everything, and to put everything in its place. We find times to work, times to play, times to learn, and times to fellowship. I'm not going to get into the details here; that's for later chapters. But I will say that, to me, the greatest benefit of scheduling is more the *process* of writing the schedule (thus examining and setting values and priorities in my life), than following the schedule that I create to the letter.

Here's where the free spirits among us may be reassured! The point of having a schedule is not to create a straitjacket that will make you feel guilty if you wriggle out of it even for a few minutes—nor does writing out a schedule mean that you are unrealistically ignoring the many curve balls that God will throw into your week! Rather, the process of writing a schedule is primarily a tool to help you notice and prioritize what is going on in your week.

Besides the above advantages, the joy of having created a detailed schedule (say, of cleaning chores as well as school lessons) is that you know what to drop when the Spirit moves you to depart from your plan. Let's say that your schedule says that you vacuum on Tuesday afternoons. Now posit that a neighbor drops in on a Tuesday to borrow a cup of sugar, but then bursts into tears, confessing marital difficulties. You draw her into your home, put aside all thoughts of running the vacuum, and minister to your friend for two hours. Most of us would agree that this unexpected opportunity to minister is likely God's priority and plan for your day!

But now, witness the beauty of having a schedule: you know that you missed that vacuuming chore. You know that you'll need to fit it in somewhere, and soon. You can quickly assess what other tasks and events upcoming will have to be shuffled so that you can get that cleaning done.

Or, perhaps you let it go for that week entirely. Well, if the next Tuesday is a brilliant, sunny spring day and you are tempted to blow off the vacuuming and take all the kids on a nature walk, I'm betting that you'll at least remember that it's been two weeks since you vacuumed. You are aware that this task is becoming a significant priority. You might even decide to vacuum earlier in the day than your schedule says, while the kids are having lunch, so that you can both get that important (but boring) chore done and follow that creative impulse and get outside.

Another hidden benefit of scheduling is that you find time slots for things (like vacuuming) that really must be done but do not seem to have value in the moment when compared with other things. Most house cleaning chores fall into this category for me, but my personal "ah ha!" moment came in connection with the mundane task of dealing with papers on my desk, specifically the daily mail and correcting my kids' seat work assignments.

Having four kids under the age of six and one on the way when I began homeschooling, the only way I could see to bring order out of the chaos in my own mind (let alone my environment) was to write up a plan that would give me time slots where babies were napping, toddlers playing, and older children doing lessons. I never really expected to follow the daily or weekly plan as written; I started by wanting to just see if I could even hope to fit everything that I wanted to get done into a single week.

Back then, our mailman came at about 11:00 AM, and I used to make sandwiches at about 11:30 AM and pray a blessing with the kids and then go get the mail from the box. The lunch break was supposed to last an hour, and then the babies went down for a nap, the toddlers for a rest, and it was prime time for me to teach the older kids to read and do math.

But, you know how it is. When you get the mail, you want to open interesting letters, look through catalogs, and file bills so they don't get lost. At this time of my life, I had a small business (the home party kind) so the mail almost always brought things that I did need to attend to in short order.

However, opening and processing the mail was not something that I had scheduled in, so the typical result was that the kids would drift away from the lunch table as I sat and digested both the meal and the mail. I would even get into answering it via my computer, make phone calls related to it, or sit at the table browsing catalogs, since the kids were basically peaceful with full bellies or sleepy heads. Thus was key time for teaching and interacting with my older children often misspent!

Now, I know that this sounds minor, and in a way it was. But it was a bad pattern. I found it easy to adjust once I realized that the consistent misstep in my days could be corrected simply by creating a scheduled time slot for reading and responding to my mail that worked better for our family.

I determined that I would not go out to the mailbox at lunch time, but rather in the late afternoon, after all lessons were done. I then could roll reading and responding to mail in with later afternoon phone calls that I had already scheduled in that time, as well as folding laundry and starting dinner preparations. In that same general time frame, my kids did their afternoon pick-up, settled into their "free time after lessons" mode, and were usually reading, playing outside happily, or occasionally watching a video.

This one adjustment to my schedule made a huge difference in my productivity as a teacher, and also in my kids' character formation and academic progress. I don't think I could have made this change if I hadn't put the work into thinking through the elements of our days and putting a structured schedule in place, so that when the problem arose I could both see the imbalance (I was not getting lessons done that required undivided attention from me) and make the needed adjustment to right it (change mail processing to a different time of day). After seeing this relationship between scheduling and structure, and having applied the lesson on a small scale, I then applied this principle to more and more decisions that I made about how my children and I spent our days.

Schedules support children by giving them structure

Now, so far in this chapter I've been focused on how schedules help us moms. Let me end this chapter by reminding you of how they affect your children.

Most (but not all) of us discover the benefits of putting infants on feeding and napping schedules when we begin building our families. While those among us who like to get up and go might have our infants napping at odd times and in car seats or portable cribs, I think we can all agree that most babies benefit from regular daily rhythms that allow for a healthy cycle of nutrition, rest, activity, and early bedtimes. (We moms especially love the last one!)

What may not be obvious to you as you come out of those infant-centered years and are now defining new patterns for your homeschooling days is that young, school-aged children thrive just as much as do infants on a regular, structured, weekly plan. Having reliable weekly rhythms that toddlers and early school-aged children can predict provides the same elements that are important to infants—and more.

School-aged children need good nutrition provided at reasonable intervals. They can go longer between meals than can infants, but their capacity to be cheerful, or learn lessons, or play quietly can be significantly affected by low blood sugar (resulting from not eating regular meals on time) or sugar crashes (resulting from meals that are "quick fixes" and thus sugar-laden).

School-aged kids need periods of intellectual activity, where their young minds are exercised, challenged, and expanded. They also need free play time (ideally outside), and creative undirected play times, during which they process what they've experienced that day and learn to amuse themselves in constructive ways. They need rest periods during the day, and early bedtimes that allow for the hours of sleep that their growing bodies require.

Children typically thrive when these elements are assembled into a routine. If they regularly get up at a set time and do the same kinds of things at the same times day after day, children tend to feel emotionally secure and content. In this kind of ordered environment, they know what to expect, their biorhythms are kept steady, and their days are interesting and varied, yet orderly and predictable. Thus are they positioned to do their best—physically and emotionally.

They don't tend to get stale unless they are cooped up for too many hours a day. Fresh air, sunshine, and some variety of scenery benefit all humans. But young children rarely crave the variety and excitement that bored adults do. Too much of what adults perceive as "everyday life" is still new and exciting to have become *blasé* quite yet.

Structures really aren't straitjackets!

Does this mean you can't ever change up the day? No! That neighbor who showed up on Tuesday afternoon changed things up: you let the kids watch a video instead of doing their afternoon pick-up and playing outside, where they would have needed your attention.

Seasonal (or weather) changes often bring welcome variations: we stay in on rainy or cold days, and decide to take nature walks instead of doing book work on those glorious spring days, or have super-fun snow days during blizzards.

For little ones, a trip to the grocery store, a walk to a nearby park, or an outing to the mall can be all the change-up they need! As they grow older, children might have after-school sports or clubs or visit friends or go on scheduled field trips or attend co-op classes or have weekly music lessons. All these will bring variety to their days, but can be kept in a regular, weekly, predictable structure.

The key here is the term "change up." I'm circling back now to those of us who are free spirits by nature, who love to go and do, and whose impulse is that the kids need to experience a broad variety of things outside the home. You might be thinking of good things, like field trips, play groups, co-op meetings, time with friends, farming or sports activities, and crafts or hobbies. Here's what I would lovingly say, however: if you don't have a basic schedule, a regular rhythm, or a clearly defined structure to your week, what you tend to then generate is a randomness, where plans are often impulsively made and followed, leading to a downward cycle of inconsistency on your part with schooling and uncertainty and an accompanying lack of motivation, trust, and respect on the part of your kids.

The moms that I have met who tend to impulsively follow their desires to "go and do" often feel chronically rushed, and often speak unkindly to their children as a result of the urgency born of over commitment. Their children do not know what to expect next, or how to meet their moms' expectations, and can grow surly, or demanding, or petulant, or exasperated and disrespectful. They generally grow in self-dependence and look to their own devices to cope with chaotic conditions. And those are just character issues.

Children typically thrive when key elements are assembled into a routine.

With academic lessons, if moms skip them in favor of trips out of the house to touch the sky, or if they don't discipline themselves to correct the schoolwork that students have done, their children will learn that they don't really have to study, or work diligently, since there is no reliable reward for their efforts (or consequence for their sloth). Nor do they feel like they progress towards a goal.

Students who don't receive corrected schoolwork back don't know if they're making errors or getting A's. They muddle through as best they can, but gaps are forming in the fabric of their knowledge of the world. Furthermore, certain academic subjects build on concepts that must be taught in order, and cannot be quickly made up. Spotty lessons compound learning difficulties for these subjects, and your kids can truly fall behind in school if lessons are regularly skipped.

And all this bad fruit can result from prizing what we think of as spontaneity, creativity, or energy, when the reality is that we are often lazy, undisciplined, self-focused, and lacking self-control. Successful homeschooling (and parenting) involves planning, consistency, diligence, and faithfulness.

There are not really any shortcuts here, but the fruit of submitting our wills to disciplined living is sweet. My favorite Scripture passages that would teach us these truths are below, for your consideration and meditation. May the Lord show you His will in these things through them, and may He grace you to grow in submission to these truths.

O LORD, you have searched me and known me! You know when I sit down and when I rise up; you discern my thoughts from afar. You search out my path and my lying down and are acquainted with all my ways. Even before a word is on my tongue, behold, O LORD, you know it altogether. You hem me in, behind and before, and lay your hand upon me. Such knowledge is too wonderful for me; it is high; I cannot attain it.

Psalm 139:1-6 (ESV)

I am the true vine, and my Father is the vinedresser. Every branch in me that ***does not*** *bear fruit he takes away, and every branch that* ***does*** *bear fruit he* ***prunes****, that it may bear* ***more*** *fruit.*

John 15:1-2 (ESV)

Older women likewise are to be reverent in behavior … [and] are to teach what is good, and so train the young women to love their husbands and children, to be self-controlled, pure, working at home, kind, and submissive to their own husbands, that the word of God may not be reviled.

Titus 2:3-5 (ESV)

14.

For everything there is a season, and a time for every matter under heaven.

Ecclesiastes 3:1 (ESV)

A Time to Plan

One thing that all homeschooling moms need in their weekly schedule is a time to plan upcoming lessons and activities. I'm a firm believer in the value of the old adage, "Plan your work, and then work your plan." As with the previous chapter on schedules and structure, I know that some of you reading these words may feel challenged (stifled, even) by this assertion, but I believe that planning is such a key to homeschooling success that I'm going to argue for it anyway. So, come: let us reason together!

First, let me define "planning your school year" in context. It is not about making buying decisions about curricula: you've already done that by the time you've come to plan. This is when you are actually looking at the curricula you have already purchased (or must create) and getting down to determining exact pages to be read and assignments to be made and completed within specific timeframes. Typically, most moms will do some advance planning, usually in the summer months before the school year starts, and then also need to carve out a set time to plan week to week. I'm going to cover both kinds of planning in this chapter.

Advance (Summer) Planning

Advance planning is, of course, only for those of us who are early birds, which—it may surprise you to learn—is the majority of us. Throughout the nation, many moms spend time online looking over web pages that display and explain curricula that interest them, then either make online purchases or wait to go to their state's homeschooling convention. There, discounts abound and one can talk to corporate reps about their products, see and touch the products, and perchance find a program never seen before.

These conventions are held from about mid-April to late June. If you are a new homeschooler, I encourage you to attend yours! Beyond the vendor hall, these gatherings offer great speakers who deliver talks that can envision and equip you for homeschooling. Also, there's great support in just being among so many like-minded folks over the course of a weekend, and you might find a mentor among those older women who attend.

However you procure your curricula, if you're an early bird, you'll have most of your core programs bought and in your home by mid-June. If you follow a traditional school schedule, you then have July and August to do planning and gathering of needed supplies before starting to teach in the fall. Summer planning can encompass a variety of activities. Below are thumbnail sketches of the most typical ones:

- If your humanities program requires the purchase of "living books" and does not offer ready-made book packages, you would spend time shopping local and online book stores for these. You'd be making decisions on how many to buy, informed by preliminary searches of your public library or local used book stores and your assessment of your child's reading speeds.
- If you purchased a math curriculum that relies on manipulatives, you may have purchased them from the same company, or need to gather common household items to use (buttons, coins, etc.). In either case, you'd want to familiarize yourself with how these manipulatives will be used as you teach,

so you'll want to look in depth at the first ten lessons or so, at a minimum.
- If you're going to be teaching a subject with which you have little familiarity—say, the history of the Ancient World, or a foreign language that you don't speak, or the exact process of teaching a child to read—then you'll want to study up, familiarizing yourself as much as you can in advance.
- Possibly your curricula needs some assembly: maybe it comes with cards that are perforated but not yet broken apart or assembled into a card box.
- Or you may need to gather art supplies like crayons, scissors, and colored paper in order to make lapbooks.
- Or perhaps the program is delivered digitally, and you'll need to print out worksheets or maps for your student during the year, and you want to get some of that out of the way.

There are more kinds of tasks involved in summer planning, but the above list covers most of it. Beyond these, there are the organizational aspects of the coming year to prepare as well. For instance, you'll need to find answers to questions like these:

- Where will your children sit and do their independent seat work? (Note to newcomers: you don't need a separate schoolroom in order to homeschool. Most children do seat work at the kitchen table or in the dining room, or possibly pulled up to the living room coffee table. See Chapter 15 on this topic.)
- Where will you sit to teach, one-on-one, with them? (Many of us choose to work at the kitchen table for subjects like math and handwriting, but gravitate towards the couch for reading aloud or discussions.)
- Where will you store school supplies? (If your children need quiet in order to study, the answer will be different than if they need your input and/or supervision. If they are younger, supplies may need to be more closely managed by you than if they are older, and can keep them accessible and organized for themselves.)
- Do your kids need a computer in order to do schoolwork? If so, how will you monitor them so that they stay both safe and productive?
- And, possibly the biggest hurdle of this kind: how will you organize the student's work?

I want to cover (and perhaps, introduce) in detail three commonly used systems of organization for student work here. They are:

1. workbox systems
2. file-based systems
3. notebook systems

Workbox Systems

Workbox systems were first popularized among homeschoolers by Sue Patrick, who still actively teaches workshops on them around the nation and sells supplies for her system. Patrick's assertion is that this system offers "an effective teaching system to reduce your organizational time and increase your child's self-control, independence and learning."[1]

In summary, you create a series of containers into which you place the daily assignments for the child. If we were talking about a Kindergarten child, one box might contain a phonics workbook with pages marked to be done. Another would contain beads and strings for him to work according to pattern cards. A third would have his math workbook and needed manipulatives with the lesson marked out. Finally, there might be a Bible lesson: a book that Mom reads aloud to him and a coloring page that he does as he listens. Of course, this workbox would contain the crayons as well. Older students using a workbox system might have detailed instructions for a writing assignment in a box, or find an educational video to watch.

The beauty of the system is that the mom organizes all materials and assignments ahead of the day, which means that her day generally goes more peacefully than if the work were not so fully organized. On a daily basis, the mom changes page markers in books and makes sure that needed "extras" (like crayons or math manipulatives) are in the boxes. It's a great discipline for moms because it keeps them current with what their children are doing while working independently.

Then, the other benefit is that the student—even while quite young—has freedom of action within set limits. He is being trained in liberty! He learns to manage his work, and own it. Within the mom's guidelines, the student chooses which workbox to do when in his day. Within limits set by his mom, he organizes his own pace and takes the subjects in the order he prefers.

There are general rules that he follows, of course. He might need to be done by

1 Sue Patrick's Workbox System, <http://www.workboxsystem.com>. Retrieved 15 November 2013.

noon (if in Kindergarten) or work to a specific class time in the week (if older) when you plan to discuss or correct his work, etc. If there are music lessons, one workbox might be simply his practice book that sends him to the piano with his understanding that he needs to practice marked pieces there for a set time, like half an hour.

File Systems

File systems are similar to workbox ones, and generally work easier with older children. Instead of boxes, the mom organizes work pages, assignment charts, and other needed student papers into file folders that students learn to access and manage.

File systems are flexible. If you have a curriculum that uses a lot of printouts, for instance, you can use them to store all the year's work in one place (printing out all of maps, for instance, into one folder and vocabulary worksheets into another, during the summer planning times). Then, during the school year, the child will visit this file weekly for his needed supplies. Alternatively, you could divide the same kinds of papers into 36 weekly file folders that each contain all the maps, vocabulary sheets, etc. that will be needed for that one week's work.

Typically, moms include in a file system a place for students to store their "work product"—completed work pages, maps, etc. There also can be files for corrected work (your feedback) that needs to be redone by the student before being permanently archived, as with Writing drafts during the composition process.

Obviously, you can use a mixture of workboxes and files, given that homeschooling curricula use a variety of supplies: some paper-based and others more bulky (e.g. art supplies and math manipulatives). And this leads us to our third basic organizational strategy: the student notebook. Let me note before describing this system that it, too, can be combined with workbox and/or file folder systems.

Notebook Systems

Notebook-based organization allows moms to create collections of materials that the student will need in order to complete his assignments (such as worksheets, coloring pages, or spelling lists) that are portable. Such notebooks usually double as a storage space for finished work.

Notebooks can be organized by subject (separate notebooks for different subjects, or tabs in one binder for different ones) or chronologically. (Tabs are for weeks of the year, and work from all subjects is stored as it is in process or completed.) Notebooks can be loose-leaf binders or spiral-bound pages with pockets for loose pages that are added.

Again, the summer months are the time when moms who use notebook systems will often print out needed pages, or even break apart workbooks in order to distribute the pages chronologically through the notebook.

As with the other systems, the detailed planning involved here helps the mom master the contents of the course of study as she plans, and frees the busy mom up significantly during the school year ahead.

Getting too far ahead

Summer planning is obviously valuable, and I recommend it. But, there are some possible pitfalls involved in it. As with any long journey, one has to plan for plans going awry! For instance, too much detailed planning too far ahead can lead to some constrictions (or a sense of wasted time and printer ink) if plans need to be changed. Illnesses (in your family or extended family), job changes, moves, or even just a jump in a child's cognitive abilities earlier than expected can throw off the delicate balance of assignments planned months in advance.

Thankfully, the last named is the most common pitfall! As mentioned elsewhere, children grow in spurts (or stair steps) with sudden changes in their abilities and working habits. A notebook that may have been packed chock full of good assignments for the year in July may be in tatters by December as a child suddenly jumps up in reading ability, or develops a sour attitude towards seat work.

Even when your summer planning efforts hold up, you'll still need a weekly slot to dot the i's and cross the t's, and be ready to teach one-on-one lessons in the week ahead. So, let's think about a weekly planning slot, and how you use it.

Weekly planning

There are some really enjoyable ways to gain a weekly time to plan, and I'm going to share just a few of them with you that worked well in different seasons of our lives over the 22 years that we were actively homeschooling.

Planning for the week ahead on Saturday mornings, away from the house, was always a welcome break for me. My dear husband, Scott, minded the children while

I usually went to the public library. There, I could browse for good books to use in the week ahead and, undisturbed for hours at a time, look over my curricula, crafts, and lesson plans for the week ahead. On my way home, if we were missing any key groceries or school supplies, I could pick them up from the stores.

As with any long journey, one has to plan for plans going awry.

Scott filled this time in different ways over the years. For a season, he just baby sat. As the kids grew older, he did elementary science experiments with them; these became the heart of our weekly science lessons. Then, when they were a bit older, he switched to marshalling them to do all of the heavy cleaning for the week (vacuuming all rugs, washing the kitchen floor and appliances, and doing the bathrooms) while I was out, which really saved my strength for the rest of the week.

I have also gone through phases where I used Friday afternoons as a reward/respite/planning time for us all. If the kids had finished enough schoolwork by Friday at around 3 PM, we all were rewarded with a trip to the public library. In this season, my youngest was about six and reading fluently, so they all generally grabbed new finds and scattered around the library. They disappeared into their new books while I browsed and planned the week to come.

Teaching Your Children to Plan Wisely

I know that most readers of this book are younger parents, but some may be newcomers to homeschooling with older children who have been pulled out of traditional school settings, so I'll share another system that worked for us.

When most of our kids became "tweens," we posted a family calendar and we bought each one a paper-based personal planner. The older boys were beginning to have music or art lessons, sports practices, and club meetings outside of the house, and do things more and more on their own—like agreeing to baby sitting jobs or volunteering for church work. We established the family calendar as our central communication tool. They had to check it before committing independently to any job or event, and record the commitment promptly after making it.

They knew that there were certain parameters that they had to maintain: rhythms of work and play. If something seemed questionable to them, we trained them to ask before committing. We also reserved the right to veto their commitments (but sought to do this as rarely as possible). This "right" goes back to Chapter 8 (Training in Liberty); there were times during the years when our older children were learning to manage their time when they made poor choices. As their parents, we needed to step in and reduce their liberty so that they wouldn't be overwhelmed by youthful inexperience.

Each Sunday evening, we would gather as a family and scrutinize the week ahead together. We then helped the kids to put schoolwork and "life" together into their personal planners.

My planning time for the week at this time was still Saturday mornings, but it got its finishing touches during this Sunday meeting as the older students' independent commitments came more into focus for me.

When is Your Best Time to Plan?

I know many women who are night owls and do their planning after the house is quiet at night. Many do it one day at a time, rather than one week at a time. Some roll planning in with their devotional times.

Planning won't just happen: we must plan to plan! So many moms struggle with homeschooling because of the daily host of little obstacles that seem to thwart our efforts at every turn. It's the pencil (or pencil sharpener) that we can't find, or the math book that's gone missing, or the library book that we need for the history lesson but failed to order in time, or the crayons that are scattered all over the living room just when we are sitting to read aloud—these are the things that pile up to form seemingly insurmountable walls in our minds or provoke low-level grumbling and complaining.

Such little stoppers are the joy stealers; they are the little foxes that eat the vines that are just blossoming in the garden of the Lord that you are faithfully tending (Song of Songs 2:15). Catch them! Pen them up! Find time in the summer months and then in your weekly routine during schooling months to take the time you need to plan, assess progress, and then plan again. To quote another cliché, "if you fail to plan, you can plan to fail…" or at least to lose some of your momentum and joy in teaching.

So, here's a practical application for you: Just when is that planning slot going to be for *you* in this season of life? Figure it out, and then share it with your family. Let them help you guard it, and make it work! It will do all of them good, and bring greater honor to your Heavenly Father as you walk in greater peace through the days ahead.

15.

home·school [hohm-skool]
verb (used with object)
1. to teach (one's children) at home instead of sending them to school.
verb (used without object)
2. to educate one's children at home.
noun
3. a school set up in the home.[1]

Looking Far (Why We Don't Need Classrooms)

One of the things that might not be apparent to you when you first start homeschooling is how to handle its physical properties—the "where do you do your schooling?" part of it. You may start by assuming that, since you always worked at a desk or table when in grade school, and learned in a classroom that was rimmed with school supplies, a globe, bulletin boards, and blackboards, that you must have a dedicated space in your home so you can create a similar classroom environment. Many of us

1 "homeschool." Dictionary.com Unabridged. Random House, Inc. Accessed 21 January 2014. <Dictionary.com http://dictionary.reference.com/browse/homeschool>.

do have schoolrooms—and love them—but if you're thinking that it's a *need* and not a preference, think again!

We were not a military family, but we moved a lot. In fact, recently I counted it up; we moved eighteen times in our first twenty years of marriage! I had all of our six kids in the first eleven years of marriage, so for half of those eighteen moves I was pregnant or nursing; for the other half, I was homeschooling a houseful. I share this background in order to explain that I had the opportunity of schooling my kids in a variety of home set-ups—some of which we rented and some that we owned. This is one part of the background I want to give you before sharing what I'm about to share.

The other part of background is this: when I was at your stage (considering and just starting to homeschool), I was doing research on homeschooling in order to educate myself. (This was in the dark ages, before the Internet, so books were my main resource.) While researching, I came across books by one of the earliest proponents of homeschooling: Raymond Moore.

Assisted by his wife, Dorothy, Moore came to his support of homeschooling by way of concerns with child development. Back in the 80's, there was a big push in mainstream education to get children into preschools earlier and earlier. This was partly fueled by the feminist movement, and partly forwarded by those who advocated earlier teaching in order to develop so-called "higher order thinking skills" in children at younger ages.

Raymond and Dorothy Moore spent years investigating the results of early education. They examined others' studies and conducted their own studies. Their conclusion was that before the ages of 8-10, children did better as students if they remained in loving homes. In fact, the titles of their books reflected what became strong convictions for them: *Better Late Than Early* and *School Can Wait* both argued for delaying formal schooling until the later time frame.

The Moores taught that child development directly affects learning abilities. They explained that small motor coordination, eyesight, hearing, the ability to focus their attention, and emotional stability all needed time and space to develop, or learning could actually become delayed later. The Moores argued that children who delayed the start of formal schooling later than the typical ages of the day would quickly catch up to their age mates who had begun younger, and also that the delayed starters would remain better learners ongoing. Finally, they wrote that children who felt safe, loved, encouraged, and valued in their own homes by their own parents had the best possible learning environment.

Now, how do these two threads from my own background—our frequent moving and the Moores' input—come together?

First, I can say from personal experience that you don't *need* a designated schoolroom, though it can be nice to have one for organizing purposes. (I started by creating school rooms in the first two houses that we lived in when I was beginning to teach my children, but found that we quickly moved out of them as we discovered our own learning and teaching rhythms as a family.)

You don't need a designated schoolroom, but it can be nice to have one for organizing purposes.

Second, if your focus is on your young children's well being, you don't need (or even want) to recreate a classroom environment in your home.

I have not re-read the Moore books in over thirty years, but I can still remember being very impressed by their arguments about children *needing* to literally "look far" daily. The Moores cited studies finding that children who were cooped up in one small room for hours, and made to do significant amounts of close work—such as handwriting, reading, and math seat work—which at the time were normal for children in preschools, were more likely to develop eye problems.

The Moores' books also highlighted for me what I'd learned in other contexts about fine motor movement needing time to develop: it's hard for preschool-aged children through first graders to cut accurately with scissors, write small letters and numbers, or do other kinds of activities that require precise, small movements of hands and fingers. In many classroom settings, the focus is on close work, and often this requires more fine motor movement than some little ones have yet developed.

And then there were what I came to call the heebie-jeebies. Most boys and some girls just *have to* move around. They are developing, and their bodies crave movement. Seat work for hours amounts to physical discomfort for these kids, and all youngsters need the benefit of exercise and fresh air as part of their daily routine. A classroom setting doesn't encourage physical movement.

We purchased a trampoline and a play gym for our back yard. (I know that many children have been injured on trampolines, so be informed of the risks if you follow our example. We had great success—and virtually no injuries to our kids or their friends in the years we were homeschooling—but everyone needs to make their own choices about yard equipment.) We also installed swings and invested in bikes. All of these helped our kids to do motions that contributed to the development of their inner ears, muscles, and eyesight.

Simply put, children need time to develop physically, mentally, and emotionally. Rushing these things doesn't help children learn better and can harm them. Those who, for educational and/or political reasons would seek to push to get children into schools earlier are still with us today. Also, there are still outspoken proponents of developing "higher order thinking skills" in children at increasingly early ages. I have one daughter-in-law who says that she feels a certain pressure from peers to put her oldest daughter—a two-year-old!—into day care "for the sake of her education." Having raised my own six children and observed hundreds of co-op kids, I see no value in pushing children to learn early.

But don't misunderstand me: some of our children develop early and are ready for reading or seat work young. As those who study gender differences will often note, this is typically the girls. My youngest girl taught herself to read at age 4! She also developed fine muscle movement early, as did my son, David, the artist.

I see lots of value in a steady, reasonable progression of small, bite-sized lessons keyed to the ability of a child to learn them, with a healthy, age-appropriate balance being maintained of mental work, rest, and play. Again, part of establishing routines of the days and weeks includes what is, for little ones, the *work* of learning their ABC's and 123's. And again, it's really important for young children to get out of the house daily, taking in fresh air and exercising, even in mildly inclement weathers.

After reading the Moores' books and doing other similar research, I decided early on that we would not coop ourselves up all day in one schoolroom, nor would I require my little ones to sit at desks and do a lot of seat work. Our studies were done mostly in my kitchens and family rooms in almost all of the houses in which we lived.

While I did *not* choose to delay all formal lessons until my children would have been in second or third grades (as the Moores recommended), I did look to change up their environments, and keep lessons short and sweet. I also went very easy on skills that had to be learned by doing close work or use fine motor skills that weren't yet fully developed.

My kids will tell you that a memorable command heard often from me in their early school years was, "Go look far!" I kept myself aware of how long my kids had been doing seat work or reading. Wanting to protect their eyesight on cold, snowy days I trained them to literally go to the sliding glass doors and look as far as they could for a few minutes when I so directed. Sometimes, I would ask them to spy things way out in the yard, or up in the trees, just to encourage far-looking. In better weather, the imperative became, "Go outside and look far."

So, where did *my* kids do their schoolwork? All over our home, no matter where we lived! Whether I set up a schoolroom or not, my kids usually read on the couch, though one preferred lying on the coffee table on his tummy, with his book on the floor, and another loved to read in the bathtub for hours. We did seat work and one-on-one lessons that required writing at our kitchen table or bar top. We did morning devotions in our living room, which involved a lot of movement to upbeat songs that I played on the guitar. Science was often done outside on nice days.

Later, when the kids grew older and I had a lot of supplies to manage, I did make dedicated schoolrooms (or libraries, as we called them) in my homes, typically using what was meant to be the formal living room. Some of the kids preferred to study in the middle of the family hubbub, but others wanted a quiet room to retreat to, so a schoolroom *was* used. But I still did most of my teaching one-on-one on kitchen surfaces, or in the dining room, where things didn't have to get put away in order for us to eat a meal, or (when reading aloud) on our family-room couches.

As long as they didn't have smart phones or computers, we also allowed our older children to study in their bedrooms. (They chose to work on the floor or beds, not on bedroom desks we provided.) Since it is never a good idea to allow unsupervised use of the Internet or phones, as they came into our home we carefully placed such electronics in places where I could see what was being viewed at any time.

To sum up: I have nothing against neatly organized schoolrooms with all the desks in a row and bulletin boards on the walls! But I do want to remind you of the physical needs of little people, and I also want to assure those of us who may be in tight spaces that schooling can be easily done without a dedicated space set aside!

16.

If evolution really works, how come mothers only have two hands?

Milton Berle

What to do with Preschoolers?

Many a good homeschooling mother has been tempted to throw in the towel because of the challenge that preschoolers present to an orderly daily rhythm. (Here I'm focusing not on the babies, but on the mobile toddlers up to the age of four or five.)

These are the little ones that are busy underfoot, constantly undoing low-lying organized shelves and cupboards, leaving a trail of toys scattered through the entire house, climbing up where they shouldn't when your back is turned, grabbing hold of sister's pencil just in the middle of a beautiful cursive "W" and then wailing loudly because he wants to do school, tooooooo!

You know. We've all been there. Even if you've not started school yet, if you have more than one child and your eldest is entering K-5, you have the T-shirt on this one!

So, the question becomes, how do we "sit at home" with preschoolers? How do we make forward motion with our school-aged children (or with adult tasks) at eye level, when little ones are so busy at knee level or regularly interfering with what's going on at table level?

This one thought, that little ones are constantly changing and growing, has saved my sanity many a time.

Part of the answer, I believe, goes back to what I've already written about establishing a quiet home, where these little people get the nutrition, rest, stability, and attention that they need at this age.

Let's assume that you've agreed with my pitch for the quiet home. Now, here you are: sitting at home and you can't seem to juggle the demands of preschoolers *and* get lessons done with your older students.

Again, the first thing I want to tell you is that you aren't alone.

The second thing I want to say is that, while there are various tips and tricks that I will share in these pages, each one only works for a short time. You will need to cycle through the general approaches that I outline, because your toddlers are growing, changing, and learning so fast. What works for a few weeks may suddenly cease to be helpful.

But, it's helpful to remember why solutions are typically short-lived. When a little one ceases to play contentedly with his toy cars, it may be that he's ready for more mental challenge, or that he needs to run around and develop his muscles.

If we sigh and say, "Oh, great! Now he's interrupting me again," we may be missing a key point: he's growing! This one thought, that little ones are constantly changing and growing, has saved my sanity many a time. It brings a point of reference and a sense of gratitude to my days, and helps me remain relational instead of overly task-oriented. (Because, believe me, when you're homeschooling a houseful, the tug is always towards getting stuff done, not stopping to smell the roses. At least, that's always been *this* Martha's challenge!)

Remembering C.S. Lewis' observation (quoted at the start of Chapter 5, "You Share Who You Are") about not seeing the interruptions from little ones as disturbing, but rather constituting the essence of the life that God is sending one day by day also gave me perspective. Our goal is not so much to pacify little ones as to seek ways that they can grow in tandem with our other goals for our family. One good approach to this is to identify a variety of *good* things that a preschooler can do in your home.

So, with those two foundational ideas firmly fixed: 1) you're going to have to keep changing up these practical tips, and 2) that's because they are growing and learning (yay!), I'll dive into details about the helpful things I've discovered about managing preschoolers.

School Toys

Most of us seasoned homeschooling moms have learned that it's a really good idea to invest in what we call "school toys." These are quiet playthings that ideally have at least a few of the following characteristics:

- The child can play safely with them unaided. (No tiny pieces to choke on, no sharp edges or breakable parts, and nothing that will mark up the walls and the furniture.)
- Ideally, the plaything has some kind of educational value. So, lots of T.V. viewing (which is passive) is not on this list,[1] but an interactive counting or coloring game on iPad or computer might be.
- If the child wants to "be big and do school," you can purchase playthings that have more parts to keep track of, or take more of your attention to supervise (like crayons, paint-with-water books, large beads that he can string, or lacing cards, etc.) These are readily available from many websites that sell educational toys for young learners.

The general idea here is that these playthings are kept away from the preschooler except during times when you are doing lessons with older siblings. Such toys are helpful aids only if the child *wants* to play with them! If he quickly loses interest because they are available all the time (and he will lose interest soon enough in any

1 This is said with the caveat that there are artistic videos (say, of ballets) and educational videos (say, travel videos that tell about people in other lands or documentaries that explain past cultures or events). Even so, my point about this being a relatively passive pursuit stands.

case, at various times and with various toys) then investing in special toys doesn't help us. It just adds to the number of things underfoot, missing parts, or broken around the house, and with the littles disrupting older children's lessons again.

Now, for the very new moms reading here, I'd like to list off some favorite examples of the school toys that we employed at different seasons.

- Quiet Books are a favorite. Their pages are felt, and they have small icons (people, animals, etc., also of felt) that the child moves around while using his imagination. You can buy Quiet Books or make them yourself. If you want to do the latter, visit Pinterest and search there. You'll find hundreds of ideas!
- Playmobil™ sets were a worthy investment for our preschoolers. Again, the trick is to allow play—and that, at a table—only during schooling hours.
- For some little ones, Etch A Sketch-type toys (where the child draws and then easily erases his art and tries again) work well!
- *Limited* and solid videos, either about parts of the world or Bible stories, can be helpful as the "spice" of the day (or as a reward).
- Getting special colored pencils or crayons that *only* get used during lesson times is a good idea, as are special coloring or paint-with-water books.
- A related idea is a deluxe sticker book on the child's favorite topic, and some girls enjoy paper dolls as well.
- For boys especially, outside or active playthings are wanted—for instance, large rubber balls, sand toys, and small scooters. (These assume that you have a child-safe back yard or blacktop for them to use.)
- Audiotapes of stories and songs were always a favorite at my house. With today's technology, your little one can use earbuds or headphones and remain very quiet indeed!
- K-4's can manipulate Play-Doh™, which is non-toxic and pretty cheap. You can make play doughs easily yourself at home, too!
- As I said earlier, some boys would delight in toy trucks and cars. Others enjoy model train sets.
- Little girls might delight in a full-length mirror, a box of dress-up clothes, and some pretend perfume.
- All kids seem to love Legos™ (and their knockoffs). Some will prefer to do the same kind of creative activity with wooden blocks.

- Some children really like chubby board books.

Here are some avenues that I would warn you against:

- Games that have lots of pieces, or are above the ability of your little one to play with independently. If you have to spend all your time managing such toys, they defeat their own purpose.
- Toys that mandate a long attention span with physical quietude or fine motor skills. (Little ones just don't sit still for too long, generally speaking!)
- Again, T.V. as a drug: used for long stretches just to keep them still and quiet.
- And finally, I would counsel you to avoid electronic toys. The stores are full of them these days, and although they might seem educational, they can drive you crazy with their noises and/or repetitive sounds and I find that they do a lot of the creative thinking *for* the child, instead of developing it *in* him. Furthermore, I have observed as a generality that many children tire most easily of this type of toy!

While many of the toys on my "recommended" list above can be initially expensive, there are ways to save money. But, first of all, let's do an attitude check: if you figure that you're in home teaching for the long haul, learn to see such "toys" as an investment in your longevity as a teacher!

Maybe you have more time than cash? You might use summers to visit yard sales and look for bargains. (My married daughter Charity and her husband do this as a date of sorts: they go out early most summer Saturdays in search of yard-sale treasures, and usually find some truly great deals!) You can also become a skilled eBay and Craig's List shopper. And, keep your eye on circulars (and coupons) from stores and websites that sell such toys because you can often pick them up on sale.

Finally, here's one last school-toy tip. After a given one has been loved enough—and ideally before it's lost its desirability—pack it away and bring out a new (or older favorite) toy to surprise and delight your little one! Chances are you'll cycle through about one per month, and if you have about five, they should last you for about one school year.

Activities

Using toys to occupy small children is not the only possible way to amuse them while still helping them to grow. There are a variety of skills that can be learned through doing normal daily activities as well. Again, if you school yourself to see these as opportunities to teach (and not just ways to control or manage) preschoolers, it's easier to make the investment of time that training requires.

For instance, morning routines (we called them "morning B's" at our house) of bed-making, bathing, breakfast, brushing hair and teeth, and Bible devotions typically take up the first hour or more of a young child's day. Require him to learn a routine that becomes automatic over the years through day by day repetition (which requires consistency on your part). He makes his bed. He washes his hands. He has his breakfast and then he brushes his teeth and hair and dresses for the day. (All of these require help at first, of course.) Perhaps he straightens his room as well. Then, he has his little Bible lesson, perhaps with older siblings.

After these, he might have special chores, if he's older (three or four years old). He might feed the family pet, or unload the silverware out of the dish washer. Smaller children can sort silverware into a drawer using a small stool, and put away plastic dishes that are purposefully stored down low where they can reach. Some children can be helpful with amusing the baby, or collecting trash through the house.

Other morning activities might include independent play outside (with some toys mentioned earlier) or quiet "bedroom time" with special school toys or a short video.

In larger families, we busy moms tend to call on the child who can do a job for us most efficiently, rather than taking time to do the harder work of asking (and training) the youngest child who can do the job to help us. But such a focus on doing chores regularly and thoroughly with little ones is important because our older children have their own lessons to do (and the older they get, the more of these there are, typically). By diligently training littles to do short, simple tasks, we both lighten the load for older children and give those little ones meaningful work (and the dignity and sense of purpose that come with it).

To keep myself and my little ones fresh and varied in their activities, I adopted a system of index cards that I kept in a jar. I wrote on these all of the possible toys, amusements, chores, or activities that I had on hand for little children: one of each per card.

As we started school lessons in earnest each morning, I got my littlest ones settled first (while the older ones got their supplies out, sharpening pencils, etc.). I would hold the jar out and have little Davey pick a card. It might say, "play in the sandbox." He might look outside and see that it was raining, and shake his head, "No!"

Okay, fine. He could slip it back into the pack and pick a different card: "draw a sailboat card for Grampa." He nods excitedly, "Yes!" Davey might not have done that one for weeks. I would get out paper and special crayons, and he'd settle into that work while I taught his older sister her vocabulary words.

Now, fair warning again before I paint an unrealistic picture for you: Davey might be delighted to start that project, and he might work at it quietly for a half an hour. Or, it might last for only five minutes. Either way, the trick for me is to not lose patience because I'm seeing the main point as either that he finish what he undertook or that he stay out of my way until I am at a good stopping place with whatever else I'm doing.

If he says after five minutes, "Mommy, I don't want to make a card for Grampa" and hangs his head, I need to be keyed into him enough to think about what's going on underneath, in his heart. Is he discouraged that he can't draw a good enough sailboat? Is he tired from being up late the night before, and I should maybe just get out a story tape? Is he wanting my attention for a few minutes so he can get his little emotional tank refilled? Is he easily discouraged and needs me to help him persevere? Did he never finish breakfast and is now really hungry and in need of a snack? My desired attititude is, "What is my little son really saying to me in that moment, and how can I best serve both him and his siblings?"

No matter what the real reason for his wanting to stop, I would probably have Davey put away his supplies as best he can before allowing him to go on to a new occupation. I might employ the jar again to jog my mind as to possibilities, or simply ask the Lord to help me see just the kind of thing that would help Davey to be in a good place.

As you can see, the quiet home model that I have described is very helpful in this area of child rearing, and to homeschooling in general. We mothers need to have margin in our days! In case this term is new to you, "margin" is the extra measure of time, energy, and emotional stability that allows us to remain flexible, keep events in perspective, and field the little annoyances that come to all mothers.

If I have overfilled my day, I will not have time to process such interruptions as indicators of my little son's needs for care or growth. When time and tasks are generally compressed (and if I add sleep deprivation from nursing babies in the night) I will feel pressured by the needs of other children and by my own miopic focus on the tasks of the day. As a result, Davey will get a smaller slice of my resources.

In a quiet, well-ordered home, there is more margin: more time to notice, to respond, or to pause in teaching older children. It's easier to be kind and gracious—like God. We image Jesus to our children, and we want to give as accurate a portrayal as possible! When we sin, margin gives us time for personal reflection, and for conviction and repentance. When we humbly express our faults to our children we speak the gospel message loudly to our youngsters, and cover a multitude of sins.

The Bible says that Christians are Jesus' hands and feet in this world, and He has gifted mothers with nurturing hearts, observant eyes, and intuitive senses that help us to notice—if we employ them—and to respond to our children as He would, in His name. This is the essence of "managing" preschoolers, and I'll go on to talk about a key element of it in the next chapter, when I discuss the crucial element of "face time"!

17.

Then children were brought to him that he might lay his hands on them and pray. The disciples rebuked the people, but Jesus said, "Let the little children come to me and do not hinder them, for to such belongs the kingdom of heaven."

MATTHEW 19:13-14 (ESV)

Face Time

This book is mostly written with moms who are new to homeschooling in mind. Of you, a majority will be parenting young children. If your eldest child is in Kindergarten or 1st grade, many moms will have two or more preschoolers or toddlers right behind. Also, many homeschoolers plan larger families (which these days means more than two, but I see average homeschooling families these days as being somewhere between three and eight children).

If you have multiple children at a variety of ages, you are going to be homeschooling a houseful! And, if that's not you, then you may be one of those moms who is more mobile, and adopts a busier lifestyle than those who have napping babies. You may also be holding down a job. Whatever your distraction might be, this chapter focuses our attention on the importance of giving your young children your full attention periodically through the day.

I call this "face time." Here's why. When I was schooling three children (K-2) and had two younger preschoolers as well, it was common that I would be home all day, and the kids would move through their regular school rhythms while the toddlers played *mostly* peacefully with school toys, or napped.

Occasionally there would be a squabble or the sound of something unusual, and I would call in to the older ones in the living room: "Nathan, did you take your sister's toy?" or "Son, are you touching that plant?"

"Yes, Mom!" came the frank reply. Pause. Then, "How did you *know*?"

"Remember, I told you?" I would tease, keeping the mood light and smiling, "I have eyes in the back of my head! Even when you can't see me, or I'm doing something else, I know what you're up to!"

This exchange would have been very common. My young children believed that, in our quiet home, I could "see" them at all times. I felt it was a harmless fancy to tell them that I had eyes in the back of my head.

Towards the end of one particularly busy day, I was putting four-year-old Davey to bed. As I bent over to kiss him, Davey stopped me.

"Mommy?" he said.

"Yes, Davey," I answered, loving the trustful look in his big blue eyes.

"Mommy, I know you were really busy today, so when I finished my drawring (he always said it that way) today, I held it up behind you so that you could see it with the eyes in the back of your head."

That was a moment that I hope I never forget. My heart constricted with love and pain. Davey kept looking at me with love and trust, but it was the moment when I realized that if my little four-year-old boy had to hold his drawring up to his mommy's eyes in the back of her head, something was wrong with his mommy's lifestyle.

I realized that I needed to make adjustments in my weekly schedule and daily rhythms so that, if Davey wanted to show me his drawring, there would be a good moment in our day when I could really look at it, interact with him about it, and be his friend, mother, and teacher for real.

"Face time" is a phrase that I coined from that defining moment in my life to mean those times when I give my undivided heart, mind, and eyes to my little ones. Face time can have a wide variety of contexts and expressions. Here's a starter list:

- talking while walking (to the mailbox, around the block, or in park lands... where isn't as important as the focus on the child)
- cuddling and tickling (bed, floor, or couch: your pick!)
- reading aloud (snuggled on a couch, propped up in bed, or sitting in a chair—the aim is attention and closeness)
- supervising (and participating in) educational games
- doing kitchen chores together
- amusing baby together
- quiet talks, prayer, reviewing the day together, etc., at bedtime

I've spent a lot of time patiently teaching, correcting, and training little ones to be compliant, cheerful, patient, and play independently during certain periods of the day, as explained in Chapter 16 ("What to do with Preschoolers?"). It's wise to do so: such disciplines are essential for your homeschooling endeavors, and good for the little children themselves. Such training yields the kind of stability and relationships that you need in order to teach academic lessons! (One can't teach children who are rebellious, demanding, fretful, or depend on you entertaining them for every moment of their waking life—especially in multiples!)

All that said and acknowledged, there's a hidden peril with well-behaved little ones. Since they are largely happy to play with the toys you provide, eat their snacks, take their naps, and leave you free to work with older kids or do needed household chores, after a bit you may find (as I did) that you neglect them. You may miss precious moments that build your family, as I did. Or, you may find that you undermine your own homeschooling efforts by tempting little ones to engage in bad behaviors.

I've long observed that, in larger families particularly, older children are often pretty well behaved, while younger ones are consistently whiny or surly or demanding or rebellious or clowns. In my book for more experienced homeschoolers (*Are We There Yet?*), I have a chapter on the ins and outs of having older children do the schooling and tending of younger siblings. This practice has definite pros and cons! But even if you are mostly in favor of using elder children as your extra eyes, ears, and hands, I wrote *this* chapter to say that God gave your little ones to *you* to parent, and they need to have regular face time with *you*!

Relationships are developed by spending time together. I will go out on a limb and say that human closeness requires both quality *and* quantity time. We homeschooling moms spend oodles of time *around* our kids, but are we really spending time *with* them—especially if our littlest ones are well-behaved?

Little ones do need to be managed so that they do not impede our efforts to teach their older siblings—this is a good thing—but I'm focused now on being careful not to marginalize little ones once they are trained. So, granted that our little ones need us, how do we work towards face time in practice, especially with older school-aged children to teach?

In my experience, it's best to fill little ones' nutritional and emotional tanks in just about the same way: small, frequent supplies. You don't have to spend all day, every day, doing face time. Rather, you need to consciously remember to *include* small moments of *real* face time several times per day as a regular feature of your family rhythms.

Below are some ways that I adjusted my daily routines after that memorable evening with Davey. (I give these as concrete examples of possible ways to apply this principle; your applications and rhythms may be totally different.)

First, I sought to use features that were already present in my daily rhythms to new purposes. For instance, I mentally teamed up daily snack times with face time as a reminder to myself. Before I changed things, I had been giving little ones mid-morning and mid-afternoon snacks, like cheese and crackers, fruit, etc. I would put the food and drink in front of them and leave them to enjoy them while I went on to the next task. Now, during morning snack, I took the time to sit with them for fifteen minutes or so at the kitchen table and talk with them about what they had been doing (or playing with) while I had been busy working with their older siblings.

During afternoon snack, which was usually right after naps, I tried to get everyone to sit together, and tried to teach older siblings to draw their younger ones out on their thoughts about life, the universe, and everything. This was a great context for one of them to ask Davey if he had any drawrings to show us all!

A second change I made was right after lunch. I had been accustomed to resting with a book, or magazine, in the half-hour between the end of lunch and the little ones' nap (or rest) time. Now, I developed a habit of having couch time read-alouds with my pre-schoolers just before I put them to bed for naps.

I will admit that in some seasons, this was challenging. With a full belly and a cuddly little warm body beside me, I often fought to stay awake and retain energy for lessons with older siblings that were coming! As my older children became able, they would clean up the lunch things for me and find their materials for the lessons I would teach while the little ones slept or rested. So, I got to sit and enjoy my face time, and had the added help of rising to find a clean kitchen and a ready teaching environment after I had put littles into their beds.

"Face time" is when I give my undivided heart, mind, and eyes to my little ones.

Another change I made was that I tried to go out for a walk with the little ones each nice day for at least 15 minutes after they got up from their naps. At this time, I had usually just finished my most intensive teaching stints with older siblings, so this walk was as much a breather for me as for them. The new element of this was that, whereas before I was content to let older siblings tend and play with younger ones while I enjoyed a catalog or letter that had come in the mail, now I made a point to be *the* pusher of the swing, or point out natural features on a walk, or play with them with a ball myself, or whatever. My focus was on the little people, not their older siblings and not my own recreation.

During afternoon clean-up times (during the 4:30-5:00 PM slot), I paired older siblings with younger ones. The elders were instructed to help, teach, and encourage their younger partners in cleaning up. This was face time for littles with their bigger siblings.

At bed time, my husband read aloud, prayed, and tucked in our kids. This was his face time! This custom was already in place when I sought to make changes, but I mention it here to say that kids need Dad's face sometime during the day as well!

And just so that no one reading this gets the idea that I'm super-mom, I did *not* get to all of these opportunities for having face time every day. Rather, these were the times in our family routines that I identified as possible times when I *could* purposefully have face time. Getting to one or two of these possible opportunities per day was far better than getting to none! As with my story of the vacuum-cleaning chore, the principle here is to identify places in a schedule when things *can* happen, so that 1) you can be sure there *are* places, and 2) so that you know when one has been missed!

As a finishing thought to this chapter, I have found that so much of homeschooling involves thoughtful, prayerful management of the bits and pieces of life. Family rhythms are seasonal: what works for a time is predictably going to change. To borrow a phrase that my former senior pastor used to love: "Constant change is here to stay." We need to get comfortable with both setting up working systems *and* periodically reassessing them so that they can be improved or replaced. We will need to both work hard to construct homeschooling frameworks and also hold them lightly, so that we can adjust them to be both strong and flexible.

It's a challenge that we're up to because of the grace of God, who called us to this lifestyle, and because we women are generally gifted at nurture, at observation, and at devising alternate ways to undertake various tasks for His glory and the good of our families.

18.

She looks well to the ways of her household and does not eat the bread of idleness. Her children rise up and call her blessed; her husband also, and he praises her: "Many women have done excellently, but you surpass them all."

PROVERBS 31:27-29 (ESV)

Managing Chores

This is another one of the more practical chapters on how to manage homeschooling with multiple kids. The principle here is that kids need to learn to be faithful in little things, so that as they grow up they will be ready to be faithful with progressively greater things. Since kids can really contribute to the family project of running what my Scott calls an "industrial strength" home, I thought I'd pass along some tips from my experiences in this area.

First, a story. My eldest son was 16, and we had just come out of the dentist's office and I was *boiling* mad. His lack of diligence in caring for his teeth had led to gingivitis, which meant extra strains on our budget and more trips to the dentist in our future. I stewed and fumed all the way to our next stop for the day: a group class with other high schoolers studying worldviews and apologetics.

When we got to the home where the class met, the mother of the house (Lucy, a good friend) happened to be standing on the front step, welcoming guests and grabbing a breath of fresh air. I slammed the car door, marched up to her, gestured at my son, and said, "He's sixteen years old! Do I *really* have to tell him to brush his teeth?!!"

Lucy blinked once. Then she smiled and said, "Yup! It's your job. You're his mother."

I stood there, stunned into silence. The truth of her words hit me like a ton of bricks. Just because he was older didn't mean that I was off the hook. He was still my son, and in my home, and I was still his mother, charged by God with training him. So, yes. If that's what it took, I still had to tell him to brush his teeth.

In the years when kids are young, the job of training them on daily and weekly chores can be both grindingly repetitive and time consuming. They need to learn good hygiene habits of brushing (hair and teeth), washing, changing clothes, etc. Then there are the management skills—making their beds faithfully, cleaning up the mess in their rooms, and putting away toys and dishes in common spaces in the home. Finally, there are household chores, like feeding pets, running and folding laundry, and putting away dishes.[1]

The more children you have, the more you need some kind of good system that allows you to give the accountability that kids need without spending all your time standing over them.

As with other chapters, I want to start by reminding you that some of these tips will work only for a season. All systems will get tiresome in and of themselves, or time consuming, and you'll want to change them up. You don't have to use my methods! By all means, invent your own applications of the principle of training your children in faithfulness to do little things. But, I'd like to give you some examples of ways that you can manage this mothering responsibility with grace—and even have some space for fun.

1 Because most new homeschoolers have mostly little kids, I'm not going to include real cleaning in this list, but as kids become tweens, heavy cleaning of bathrooms and kitchen floors, vacuuming effectively, and dusting are life skills you'll need to teach.

Chore Charts

You can buy or make chore charts. These are basic charts that list the names of your kids down the first, left-hand column and the chores as headers across the top. Such a chart may be either printed out daily (using a home computer) and posted, or laminated for repeated use. They can checked off with a pen or with dry-erase type markers (if laminated), or some purchased versions have stickers and stars that can become rewards for completed chores. Most of us post these charts on the family refrigerator.

On such charts, list all the chores of the day or week (depending on how you set it up). The key thing is to train your children to faithfully check off their chores as they do them. This means that you can look at the chart at meal times and see if anyone needs to get something done before they sit to eat. If so, sweetly remind the miscreant of his remaining responsibilities, and require that the chart be completed before his meal can begin.

The more children you have, the more you need some kind of good system.

Variants on the posted chart include printing off copies for student notebooks, using white boards (or blackboard paint on walls), or sliding the daily printed copy under the clear plastic that you bought to cover the pretty tablecloth that goes with your decor.

Parenthetically, such plastic can be bought at any fabric store. They not only save wear and tear on a fabric tablecloth, but you can slide all kinds of things under them *and* use dry-erase markers on them! I have put the week's maps, the current memory words, spelling lists, etc. under such plastic tablecloths for years!

During one season, when I was tired of being the chore police, I asked Scott to check off the list each evening at supper, and then deal out consequences for chore dodgers right after the meal ended.

This lasted about two weeks, as we quickly saw that it took most of dinner for him to drill six kids on their daily lists. Then our evening time as a family began with a line up of those who had transgressed to receive their consequences in the bathroom. The overall effect did not contribute to a pleasant family night together, so this is one of those "don't do what I did" pieces of advice. I soon took up my role as chore manager again, asking God for renewed patience and strength for the task.

Chore Cards

One of the most successful chore management systems we ever used was one that involved chore cards. I got a host of 3" X 5" index cards in colors and put a picture (for non-readers) or word on each one to represent one chore per card. The cards' colors indicated whether the chore was a "before breakfast" (yellow), before lunch (red) or before dinner (blue) or after dinner but before bed (green) task.

Each child had two pockets (at first created from card stock and mounted on poster board, but later made out of fabric). The lower pocket was the "to do" pocket; the upper one was the "all done" pocket.

Daily, children came in, shuffled through their cards, did the indicated chores, and then shifted the completed ones to the upper pocket. While assembling any given meal, I could look over to see if all colored cards from that time slot were completed and, if not, could call the dodgers in to do their chores before the meal began.

One of the greatest features of this system was its flexibility. With charts, I always felt that the maintenance of the chart itself (printing, erasing, reprinting, tweaking, etc.) took up a lot of time. Plus, the little ones couldn't read, so I had to help them. With cards, I could add or take away a card with great ease, and those that we repeated day to day and week to week were always ready and never needed to be recreated!

I have seen variants on this theme using Post-It® Notes, magnets on magnetic white boards, popsicle sticks in mason jars, etc. You can find a host of creative applications for this principle on Pinterest by searching for "chore charts for young kids" (or "older kids," if that's your need).

An occasional change in the method of delivering these necessary chore reminders will be welcomed by your children as you and they work on this crucial training together. Below are some systems that lasted less time, but did offer a good change up for our family.

Awards or Point Systems

For a season, we were all so sick of simpler chore management methods that we tried a system of points. Scott and I decided to harness the children's competitive spirits and attempt to build *esprit de corps*. We got onto the Internet and found websites that sold inexpensive promotional materials, icons, patches, etc. We then devised such awards as "most diligent" and "best encourager" and "most faithful in little things," etc., and bought appropriate awards for each one.

Each week, the kids were given points by their parents towards these awards. The process was helpful to Scott and me because it trained us to look for the things that the kids were doing right, and verbally exclaim, "Ah! A point for Nathan! I heard you encouraging your little sister just now." And then we'd march to the point counter on the refrigerator and make a mark in the appropriate spot.

At the end of the week, at supper, we had an awards ceremony, where Scott would read the title of the award, and then hand the token to the winning child and encourage him verbally. It was a really happy time (in contrast to the check-off list with consequences model that I described earlier).

The main drawback to this approach was the time that it took us each week to keep up with points. Secondarily, there were no built-in consequences (except losing the competition) for those who failed to do necessary chores. After a very short while, we realized that (especially for the girls) the competitive forces just weren't that strong, and training was more undone than done using this system.

Still, I include it here because you might want to try this approach for a season as a positive change, or even to kick off the school year and get into the flow of regular chores after the summer break. Also, in some families who are suddenly taking their kids out of school settings, it's a kind and gentle way of easing them into the realities of good home training!

And, too, though this system may be lacking in consequences, it is strong in training us as parents to verbally encourage, and encouragement is no small thing. So, I do recommend that you look for ways to include a strong element of noticing what your children are doing right, then encouraging and rewarding them for it! I have found in life that the proverb "you get what you spank for" has a counterpart: you also get what you encourage for (especially as your kids get older, past the point where a spanking is as appropriate).

Conclusion

Lucy's words to me that day were the wounds of a friend. I did need to keep exhorting, training, and holding accountable my eldest son for a discipline that should have been better trained *by me* when he was younger.

As mothers, we do bear most of the weight of devising and administering a system by which we can adequately and faithfully manage this training. It's part of homeschooling, and it's another way that we pass on who we are and how we live!

19.

Know this, my beloved brothers: let every person be quick to hear, slow to speak, slow to anger; for the anger of man does not produce the righteousness of God.

JAMES 1:19-20 (ESV)

Questions, Categories, and Consequences

This chapter is as much about parenting as it is about homeschooling, but, as I've said previously in this book, homeschooling is parenting concentrate, so that shouldn't surprise anyone. The pith of this chapter is about looking to discern the underlying reasons of the heart that give rise to various unlovely behaviors in our children. It's not original with Scott and me[1] but (like Gregg Harris' teaching on

1 We first heard this teaching from Dr. David Powlison when he visited our church as part of a teaching team for a Small Group Leaders' conference. Powlison is a senior faculty member at the Christian Counseling and Education Foundation (CCEF), and was applying this verse to ministry to Care Group members. My husband, Scott, then re-applied it to be useful in parenting.

training in liberty) it became foundational to our homeschool and parenting over the years, so I wanted to pass it on here. But first, to lay a foundation, I want to stress the value of learning to ask good questions.

What's a Good Question to Ask?

One of our favorite family stories happened near the end of my homeschooling journey. I was annoyed with the arrangement of furniture in my bedroom. Every day, I felt unsettled by its lack of grace and balance, but I couldn't really pinpoint why. One night, all three of my adult sons were over for dinner, and I asked them to come upstairs for a few minutes and help their dad move the furniture around. We had a king-sized bed, two end tables, a chair, and two bureaus in the room.

Over the next half hour, the guys began to sweat as we moved that room four whole times, putting the bed, dressers, and end tables in four different arrangements in the room. At the end of the time, the room was back to where it started and it *still* bugged me.

As I stood and pondered, my son Mike asked me, "Mom, what *really* bugs you about this arrangement?"

I thought for a moment, and then pointed to the dresser near the door. "I think it's *that* dresser," I responded. Without a word, Mike picked up that dresser and carried it from the room.

"Yes! That's it!" I yelled to him, "SO much better!"

Mike walked back in and said aloud to no one in particular, "Note to self: in the future, before moving furniture, find out what's really bugging Mom."

Since that day, this question ("What's *really* bugging you?") has become a useful one for everyone in our family. Quite frequently, when one of us is unsettled, another of us will look fixedly at her and ask, "What's *really* bugging you?"

It's a good question because it is open-ended, yet it asks a person to examine and express for you what's going on under the surface, where you can't see. For a parent, it's the kind of question that keeps us from assuming that we know already all that our children are thinking or feeling. *That* is almost the definition of a *good* question.

One of the most powerful aids to both teaching and parenting is a skillfully asked question, for a variety of reasons. Questions invite responses. Questions ask for information. Questions provide an opportunity for us to try to untangle what we *really* believe. And, unless they are thinly veiled demands for action or responses, questions position adults as humble listeners so that we can gain needed insights that we would otherwise lack.

Answers to such questions can become windows into our children's minds and hearts, and are therefore precious and valuable. If we listen carefully, we can get way down deep—but we have to win trust first.

As a parent, especially of young children, I am a much more sophisticated thinker than is my child, and I should be a more mature Christian as well. It is easy, therefore, for me to outdo my little one in verbal expressions of thoughts and in processing actions theologically.

This superiority can easily tempt me to pride: contrary to the clear teaching of Scripture,[1] I can begin to think that I know what's going on inside my child's heart or mind without asking him anything, when in reality, I am guessing based on limited information.

Note to self: in the future, before moving furniture, find out what's really bugging Mom.

So, as an example, let's say that my son barges into a quiet family room and speaks loudly and angrily to his sister. If I immediately voice my guess (or more likely, my judgment) as a statement (or rebuke), like "Hey! You know better than to speak angrily to your sister!" without any inquiry, I have closed the door to entreaty or confidences, and opened the one to defensiveness or anger. If I instead choose to humble myself and pose my guess as a question, I may find that I guessed right, but more often, I find that I was unaware of the child's thoughts and feelings.

So here's a parenting tip: when you see your child misbehaving or struggling, instead of telling him what's wrong with his heart motives or actions, try asking a very open-ended question like, "Hey, there. What's up?" And then control yourself long enough to listen without interruption. (It's hard.) Pray while you listen: the LORD sees your child's heart and can help you understand both him and how you can best serve him in that moment.

1 See, for instance, 1 Kings 8:39, 1 Chronicles 28:9, Psalm 7:9, Jeremiah 17:9-10, Acts 1:24, and 1 Corinthians 2:11.

Your child may surprise you with his version of what is up. He might be hungry and cranky (and his sister is behind times making lunch for the family). He might be fearful or anxious (thinking she's been in his room messing with his pets again), or he might have just been wronged or slighted by a neighbor child (who is a good friend of his sister, so he figures it's her fault).

All of these circumstances could lead to an angry outburst as he's just entered the room. All of them will need your instruction in response. But before you rebuke him for his angry tone, you'd be wise to ask a few open-ended questions in a friendly voice and find out what's really bugging him!

Developing Biblical Categories and Consequences

Once you've heard a child out, 1 Thessalonians 5:14 gives parents useful categories to think about when addressing children who are not in a good place. Paul writes, "And we urge you, brothers, admonish the idle, encourage the fainthearted, help the weak, be patient with them all." Let's look closely at this verse and identify some categories.

Categories and Consequences

Not all misbehavior stems from the same wrong heart attitudes. Indeed, if you read this verse closely, you'll find that sometimes people don't act the way we think that they should from inability, rather than bad attitudes or motives. As you can see, Paul identifies three distinct roots of trouble: there are the idlers, the faint of heart, and those who are weak. Let's examine these three terms.

The first one translates the Greek word (ατακτους) as "idlers" in the ESV and others. This word has several nuances. More literal English translations of this word are "out of line" or "unruly." (You may also know that a literal translation of "to sin" is "to miss the mark.") The unruly person is sinning *willfully*, and this verse directs the leader to *admonish* him. What does "admonish" mean? A synonym would be "rebuke." Literally, this word (ουθετειτε) means "put in mind," and the KJV translation renders it "warn."

So, we are to strongly verbally rebuke and instruct the unruly ones among us who are missing the mark. Let's take a homeschool example for this principle. Let us say that you have a child who is taking an unreasonably long time to do his math workbook page of problems. Pretend you have already asked him some careful, patient questions and made sure that he does in fact know how to do the work, but he doesn't want to, and is making no effort at diligence or self-control.

This verse would direct you to admonish him: you would firmly require him to finish his math work in a reasonable amount of time, or else he would receive disciplinary consequences.

In such a situation, I used to use a kitchen timer (since we didn't have smart phones back then). I set it in front of the dawdler and said kindly, "Sweetie, you know how to do this work. If you don't get it done by the time this alarm sounds, there will be a consequence." Then, I would leave him to it. (In our house, a consequence was a spanking, which we believed to be the biblical response to unruly children, according to Proverbs 13:24, 22:15, and 29:15, among others.) Giving the unruly child a reproof that is backed up with sure, biblical consequences is usually an effective way to train.

But it is not always the case that our children are unruly. Sometimes, they are faint of heart, which means either timid or discouraged. They lack confidence in themselves or their leaders. This is where it is a good thing that you train yourself to ask questions about why he's not getting his work done! Good, open-ended questions that invite confidences are ones like these:

- "What are you thinking about?"
- "Are you having any problems with that math work?"
- "What's up?"

Listen hard for the answer. Pay attention to body language. Does your child look unruly or downhearted? If the latter, you need to find out why. In a quiet home, this is always easier because you have time to gently pull away the confusing covers that a child may have inserted as protection and get down into his heart attitudes. Please don't assume that he's just lazy or rebellious! Perhaps he's downhearted or discouraged, and just doesn't know how to express himself.

In the academic context, with the same math seat work example, perhaps your careful questions reveal that the child hasn't learned his basic addition tables well enough to do the work in what would, for another child at his stage, be a reasonable amount of time.

He is fainthearted because he knows that each problem is going to be a tussle for him to figure out by laboriously counting out on his fingers. In this case, a rebuke and a timer are not going to be the right responses.

Ask yourself if he has a good foundation. In this example, has he mastered elementary math concepts that are necessary to the math lesson at hand? Look at yourself, and your lessons thus far, and evaluate how you can best encourage your son. Possibly you need to take some responsibility: "Son, I see that I haven't really made sure that you know your addition facts well enough to do this page easily." Then, cheerfully put the math workbook away and get out the math flashcards, telling him that you know he can do the first half of the deck just fine, and soon will know all of them. Then, he can return to the work page!

Children are, by definition almost, weak.

This orientation could overlap with our third category: Paul advises us to "help the weak." Children are, by definition almost, weak. Generally speaking, they are little, untaught, inexperienced, and unable to discipline themselves. They have few natural defenses. This is why God gives children parents. It is our job to help them to grow strong, but they aren't there yet!

Weakness can result from so many different things. Consider a child's lack of physical strength or height, such as is needed to complete a simple action like opening a jar of pickles, or reaching a glass on a high shelf in order to get a drink of water. In cases like this, kids simply need the help of a grown-up.

My husband used to say to our small children, when he found them in situations where they needed adult help, "Hi, Son. What's going on? Oh! You need a glass from the shelf? Better use a grown-up!" And then he would reach for the glass and hand it down with a smile.

Children may be emotionally weak: perhaps dogs have frightened them in the past, or they imagine that there are monsters in the closet after dark, or they are afraid that they will get lost in a store. There are a host of fears and phobias that underlie the typical weaknesses of childhood. (One of my teen-aged daughters got the idea that formal logic was a type of black magic—and at first refused to learn it!) To us, their fears may seem silly, and we can be tempted to be impatient with them for chronic fearfulness as time goes on. But these are expressions of weakness that are very common with small people.

Our kids can also lack social graces. They can be quite weak in their ability to be tactful or considerate. They can sometimes express strong, unrestrained emotions, and other times be clueless as to what's churning inside themselves. They often lack patience with others who trouble them, or are different than they are.

To return to the math lesson for an academic example, your son's weakness might result from his not knowing his addition tables, but it could be that his fine motor skills have not yet developed and he thus dreads writing out answers that he does, in fact, know. In such a case, the child is physically weak in that he finds it hard to write small numbers in the proper places.

Weakness wears so many masks! A child's eyesight might be weak: he might need glasses and you don't yet know it (as happened with my husband until he was in second grade). Or your child might be tired because he stayed up too late the night before. Now all he wants to do is put his head down on that math book and drift off to sleep!

Or, perhaps his weakness results from the fact that he's stayed still too long that day and his little body is just itching to be up and active. If he had a play break outside for 15 minutes, he'd be able to concentrate on the math work and dispatch it quickly, but right now, all he can think of is to look longingly out the window and try to keep his twitching legs under control.

As you can see, part of being a homeschooling parent is to become a skilled diagnostician of the heart. This takes both practice and humility! The Bible teaches us that "The heart is deceitful above all things, and desperately sick; who can understand it?" (Jeremiah 17:9 ESV). If our grown-up, somewhat sanctified hearts aren't completely pure, and we don't understand fully them, how much more true is this for an undeveloped little person?

Furthermore, we should be mindful that we are not God, who alone can accurately read hearts the first time, every time. This verse teaches us that no one but God knows the depths of our children's hearts. Our job (and privilege) is to seek to learn what we can about our children's hopes, dreams, wishes, fears—and sins—so that we can *help them* to deal with these *as fellow sinners* who stand in need of a Savior.

How can we do good to our children when they are unruly, fainthearted, and weak, and thus daily present obstacles to training in godliness and the teaching of academic lessons? 1 Thessalonians 5:14 has good advice: "...be patient with them all." It is when a person is most unlovely that he most needs to be loved!

Jesus is our model. He is fully formed; He is perfect. Yet, His glory is that He is the giver. In Psalm 18:35, King David writes for us all: "You give me your shield of victory, and your right hand sustains me; you stoop down to make me great" (NIV). Other translators make it "...your gentleness makes me great" (ESV, NASB).

God, who is much more our superior in every way than we are superior to our children, shows us how to "be patient with them all." We are to take the time to understand, and then to help them to understand, what is going on in their hearts and minds. We are to pray for them and seek God for insight into their hearts, since He searches and really knows them! We are to patiently teach lessons, and often reteach the same lessons.

Sometimes, teaching looks like rebuke; it has the sting of correction. So the Lord does with us! Sometimes, it looks like encouragement in the face of despair or trial. So the Lord does with us. Sometimes, it looks like coming alongside and helping our weak children and helping them with the tasks of life; so our Savior does with us.

> *Surely he has borne our griefs and carried our sorrows; yet we esteemed him stricken, smitten by God, and afflicted. But he was wounded for our transgressions; he was crushed for our iniquities; upon him was the chastisement that brought us peace, and with his stripes we are healed. All we like sheep have gone astray; we have turned—every one—to his own way; and the LORD has laid on him the iniquity of us all.*
>
> *Isaiah 53:4-6 (ESV)*

SECTION FOUR

As You Walk Along the Way

I am always doing that which I cannot do, in order that I may learn how to do it.

Pablo Picasso

I did promise that there would be practical tips and "how to's" included in the pages of this book. You're not always *sitting* at home! You are busy! In this section we take up the next part of our Deuteronomy 11:19 passage: "You shall teach [My words] to your children, talking of them when you are... walking by the way..."

My goal for these next few chapters is to give you more practices than principles, but the latter have made their way in here, too, since I find that when principles underlie practices, the practices last longer and work better. My focus for this section is those practices (and principles) that we use as we go about the everyday tasks of homeschooling.

Since homeschooling is more than just teaching academics, you'll find quite an assortment of topics here. I start by noting the God-given differences between little boys and little girls. I then progress to the important idea that different people learn best through different senses, or experiences, and, since this chapter is pretty long, proceed to take another chapter to tell you ways that you can use this insight wisely when teaching your children From there, we progress to the importance of storytelling.

After this, we are ready to think together about the broad categories of curricula—plans of study—that are commonly marketed to homeschoolers. I then finish the section with chapters on the importance of trudging as part of educating our children, and the fact that we teachers must dare to make choices. Then, I'll wind up addressing two very commonly asked questions: "What about memory work?" And: "Why do crafts?"

My discussions of these topics are hardly exhaustive! I seek to paint with a broad brush as we continue to visit together through these pages. While there is detailed "how to" information, I've mostly set down examples of paths of the journey you can try if they appeal to you, or places I've visited that I'd rather not see again!

I'm praying that what I have to share will give you vision and that sense of direction that comes to us when we have seen our mothers at work, and so have some idea of how a task—like cooking a Thanksgiving turkey or sewing on a button—is to be accomplished.

20.

So God created man in his own image, in the image of God he created him; male and female he created them.

Genesis 1:27 (ESV)

What are little boys made of?
Snips and snails, and puppy dogs tails
That's what little boys are made of!
What are little girls made of?
Sugar and spice and all things nice
That's what little girls are made of!

18th Century Nursery Rhyme

Gender Differences

Guess what? Boys and girls are different. Seriously! They are really, *really* different in each and every cell of their body, in the ways that their brains are wired, in how they process information and emotions, in their drives and impulses, etc.

Furthermore, many (if not most) of these differences are hard-wired into them. No amount of socialization can make them change, though you can achieve a thin veneer of similarity between them if you *really* work at it. But, it was God's idea to make men and women complementary (as we noted in Chapter 11 when discussing marriage relationships): both of the sexes created in the image of God, but both imaging different aspects of God's communicable attributes.

The reason I wrote this chapter is to alert you to the ways that gender differences affect parenting and homeschooling. When I was homeschooling, we did not have the benefit of much research—at least, not that had been publicized in laymen's terms. Also, I was homeschooling in the glory days of the feminist movement. Back then, a joke went around that was so telling of how feminists were trying as hard as they could to convince little boys and girls that they were the same that I wanted to reproduce it here. Though it's older, the underlying sentiments still affect cultural norms on how girls and boys are raised and educated. See if you can identify tendrils of thought that you have encountered as a parent and Christian in our world today.

> *The teacher of Kindergarteners was leading a discussion about what the children would be when they grew up. One boy wanted to be a fire-fighter, like his dad. That got an affirming nod from the teacher. Another boy wanted to be a doctor, like his neighbor. That, too, was encouraged.*
>
> *Then, little Suzie had a turn: "I want to be a mommy, like my mommy, when I grow up."*
>
> *The teacher frowned, and gently said, "But, Suzie, you can be anything you want to be when you grow up." Suzie looked surprised, and a little mystified. "Try again, Suzie. You can be anything."*
>
> *Suzie felt a little shy, but she took courage at her teacher's smiling nod of affirmation and said, "Then, I'd like to be a teacher, or a nurse!"*
>
> *Again came the frown, and a tiny shake of her dear teacher's head. "Suzie: you can be anything you want to when you grow up. Anything!"*
>
> *Suzie got dreamy-eyed. She smiled a big smile as light dawned and she repeated the magical word, "Anything?" Her dear teacher nodded again. So, Suzie boldly and decisively said to the class, "Then I want to be a horsie when I grow up!"*

This joke captures so many of the nuances and intentions of those who have fought to persuade others that humans are unisex beings. Let's examine it carefully together.

First of all, boys who wanted to be like their dads, or other skilled men, were affirmed by society, as a norm. They also were affirmed for wanting to grow up to be professionals; no worries there. But, little girls should *not* want to grow up to be at-home moms like their mothers, nor were the traditionally accepted professions for women seen as good choices for little girls' aspirations either. Nope: the acceptable answer for Suzie would have been that she wanted to grow up to be the president of a corporation, or a lawyer, or a dentist, because these were roles that society had traditionally given only to men.

These views were all *very* clear to me when I was raising and homeschooling my three boys and three girls. In fact, this was one of our conscious reasons for taking the homeschool journey: we wanted it to be a viable and encouraged option for our girls to choose to "only" be wives and mothers!

All of our girls are today college-educated; we are not against higher education or women going into professions. Neither do Scott and I feel like girls and boys differ innately in their abilities to learn skills and information and perform tasks that are in keeping with their gifts, talents, and physiques. But, our boys and girls *were* differently made and differently oriented from their cradles up. We wanted those differences to be allowed and encouraged, so this was one reason why we homeschooled.

As I say, gender differences have been studied much more carefully, and the body of research is far larger now than it was thirty years ago. I would like to recommend (with caveats) a book that collects a lot of research in one place, organizes it, and then interprets it in layman's terms (but not Christian ones). It is entitled *Why Gender Matters*, by Leonard Sax.

Sax is a family physician and psychologist who has become an expert on gender differences. Chapters of the book include such topics as how male and female brains are wired differently to process both emotions and information, the significant differences in how boys and girls look at taking risks, how boys and girls fight (and do or don't reconcile afterwards), and how they react and respond in traditional school settings to teachers and lessons.

Homeschoolers have the ability to put our children in situations that are best calculated for their success.

The book is a great read, in and of itself. My husband and I had several light bulb moments about our marital relationship while reading it aloud together. We also got pushy (very unusual for us) with our adult kids, saying that those of them who were now parents really *needed* to read this book.[1]

I'm going to share with you just a few examples of gender differences that Dr. Sax highlights to show you why I felt that this topic merited a chapter here as we get started with the more practical topics related to teaching in the homeschooling context. Let's start with the research that demonstrates that boys' brains mature in a different *sequence* than do girls'. Sax writes:

> *It's not correct to say, "Boys develop along the same lines as girls, only slower." The truth is more nuanced... researchers found that while the areas of the brain involved in language and fine motor skills mature about six years earlier in girls than in boys, the areas of the brain involved in targeting and spatial memory mature about four years earlier in boys than in girls. These researchers concluded that the areas of the brain involved in language, in spatial memory, in motor coordination, and in getting along with other people develop in a "different order, time, and rate" in girls compared with boys.*[2]

Think about this remark in relation to the ongoing push to teach "higher order thinking skills" earlier and earlier to young children. We would expect girls to be far more successful than boys at any kind of seat work that involves fine motor movement—cutting and pasting, coloring in the lines, handwriting, drawing, etc. The little girls will excel at these educational activities!

In what will the little boys excel? Target practice...(but how do we fit that in?) and spatial memory! Hmmm. How exactly do we translate *those* into early achievement that can be recognized, rewarded, and checked off in little boxes?

As classroom teachers, we don't. As homeschoolers, we can adjust our expectations for our boys with close work. We can also find ways to approach lessons such that little boys' early skills will shine. (For more on that, see the next two chapters of this book!)

1 I must here offer just a few brief caveats to my recommendation of this book. First and foremost, psychology as a discipline is most useful in the *observation* of behaviors; it is less so (from a Christian perspective) in offering fixes for undesirable behaviors. Dr. Sax does not offer biblical solutions for the problems that kids encounter because of gender differences in our modern schools and society. Secondly, the book has been criticized as flawed by some of Dr. Sax's colleagues, so you may want to check out his webpage for corrections that he himself has made, after it was published in 2005.

2 *Why Gender Matters*, by Leonard Sax. Three Rivers Press: United States, 2005, p. 93.

This one dissimilarity leads us on to the differences between how boys and girls do at verbalizing thoughts and emotions. Dr. Sax writes:

> *In young children ...researchers found that negative emotional activity in response to unpleasant or disturbing visual images seems to be localized in the amygdala (a...primitive area of the brain). That may be one reason why it doesn't make much sense to ask a seven-year-old to tell you why she is feeling sad or distressed. The part of the brain that does the talking, up in the cerebral cortex, has few direct connections to the part of the brain where emotion is occurring, down in the amygdala.*
>
> *In adolescence, a larger fraction of the brain activity associated with negative emotion moves up to the cerebral cortex. That's the same division of the brain associated with our higher cognitive functions—reflection, reasoning, language, and the like. So, the seventeen-year-old is able to explain why she is feeling sad in great detail and without much difficulty (if she wants to).*
>
> *But that change occurs only in girls. In boys the locus of brain activity associated with negative emotion remains stuck in the amygdala. In boys there is no change associated with maturation. Asking a seventeen-year-old boy to talk about why he's feeling glum may be about as productive as asking a six-year-old boy the same question.*
>
> *Emotions—both positive and negative—are processed differently in girls' brains than boys'.*[1]

If you have both sons and daughters, knowing this can save you a lot of frustration when parenting! It's so tempting, when a boy doesn't share what he's feeling easily, to jump to the conclusion that he doesn't *want* to share, or that he's punishing us by holding out on us. (This is especially true when we moms are doing most of the parenting, while Dad works full time. We are typically so *good* at articulating *our* feelings that we don't stop to ask whether our boys might really not be *able* to verbalize what they are feeling, or why they feel as they do.)

1 Ibid., p. 29.

And this relates to schoolwork. Why is it proverbial that adolescent boys don't seem to readily share during discussions about how a story read in Literature class made them *feel*? Perhaps its because this is something much harder for your son to do than it is for his sister!

Let's consider one more example: a study about things that day-old baby boys and girls like to look at, and why. Dr. Sax, after outlining a study, writes:

> *The retina is that part of the eye that converts light into a neurological signal. The retina is divided into layers. One layer contains the photoreceptors, the rods and the cones. Rods are sensitive to black and white. Rods are color-blind. Cones are sensitive to color.*
>
> *Rods and cones send their signals to the next layer, the ganglion cells...*
>
> *Suppose you give crayons and a blank sheet of paper to young girls and young boys. Let them draw whatever they like. You'll find that girls will prefer colors like red, orange, green, and beige, because those are the colors that [their specialized eye] cells are prewired to be most sensitive to. Boys prefer to simulate motion in their pictures. Boys prefer colors such as black, gray, silver, and blue because that's the way their [specialized eye] cells are wired.*
>
> *Studies in young children have demonstrated that girls are better at tasks involving object discrimination—answering the question, "What is it?"—whereas boys are better at tasks involving object location— "Where is it?"*[1]

Sax continues with this discussion by summarizing in his next section subtitled "girls draw nouns, boys draw verbs." If young children are asked to draw a picture, girls will draw houses, themselves, and smiling faces of people (perhaps a picture of themselves in front of a house with flowers, or of themselves and their parents, using reds, browns, oranges, and flesh tones). Girls will be able to describe their pictures in detail, and the teacher will be able to recognize what they're describing easily.

Boys will draw a black and white scribble (trying to connote action) and gleefully

1 Ibid., p. 19-22.

tell the teacher that it's a rocket colliding with an asteroid in space. There will be no people, or faces, and almost no color in their typical drawings. Teachers of young children—who are often female—will not typically be thrilled with such drawings, and uninformed mothers in homeschool settings may not be, either! But the boys are expressing their God-endowed orientations just as much as are the girls! The wise parent-teacher will look for what the boy is getting at, rather than dwelling on the fact that this is not as familiar (or recognizeable) as pictures that little girls tend to draw.

Now that I've given you these three detailed examples, I hope you'll look back at some of the other topics I listed that Sax covers in his book (bottom of page 187). Boys and girls differ in their basic approaches to so many aspects of life, and schooling can be profoundly affected by the differences. As homeschoolers who are "in the know," we have the ability to put our children in situations that are best calculated for their success.

It is not coddling a boy to admire his drawing on its own terms. It is not fair to assume that a boy is holding out on us when he simply can't put into words why he's sad. It shouldn't surprise us that boys want to take risks, while girls avoid them. That's how they're wired!

Here's one last example. A boy typically feels that it's shameful to ask a teacher for help until he's exhausted all his own resources—beating his head against a problem is, for him, the instinctively right course. With the solution comes a sense of accomplishment, victory, and glory! Girls feel like it's silly to reinvent the wheel. If someone knows how to do something, ask! Why beat your head against a problem when one can just ask a teacher for help. Isn't that what the teacher is there for? To teach us?

Which is the right approach to a given problem? Well, it depends. What's the goal? Do we want our child to arrive at a solution in the fastest possible time, or is there merit in him trying to figure out his own solution before asking for help? What are we building in our son? Later in life, when there's no one else to ask for help, will this future worker and father be able to figure out similar problems (or bigger ones) or will he have been conditioned to just give up?

The conflict between men and women in approaching a situation where they are lost is almost proverbial. Women ask for directions and men don't. Women often become contemptuous of men who try to puzzle their way out of such situations.

Should moms teach their sons to (essentially) always ask for help, and berate them for prideful behavior when they don't? We teaching moms are women, so I believe we should be careful not to require our sons to do or not do things simply because they would be our first instinct—at least, not without first asking whether this is one of those things that is equally appropriate for boys and girls to do as humans!

Pulling back out to the big picture on this topic, recognizing gender differences should clue us in to the dynamic that we, as mothers, will spend a vast amount of time with our sons, but we are not men. While mothers will do the majority of teaching young boys, I argue that we can do a better job by recognizing (and learning details about) gender differences, and then parenting boys on their own terms.

This is where dads, too, can strategically invest themselves in the homeschooling journey, especially as boys grow to be teens. For instance, when there is friction between mothers and sons in the homeschool setting, a dad's counsel is especially valuable for us teaching moms, since we tend to become irritable, judgmental, and self-focused when our sons' ongoing behaviors exasperate us.

Perhaps it is we who need to change in some areas, by learning to marvel at, and value, the God-ordained differences between the sexes, and then seek to adjust our teaching approaches and expectations accordingly! Our husbands can help us understand the male point of view, but we need to humble ourselves and listen in order to take full advantage of their wisdom.

21.

Tell me and I forget, teach me and I may remember, involve me and I learn.

Benjamin Fraknlin

Why Modalities Matter

Whether you are a new teacher or a seasoned one, we all need to broaden our horizons from time to time. This chapter seeks to impart vision for using less-traveled paths of teaching. Together with the next chapter, we're going to think together about the ways we take in information, and how we can use the strengths of our homeschool environments to facilitate a variety of approaches to learning.

The most common forms of information transfer in traditional schools are books and lectures. Generally speaking, students read a variety of books at different ages as they progress through K-12—early readers, picture books, chapter books, textbooks, and stories (also called literature). Some homeschooling programs use what we call the classics, the Great Books of Western Civilization, to involve older students in the

Great Conversation that has been going on among humans since the dawn of history. (See more on this in Chapter 24.)

Books are good and useful tools for imparting knowledge, and the combination of pictures and text in many books are effective, but as homeschoolers, we have the opportunity to take students beyond books (and the limitations of a traditional classroom). We are able to give them a much broader education than we probably had growing up.

At first, this might seem to be almost a contradiction in terms: how can we, in our own homes, where our children are usually limited to one teacher (us) for all subjects, provide a broader education than that of a vast school system? Let's explore.

Educators talk often of learning modalities, which is "eduspeak" for the three main ways that human beings take in information. We use our eyes, our ears, or our touch (broadened to include experiences) to do visual, auditory, and tactile (or kinesthetic) learning.

While everyone uses a combination of eyes, ears, and touch to learn, most of us are wired to prefer one of these modalities above the others. Our preference may change or expand to include another modality as we grow older—several of my children started out strongly "ear" or strongly "eye" learners, then gradually became more "ear-and-eye"—but when we are young, we often tend towards one primary modality.

Some most easily remember what we see or read. Others can practically recite the sermon we heard last Sunday, or pick up lyrics to new songs with very little effort. And then there are the "show me" people—those who learn best by doing something after seeing it done, or who itch to take things apart or "try for themselves."

As homeschoolers, we have the opportunity to take our students beyond books.

Obviously, as adults, most of us can learn in all these ways, much of the time. We have our favorites (often unconsciously), but the majority of homeschooling moms learned to learn primarily through books as we went through traditional schools, or even in homeschools. As adults, the less-preferred modalities tend to atrophy from disuse, or they find other ways of being expressed: in activities such as pick-up football or basketball games, cooking classes, dancing, painting, or quilting group.

For instance, have you ever met adults—I know several—who, when you talk about the latest greatest Christian book in glowing terms, seem to glaze over and look uncomfortable? They usually mumble something like, "I just don't read." Or, "I don't get anything out of books." And then they change the subject.

For many adults who tend strongly to learn through touch rather than eyes, or had early visually-oriented disabilities, traditional school systems were a torturous ordeal because the classroom approach has a hard time providing educational alternatives to their primary tool: book learning. As homeschoolers, however, we can provide those alternatives!

Now, as you're reading this, if modalities are new to you, you're probably wondering, "Which kind of learner am I?" This is a great question, and worth exploring, so let's do a little test.

Pretend that we're standing (just you and me) opposite one another and talking. (Actually stand up if that helps!) Suppose I asked you "What does the front door of your house or apartment building look like?"

What would you say? (Please put down the book and describe it, aloud, right now, before you continue to read.)

* * * * *

Think now: Did you look up, straight ahead, or down as you considered how to tell me about your door?

Did you speak about its colors, materials, or characteristics of use—such as, "It bangs or sticks whenever we use it"?

Usually, visual ("eye") learners look up while describing the door: its colors and/or decorations. They'll be seeing it in their minds as they're talking, and may want to gesture in order to help you visualize it, too.

Auditory ("ear") learners tend to look straight ahead, and describe a variety of the door's features. Some include noises associated with the door, if these are notable. Generally, verbalizing all experiences (visual, tactile, emotional, etc.) is easy for auditory learners. They think better when they talk out loud.

Tactile ("touch") learners usually look down, often gesture while describing, and may focus on characteristics of the door's texture/materials or use: Is it metal, wood, peeling paint, or two-part, with a screen? Does it squeak, stick, or bang when being used? Do they experience a sense of welcome or dread when opening the door? They'll tell ya, usually!

Now, that's hardly a determinative test, but it is interesing. There are a host of possible indicators for what your primary modality might be and, of course, adults tend to exhibit mixed modalities: audio-visual, for instance, is very common.

So let's try another one: When returning from a party, what do you tend to first describe in giving an account of it to those who were not there?

- The decorations? What people wore? (visual)
- The conversations that you had, toasts that were made, or jokes that were told? (auditory)
- The activities, games, or socially-oriented incidents: the "what happened"? (tactile)

Now, it's true that some other personality traits will play into this party indicator test. Are you an "extrovert"? Then you might recount what was said, rather than the decorations, for instance, even if you are a primarily visual learner. Are you an "introvert"? Then you might describe events, even though you are an auditory learner, because you are a watcher and don't have lots of general conversations: yours tend to be deeper and more one-on-one. Still, you might glean from this little test.

Now it's time to think about your kids, each of them. Make a copy of the worksheet on the next page. Jot their names down on the left side of your paper, and opposite each name, see if you can list whether they learn best through their eyes, ears, or touch/experiences. If they clearly use more than one, try to list primary and secondary ones. (There are more questions below to help you parse this out listed below the chart if you need them.)

MODALITY WORKSHEET

Kids' Names:	Primary (preferred) Modality	Secondary Modality
______________	____________________	____________________
______________	____________________	____________________
______________	____________________	____________________
______________	____________________	____________________
______________	____________________	____________________
______________	____________________	____________________
What about YOU?	____________________	____________________

More Clarifying Questions to Help You Sort Modalities

When you want to learn something new, how do you like to go about doing it?

- Go to the library or Internet to read how to do it? (visual)
- Call someone on the phone to ask them for information, or their experience, or advice? (auditory)
- Find someone to show you how to do it? (tactile/experiential)
- Listen to/watch an audio or videotape that both explains and demonstrates? (audio/visual/tactile combination—which is why it's so effective!)

Consider (and add to/modify what you've already written on your copy of the worksheet) the answers that each of your kids might give to this same question if they are old enough.

Here are more indicators:[1]

- Would you rather read a book silently to yourself (visual) or listen to it read aloud—live or on tape (auditory)?
- Which would you choose to do when given free time: read books (visual), listen to music or teaching tapes (auditory), do active pursuits/crafts (tactile), or watch TV (mixture of audio/visual)?

1 None of these are "purely so." For instance, an auditory learner may prefer to read silently so that she can "listen" to the words in her head. And a visual learning may want to look at her handwork while being entertained by books on tape. Take these indicators as helpful, but not determinative!

- When you return from church, what are you interested in discussing, or what do you most easily remember?
    - The clothes that others were wearing, or how tired/sick/happy some people looked, or the decorations at church? (might indicate visual)
    - Recounting and discussing the sermon? (auditory)
    - The events of the day: how the Lord moved and what happened in church? (tactile/experiential)

For each member of your family, if you're clued in to these and other telltale signs, you can pretty quickly figure out the strongest modalities through which you and your kids learn. The main points here are: 1) that though there are three basic ways to take in information, we all usually favor one and 2) we aren't purists. We all use a combination of all of them to some degree, but favor one by inclination.

If this idea of modalities is new to you, it might also be a new concept that *we tend to explain, share, or teach others in our own preferred modality.* This is not surprising: we want others to gain knowledge as easily as possible. To us, our preferred modality sure seems like it's the easiest! But after learning that our kids also have modality preferences, and that their primary modality may not be just like ours, we see that we might need to make adjustments in how we teach.

Here's an example from my life. I personally struggle to learn math and am primarily an auditory learner. It takes all my concentration to do math, so listening to something on tape while I do it drives me crazy because I want to listen rather than figure out sums, so the tape divides my attention. But, during our late homeschooling years, two of my kids claimed that listening to story tapes while doing math improved their scores, because math was easy for them and a story tape in the background gave them enough to occupy the unused part of their minds so that they did not make unnecessary mistakes through sheer boredom.

Knowing about modality influences on the learning process, I was open to the differences that might exist between us, so we did experiments. Sure enough: these two did math homework faster and better while listening to story tapes (namely *Adventures in Odyssey*).

Was it *my* preference that they study that way? No! I couldn't imagine learning math while listening to an interesting story that was wholly unconnected. But did I yield to the evidence and allow it? You bet! The goal was learning, not doing it my way.

Not only are some of your kids different from you in their modality preferences, but they are also probably not all alike each other! One may be bookish and enjoy using pencil and paper (and thus be quite easy to teach using traditional approaches). Another may be always on the move, and easily bored with book-centered approaches, thus indicating that learning is easiest for her through tactile approaches.

Parents who teach the bookish child first may naturally assume that the active tactile child needs to be disciplined (or drugged) into conformity. While such active behavior (or an inablility to learn from books) can indicate a learning disability, it may also be that the child is wired differently from her older sibling, and a wise teacher will look for different avenues for presenting lessons.

I have one friend who experienced exactly that dynamic: her oldest son is a bookworm, but his two-years-younger brother never picks up a book by choice but competed successfully in regional-level gymnastics. My friend wisely recognized that her sons needed different approaches. She gave her oldest a rigorous high school education with plenty of thick, difficult books (which he loved). Her second son received a solid (rather than rigorous) education, in which she challenged him to read the occasional difficult book, but tended more towards the middle of the high school academics road that left plenty of room for gymnastics training.

Her sons are now in college, and she was recently stunned to hear that her second son had actually chosen to pick up a book by choice! This demonstrates that, as our children grow, they really do change. But we need to be patient with them (and affirm wholesome differences between them and us and between siblings). The goal is to try not to frustrate, belittle, or frighten them in ways that drive them away from learning. Though school always involves some stretching for every child, we can make it more enjoyable for them to learn by paying attention to *how* our children learn easiest.

So here's what's important for us to recognize as homeschooling parents: because we personally lean unconsciously towards certain modalities, we can be unaware of the need for (and joys of) using a variety of approaches (some of which we don't ourselves prefer) to academic subjects. Furthermore, we can be quick to judge, condemn, and punish the "different" child, or even just ignore possibilities for teaching in a new way. We need to walk humbly and carefully here!

Many new homeschooling parents aren't aware of this dimension of teaching and learning. Even veteran teachers get into comfortable ruts and slog along, teaching in increasingly uncreative ways instead of looking for ways to change up their teaching and keep learning fun and interesting in our home environments.

Again, from my own life: I love to read, but I tend to retain information longest when I learn through my ears, and tactile learning is hardest for me. So it's not surprising that I like to teach by first assigning books to my kids to read so they have background information, then do the actual teaching by discussing them aloud. That way, I can gauge what they've retained, and lead them to places that they can't go on their own. To me, it's easy, tidy, and—in my personal experience—highly effective.

Taking time to recognize modality differences is important on a number of levels.

Given my modality preference, then, it won't surprise you to learn that during, my homeschooling years, I most frequently avoided opportunities for my kids to learn by doing. For instance, left to myself, I hardly ever got around to using messy and time-consuming crafts that took hours to prepare, and seldom went on field trips that required the efforts of planning, packing up the kids, following directions to get to the place, shepherding them through public places, etc.

However, when I learned about modalities and the importance of including variety in the academic diet, I embraced ways to get these elements into my kids' homeschooling. I formed two different co-op groups over the years (mostly because we moved) almost for the sole purpose of giving my kids the opportunities to do tactile/experiential learning that I knew we weren't getting to on our own. We also invested in art lessons.

It turned out to be a good thing I embraced these modifications to my preferences, since two of my kids became professional artists: one in fine arts and the other in graphic design. But, to demonstrate the variety under one roof, and where God took them, I'll share that another of my kids grew up to become a team leader and IT systems engineer who has worked primarily for defense contractors. One (the fastest and deepest reader of them all!) loves his job driving a truck for UPS. One has become a professional writer and curriculum designer. My youngest girl got her dream job as an executive assistant to a pastor. Four have, at one time or another, been teachers. All are so different from each other!

Taking time to recognize modality differences is so important on a number of levels. First, what I'm communicating here may explain frustrations in your homeschool that will mystify you as you get underway with your journey. When we do our best to teach according to our preferences and our children don't get it, we can fumble in the dark, and be tempted to impatience, misunderstanding, and judging our kids. We increasingly think of them as being resistant, uncooperative, or unable to learn. While learning disabilities may be present, sometimes a simple shift to a different modality will make a world of difference!

Your child may delight in messy, tactile learning and become the willing student of your dreams by a simple change from learning only through books to learning partly by doing. If you have an auditory child who struggles with his spelling workbook, you might find that he does far better when allowed to dictate his spelling words into a dictaphone, then listen to replays of the tape. (There is probably a digital app for this as well!)

While you probably can't (and shouldn't) customize your children's lesson to their preferred modalities entirely, at the very least, understanding that you and your child are simply wired differently by our Creator can help so much with creating a healthy learning environment! And, making reasonable adjustments to try to provide something for each child's primary modality isn't a quick fix that takes you through all of your teaching career because you will still need to help your kids to develop some proficiency in all three modalities. But simply knowing that these real differences exist can smooth many formerly strife-ridden days of mutual frustration.

Beyond easing tensions, recognizing and affirming modality differences is important because we recognize and affirm the God-ordained differences between human beings. This enhances humility and mutual respect.

Furthermore, providing for a variety of modalities will ultimately help get us to the real end goal—learning—as we will talk about in the next chapter. As I've said, but it bears repeating, understanding and embracing modality preference differences are important to our effectiveness as home teachers. In a traditional school, your child would encounter a variety of teachers who would each tend to present information from his or her strongest modality. The child wouldn't be taught by a single teacher for his whole school career, so chances are good that he'd have one or two teachers who would naturally be "on his wavelength."

However, since you are the only (or primary) teacher and educational director that your child will have for years on end, you can see that it's important for you to work hard to learn each of your students' God-given strengths, and utilize them effectively, while, of course, stretching your child to grow in other modalities as well.

At the start of this chapter, I wrote that we homeschoolers have the chance to broaden our students beyond what traditional classrooms are able to offer. This is because we are, essentially, tutors. Traditional schools must "mass teach" large groups of students, and find ways to do things as efficiently and cheaply for those large groups as possible. So, they are limited: they can't typically tailor lessons to a child's primary modality.

We homeschoolers, by contrast, teach one or two students at a time, (or perhaps a handful of students if we are part of a co-op), and we can individualize their instruction a great deal. For example, if your child is primarily an auditory learner, he can listen to many books on tape, rather than using his eyes, to learn the great stories of history. If you have a young tactile learner, modeling pyramids might better cement his understanding than reading about them. The idea of using recordings to learn spelling given earlier also fits here.

Cluing into the variety of ways people learn can give us new creativity and energy as teachers. We can seek to broaden the spectrum of approaches we use for teaching, thus make learning more fun and interesting for our kids.

Would you like to gain a vision as to how to put all this theory into practice? I've included many details in the next chapter.

22.

Education is what remains after one has forgotten what one has learned in school.

ALBERT EINSTEIN

Lesson Planning with Modalities in Mind

Having discussed the importance of recognizing our own and our various children's learning modalities, I'm now going to discuss a variety of approaches to one sample lesson topic. I hope to show you how lesson planning can grow rich and varied when we keep in mind the variety of modalities we discussed in Chapter 21.

I'm going to break these approaches down by individual modalities, then broaden out to include mixes of modalities for each approach. Remember, in the real world, most modalities are mixed, so there's no real need to be purists about this.

Our sample lesson topic will be an introduction to the history and culture of modern India.

Visual Learning

Let's start with visual learning, which is the most commonly used modality in traditional schools, and is the modality from which you probably were primarily taught. Let's go back to books.

In terms of modalities, books are visual aids. The reader takes in information through his eyes, enhanced by his own personal imagination and experiences. On the pages of a book, the students may find pictures, but the older the reader is, the more he will see simply printed words.

So, if we want to learn about modern India, our natural tendency would be to have our students read a book. The words will tell him facts and paint pictures in his imagination. The fluidity with which his mind can absorb these words through his eyes, and the amount of context he has for the topic already, dictate the amount and ease with which he learns from printed words.

But now let's think beyond printed words for a moment.

When introducing a new topic, or era of history, or culture, I have found that my older, high school aged students often really benefit from one of their younger sibling's picture books on the same topic! There's the old saying that "a picture is worth a thousand words," and it's true. Picture books for younger students tend to both distill the main ideas of the subject (using simplified vocabulary), and show the subject matter through pictures. Older students who, for one reason or another, are not strong in reading words can often gain the main ideas of a subject through looking at a picture book.

In our example of studying modern Indian culture, imagine how useful picture books would be. Without reading a single printed word, visual learners can take in the distinctive ways that modern Indians look, the clothes they typically wear, the foods they like to eat, the housing they live in, the kinds of parties they have, the look of their places of worship, the landscapes they see each day, and the degrees of wealth and poverty that are typically found in an Indian city. All this information can be quickly absorbed by looking through a simple picture book on Indian culture in modern times, even though a student might be "too old" for the book!

Now let's continue the theme of visual learning, but look beyond books. How can we use the Internet for visual learning? There are thousands of web pages about India that contain both text and pictures. Also, different sites will present varying genres that your student may enjoy: instead of the purely informative style of a textbook, he might find journalistic articles, first-person narratives that describe daily life, advertisements that reveal the interests of modern Indians, etc.

Some web pages will include videos, which broaden our scope to include an auditory element in this visual learning. Your child might view a traditional Indian folk dance, a modern Indian leader's speech, or archived news reels of key events from the history of modern India.

Note that, here we are also introducing mixed modalities that enhance one another: the folk dance will include traditional Indian music; the historical event clips will include audios of speeches that display concepts that were important to the history of modern India. Pictures, motion, and sound all contribute to the depth of understanding that your student has now gained from primarily visual (or audio/visual) presentations.

Along these lines, think of films, another audio/visual teaching tool. There are travel DVDs available at your public library. There are also fictional movies that are set in India, and available via services like Netflix that, while not primarily intended for teaching school children about the culture of India, can be well used towards that end! For example, one could watch *Ghandi* (a well-made movie about the life of the leader who secured India's independence). In using such resources, you can not only learn about a leader's life, but discuss what biases the filmmakers have of the topic, since all such films are selective.

There are even more visual displays (mixed with other modalities) to access! Think of attending live plays, or taking field trips to local museums, which is experiential learning. Some museums have exhibits that can be touched and handled, so now we are mixing in the tactile modality with visual learning, and again, both are enhanced.

Before leaving visual learning avenues, I want to note that, even if you yourself are not wired to be primarily visual, you probably had to adapt to visual learning as you went through your traditional school experience. While your children can adapt likewise, there's not as great a need for them to do so within homeschooling, since you can tailor lessons to their preferences—and yours!

However: a word of warning is in order. Since our culture relies heavily on visual communication, especially for higher education, all students should become skilled at learning independently from books and other printed materials (and computer interfaces), even if you would prefer to teach your children primarily through tactile projects or read-alouds.

Auditory Learning

Let's explore ideas for those homeschool students who learn best through listening. What kinds of creative auditory approaches can we incorporate into their lessons?

Music all by itself is an auditory medium. All cultures have distinctive music, and students who study these differences are broader in their understanding of the world than those who do not. Think of dance tunes, protest songs, or the current pop music that reveals a lot about an era's youth culture. Music can introduce students to the themes, passions, and delights of a culture or an era.

For instance, have you ever listened to traditional music from the Middle East? The reedy, atonal, and almost seductive tones are completely foreign to my ear as a Westerner, and always remind me how very different than mine was the culture that my Savior experienced while on earth. When Jesus says that the Pharisees are like children in the marketplace—they neither dance to a happy tune nor mourned with a sad one, I hear again the wild Middle Eastern music and remember: it was a very different culture, but humans are the same everywhere! Amazing! This broadens my understanding of the Scripture passage and enhances my knowledge of the Savior. Music does the same for your students studying all kinds of foreign cultures, near and far.

Speeches, also, are primarily auditory events. Your students probably hear a speech every Sunday: we call it a sermon. Learning to listen well to a logically-organized sermon is a skill that all students can hone. (A good way to start is by asking them to outline the main points as they listen each week.) Returning to our sample lesson on modern Indian culture, your student may listen to speeches from history online, or even view modern India's parliamentary proceedings via international television.

Live lectures are stock-in-trade for teachers in traditional upper-school classrooms, and you can use them at home, too, to give variety to your older students' more independent-study routines and delight your auditory learners. There are also recorded lectures on a variety of subjects that can be accessed at your public library or online. Your student can listen to these independently.

Storytelling, especially by someone who witnessed events, can be a powerful tool in homeschool studies. While you are studying modern Indian history, do you have a neighbor or friend who came from India, or perhaps visited India, or experienced any of the history you are studying? Do you know anyone who has been a diplomat or soldier in India? He or she could come and talk to your kids about their experiences there, giving them a wealth of information! Accessing "living history" through stories is a wonderful way to broaden your lesson plans.

Reading aloud is a terrific way to share any kind of story and teach anything from history to literature to geography. It's a pleasant, companionable way to take in information and employ the imagination as well. When done as a regular practice, reading aloud together builds family memories and unity. You come to share a common set of plots, vocabulary, and "in-jokes" that bond your family relationships tighter together. Plus, it's just plain enjoyable to listen to someone read aloud well! (Asking your children to read aloud by turns also helps them to develop this valuable skill.)

For those of you who have weak readers or spellers, it could be partially because they are primarily auditory or tactile learners. You may be able to help such children learn easier by teaching them some study tricks that use their ears or hands. I've already mentioned the idea of speaking spelling words or spelling rules aloud into a recording device; the same technique can teach all kinds of vocabulary words, science terms, math formulas, and foreign language conjugations.

All Scripture memory (or any kind of memory work) may be easier for auditory learners to accomplish using verbal repetition; or, especially for younger children, Scripture and other memory work can be learned by singing them to simple tunes. Many professionally-recorded Scripture memory songs are available to us as well. My adult children—aged 23-33, presently—can and do still sing Scripture memory songs that they learned at ages 3-5 from listening to such audiotapes! Many resources also put other memory facts, such as lists of presidents or states and their capitals, to music.

Once anything has been memorized, whether a Scripture verse or a list of facts, or a poem, or a scene from a play or story, or really anything at all, it is valuable to allow the memorizer to perform his work by reciting it to an audience. Grandparents, other siblings, and his dad, to name just a few, may be glad to act as audience members. The student will receive a tangible reward for his hard work, and the deadline of a performance date will motivate him to finish the project of memorizing.

Finally, the element of "teaching what you have learned to another" by reciting to an audience will help to solidify the student's memory work. (Did you know that typically we remember something far better if we not only study it but also immediately use, perform, or teach it to somebody else?)

Learning by touching or doing

What are some tactile, or experiential, approaches to learning that we homeschooling teachers can introduce?

Hands-on projects are my favorites of this category. Children enjoy learning by doing, and often remember what they learn better for having used their hands. Scale models (of varying complexity) are great projects for slowing students of all ages down and getting them to really comprehend the details. Homeschooled children have more time than do traditionally schooled ones, since they don't have to wait for other classmates after completing assignments. They can thus go deeper into a subject.

For instance, how *does* a modern Indian farmer's cart harness fit his bulls? If your student builds a scale model of a traditional Indian cart and bulls (which are still in use today), he'll have to find out!

What is the furniture in a traditional upper-class, modern Indian home like? What are the colors, the shapes, the details of carving? How comfortable is it to sit on, and how high off the floor do most Indians sit? These are the kinds of details that modeling common aspects of Indian culture helps one to notice and remember.

Maybe these things don't seem important for a modern American student to know (when will he ever have to harness a bull?), but details are important to the *fun* of learning, and growing to appreciate details is part of the process!

Your student can find this kind of information by looking carefully at a book's picture that is detailed enough, but there is something about doing a model that really makes this kind of detail stick.

Labeling blank outline maps is similar. For most students, when they look in an atlas to pinpoint a city on a map, then label the same place on their own blank outline map with their own hand, they slow down and really note the relationship between the city and other features (natural and man-made) on the map—which they must do in order to place it accurately on their blank map. Students usually remember that city's location far longer after labeling themselves than they do if they had simply looked to find the location in the atlas and then moved on.

When introducing a major geographic area to students, like the Middle East, or Europe, or the Eastern Seaboard of America, it's a good idea to have students do salt maps of that area. Using a simple dough that's easy to mix at home, kids study closely the natural features (mountains, rivers, coastlines) of the area as they model it. Alternatively, why not make such maps out of cookie dough, and eat them when done?

Tactile learning helps to make the lesson stick! In our sample lesson topic, students could make a salt map of the sub-continent of India while you read aloud to them from the encyclopedia or a website about the unique climates that shape life in different areas of modern India.

Lesson planning can grow rich and varied when we keep in mind the variety of modalities.

Let's think about field trips. As they say, "Travel is broadening." It may not be possible to visit India, but all field trips are educational experiences that broaden our kids and help them become more mature thinkers, seeing the world from more than just their own point of view. Do any nearby museums display aspects of Indian culture? Or, think smaller: again, do you know any neighbors or church members who are from India, whom you might visit either in their home or worship center with your children?

Leaving aside our Indian example for a moment, for your youngest students, it is a worthy investment to make visits to everyday businesses into field trips, because going behind the scenes of things that we adults take for granted can greatly expand a child's comprehension of an industry he may not understand. For instance, how are the canned goods made that he consumes daily? Or toys? Or computers? Or cameras? How do rice or milk or blueberries reach your table?

Visiting a factory, fire house, farm, or car salesman opens up new vistas, especially for students in younger years. Of course, you can read a book or watch a documentary about such things, but visiting puts things in a new light, and kids simply remember field trips longer. Also, though you may not be sure whether your local factories or firemen accept visitors, it isn't rude to pick up the phone and ask!

Taking a major summer field trip from home and visiting a famous place—in the

U.S., such as homes of American presidents like Jefferson's Monticello or Washington's Mount Vernon—or full-scale historic replicas like Jamestown, Williamsburg, and Plymouth Plantation, can give great context to all historical or literary studies of early America.

When we were preparing to study the westward expansion of Americans in the 1800s, I took my six kids (then aged 6 to 16) on a summer cross-country drive that we'll all never forget—especially since we broke down in Ogalala, NE! As we opened books about covered wagons that fall, my kids had in mind the vast expanses of flat lands of the mid-west with their big sky overhead, and the awesome wall of the majestic mountains that were the Rockies.

Shifting gears: there's another way to do tactile learning. Try cooking and eating cuisines from other cultures! This is tremendously broadening and a fun break from book learning. Have your children eaten oxtails, or head cheese, or fried ants? These are all delicacies in other cultures!

If studying modern India, why not explore the diet and tastes of modern Indians as part of the experience? What do Hindus eat, or avoid eating, and why? What is the diet of the very poor of India, and how would it feel to eat like that for a week or so? Do Buddhists' diets differ from Hindus'? Why?

In the same vein, but on a different topic, you can also dress up in traditional Indian costumes, such as would still be worn to a modern wedding, and have Indian cuisine, while sitting as Indian people would, near to the floor.

Tactile learning could also involve trying things like Indian folk dance and Indian art forms to gain appreciation for the skill that others have. When my high school students study the Ancient World, I like to allow them time to attempt to reproduce many ancient handcrafts, like making models of Egyptian pyramids, or painting Cretan frescoes, or carving Assyrian friezes, or assembling Etruscan mosaics. Such older students tend to have developed a certain superior attitude towards ancients, which can affect the way they perceive holy Scripture. Doing these simple crafts can teach new respect for the skills of these "primitive" people who accomplished such amazing works of architecture and art with so limited an array of tools and technology!

You can broaden this idea of tactile learning to include showing a student how to do something, then coaching him while he learns to do it well. Moms, think of sewing or cooking skills, learning to shop for the household, budgeting, etc. Dads, think of sports skills, building things, maintaining a car, or teaching your area of vocational skills, or (for both sexes) learning to use various computer programs, how to change a tire, and how to ride the subway. There are many kinds of things for which a "show, then tell" approach is the most effective one.

And speaking of vocations, for older students, experiential learning can include trying out a profession. For instance, if your daughter wants to be an artist, visit artists and let them share their views on the best route for your daughter to take to fulfill her dream. If your son wants to be a journalist (like one of mine thought he did) send him to a Journalism Camp. When my son discovered the nuts and bolts of this profession, he quickly changed course—which is learning!

Down the road, you will find that internships for high schoolers are valid educational tools. Plan to allow your older son or daughter to spend time in an office, a food store, or a fast-food restaurant. Let him work a construction job in the summer, or let her work for free on weekends with a movie producer, as did my niece one summer.

Some students will find that they didn't really understand the vocation that they thought that they wanted to do and change course. Others who intern may find that they love the job, and might meet the perfect mentor to help them get a great start and form a lifelong friendship!

For some kids who are currently disinterested in studying—they don't see the connection, for instance, between Geometry and "real life"—either a job digging ditches for the summer (one alternative to getting an education) or an internship in a field they love (for which geometric knowledge is a prerequisite) might provide fresh motivation!

Going back to mixed modalities, composition (or "Writing" as it's often termed) is a tactile and visual exercise which may also involve an auditory element if the student reads his paper aloud as he proofs it (or to an audience, once it is finished).

In its simplest form, writing aids retention, as with taking notes. This is the same basic dynamic that I just discussed with modeling or geography work. In its more advanced forms, writing involves complex thinking and also putting words together to both express ideas and persuade others. In its most advanced form, writing does all of the above *and* both pleases and moves the reader.

Writing is a kind of learning that is crucial to building the Christian thinkers, theologians, apologists, and cultural communicators of tomorrow. On a simpler level, it is important for all Christians who want to be able to communicate love in thank-you, encouragement, or sympathy notes.

Writing is also used in the process of creating presentations, which use all of the modalities. The "show and tell" part of giving them is tactile and auditory, but creating them is also a visual exercise. Speeches, mini-reports, or creating and explaining a visual component like a display board, etc.—all these are forms of mixed-modality learning that could be used in pursuit of our sample topic of modern Indian culture.

This is an easy addition to any curriculum! The process of assembling ideas, arranging them cogently, and then presenting a finished written and/or oral form slows the student down, makes him think about his subject, and then includes the motivation to make the topic his own.

Obviously, there are more ways to mix audio and visual with tactile learning: music enhances doing a dance, and a manual on car repair sure will help your student find his way around an engine better. In fact, most combinations of modalities enhance learning.

Conclusion

There's no magic in the modalities themselves. Rather, it is when we keep the modalities in mind as we take our homeschooling journey together, and seek to serve our students by employing different ones to both aid learning and retain teaching creativity, that they come most sharply and helpfully into focus.

23.

Violet saw a Santa Claus on our walk today. She said, "Ha! Who dat guy?!"

So I told her that there's a story about Santa, who gives presents to kids at Christmas. She said, "Dat's true, Mommy, but God gave presents to Jesus."

And there you have it.

CASEY SOMERVILLE

Tell Me the Story Again!

As parents, we have a unique privilege: for good or for ill, we shape young minds and souls. One of the most powerful tools that we have for this work is storytelling.

We tell stories all day, of course, with our reactions and responses to the events of life that confront us. As I wrote in earlier chapters,[1] our impressionable youngsters are watching us all day long. Day by day, week by week, and year by year, we are unfolding a story about God. We are telling our children our version of who He is and what He is like. This is unavoidable (and can be a painful truth or a joyful one, according to our daily choices), but I want to focus on a different, related thing in this chapter. Beyond the unconscious storytelling that we all do as parents, we can also

1 See Chapter 5 (You Share Who You Are) and Chapter 7 (Cross-Eyed Parenting).

choose to tell stories as we walk along the way in homeschooling.

We know that stories have great influence on the way people view the world. Solomon used proverbs to communicate wisdom. Jesus used parables to convey timeless truth about the Kingdom of Heaven. Aesop used fables to teach morality in ancient Greece. Stories matter. They engage not only our minds, but affect our hearts and shape our worldviews.

It is for this reason that we want to be careful to tell our children true stories—not in the sense of telling only non-fiction, but rather in the sense of telling truth about God, His world, and humankind, whether we use fiction or non-fiction as a vehicle. In Isaiah 5:20 (ESV), we read this somber warning: "Woe to those who call evil good and good evil, who put darkness for light and light for darkness, who put bitter for sweet and sweet for bitter!"

Little children are easily deceived; this is one reason why such well-intended hoaxes as Santa Claus, the Tooth Fairy, and snipe hunts can be so much fun to perpetuate. Their big eyes full of wonder, their simple faith, and their great delight in figures of the imagination, may beguile us into thinking we are doing no harm as we string them along. But, take care! Jesus said,

> *Whoever receives one such child in my name receives me, but whoever causes one of these little ones who believe in me to sin, it would be better for him to have a great millstone fastened around his neck and to be drowned in the depth of the sea.*
>
> *Matthew 18:5-6*

I have no desire to kill either your joy or your little ones' delight in believing in Santa Claus or the Tooth Fairy, but at the same time, it's worth thinking through whether you want to make withdrawals from your child's trust bank in order to promote these kinds of stories. I think that my daughter-in-law Casey was wise to tell her two-year-old Violet that "there is a story about" Santa, rather than "there really is a Santa."

Think about this tradition for a minute with me. Santa is a man whom your children never see, but who you tell them is always watching them throughout the year. You say that he is coming back soon (once a year), and you tell them that he will reward or punish them according to whether they've been "naughty or nice."

And one day, your child will find out that you were fooling him when you told him solemnly that he had better watch out, and better not cry! It isn't much of a leap for a disappointed child to say, "Fool me once, shame on me. Fool me twice, shame on you!" Might not his little mind begin to wonder if the stories you tell about Jesus—whom you *say* is alive, though he can't be seen, and whom you *say* is coming back, and whom you *say* is always watching to see if he does right or not—might he not wonder if *these* stories about Jesus are true, or are just another hoax?

Anytime we ask for another person's trust, and then prove ourselves to be untrustworthy, our credibility takes a hit. Since we are flawed and sinful, the trust banks that our children have in us are going to take some hits in any case, but I've always felt that I should be as careful as I could be to keep my children's trust. I've tried really hard to never tell them a lie, and to always keep their confidences when they were entrusted to me. I saw these as precious, and guarded them carefully. I sought, where I could, to make deposits to my children's trust banks instead of withdrawals. Trust is often the basis for love and openness in children that make parenting a lot easier, and of course I wanted to preserve those things.

But as sweet as my children's love and openness were to me, the main reason why I wanted to gain their trust was so that when I told them true stories, I would be believed. Of course, the most important story that I wanted to tell them was the Gospel story! It is this one above all other tales that is the most exciting, the most true, the most precious, and the most attacked by the world, the flesh, and the Devil. In order for my children to be saved, they would have to not only believe, but put all of their trust and confidence in this strange and impossible-sounding story, even when opposed or mocked for believing it!

Speaking of stories and the Gospel, there is a story I love from the life of renowned English preacher C.H. Spurgeon, who lived in the 1800's. It underlines for me that there is no better story to tell than the Gospel, and shows excitement of "telling it again" through multiple generations within the same family:

> *C. H. Spurgeon had been announced to preach at Haverhill in Suffolk, and—an exceptional incident—he was late in arriving. So his grandfather began the service and, when the expected preacher did not arrive, proceeded with the sermon.*

> *The text was "By grace ye are saved." He had gotten some way into his discourse when some unrest at the door made him aware that his distinguished grandson had arrived.*
>
> *"Here comes my grandson," he exclaimed. "He can preach the Gospel better than I can, but you cannot preach a better Gospel, can you, Charles?"*
>
> *Still pressing up the aisle, his grandson replied, "You can preach better than I can. Please go on."*
>
> *His grandfather refused, but he told him the text, explained that he had already shown the people the source and fountainhead of salvation "grace"—and was now speaking of the channel of it "through faith."*
>
> *The younger preacher took up the theme and advanced to the next point—"but not of yourselves"—and was setting forth the weakness and inability of human nature when his grandfather interrupted, and said, "I know most about that." So for five minutes he discoursed, and then his grandson continued again, having his grandfather's whispered commendation "Good! Good!" as he warmed to his subject, until at some special point the old man ejaculated, "Tell them that again, Charles."*
>
> *Ever after, when Charles recalled the text, there came to him with recurring force the words, "Tell them that again."*[1]

As with Charles Spurgeon and his grandfather, the love of the old, old story does unite Christian generations. If you are blessed with believing parents (as my husband is), then you know the joy of hearing your parents tell God's story to your child. You can rejoice as the beauty of God's wisdom and the accounts of His mighty acts are passed on one more time, with love and reverence, as yet another generation is raised to grace.

We do well to read Bible storybooks with our young children, often in the morn-

1 *Charles Haddon Spurgeon: A Biography*, by W.Y. Fullerton, <http://www.spurgeon.org/misc/bio1.htm>. Retrieved 2 January 2014.

ings as devotions or in the evenings as we put them to bed. But we can find more ways to make themes of the Bible come alive to our children. One is by asking others to tell their pieces of God's ongoing story, which is still unfolding today.

You do this by developing a habit of prompting guests, grandparents, and church friends to tell their testimonies to your children. A good time to do this is when sharing a meal together. Most Christians of any age will enjoy the opportunity to tell your children how God worked in their life to bring them to Himself, even if they start out shyly.

Of course, if they are deeply ashamed of their past and afraid to soil your children with the story of their own sins or sins done to them, that is something to consider. Yet even then, if possible, I would encourage you to consider with them whether they might find an age-appropriate way to tell the story. First of all, God's amazing grace will shine all the brighter for the dark contrast (which, again, need not be given in any detail). Second, your child will come into contact with the evils of mankind sooner or later, and when he does, wouldn't it be valuable for him to know some true stories about how God has saved real people from those evils?

We tell stories all day, of course, with our reactions and responses to the events of life.

Sometimes, the story may not be dramatic, but that's important for your children to see as well. There are times when God's grace dawns in a human heart gradually and slowly, like a gentle summer sun. Other times, He uses tempests raging with thunder and lightning when bringing a soul to Himself. But whether dramatic or not, all salvation stories glorify God and display His wisdom, love, and mercy. They tell us who God really is: the Good Shepherd, who goes after His sheep! And they tell us of ways that God deals with His people, from miracles to trials, in love and wisdom. We learn that we are not alone in our thoughts and feelings, or in our sorrows and joys. Others have walked where we now are, and found God there.

Returning to the Scriptures, it's important to tell the Bible message as a story because we can always find ourselves in that story. The history of the human race is at once simple and complex. One can make an academic career out of studying a single era of it, and many professors have done so! One can also summarize its major themes in a single evening. With young children, you'll want to identify those central themes and keep things simple.

You might do it like this. "Son, there are good and evil in the world. Evil has had its day, and people choose evil apart from the grace of God. But He knows we need help, so He sent a Savior to die in our place and take our punishment. Death could not hold Him, though, and He rose triumphant and rescued all who called on Him. People are still sinning today, but some are also calling on Him today, and being saved, changed, and used by Him in His world. He is always showing Himself to be the biggest, brightest, most *important* person in the universe. He loves to display the glory of His Son, who is God above all! He loves to love us, too. He doesn't need anything from us, but He loves to give, and to teach people how to treasure Him above all because He designed us to be happiest when we love Him most. We owe everything to Him; our lives are all about Him."

We all want to teach our children to do right and avoid heartbreak and pain. We want them to learn to be diligent, obedient, and wise. To this end, we often teach memory verses that highlight good conduct. There's nothing wrong with this, but an additional good way to make the teachings of the Bible come alive is to look for the themes of the old, old story in any historical event one chooses to study.

For instance, you can ask your children (especially as they grow older and wiser) to relate to the feelings that others from bygone eras may have felt. Can he relate to such feelings as the fear that civilians have in war times, or sadness after being physically injured in an accident, or joy in a battle won against evil, or the nobility of parental sacrifices during the Great Depression?

Asking a child to imagine himself in the stories of bygone eras—and what his thoughts, feelings, and reactions to the circumstances would be—gives him a deeper sense of being connected with what God was doing in earlier times, as well as giving him perspective on his own life. The history of the world is one long story, and the Bible is God's commentary on it. This is one good reason why we study history.

More broadly still, when we seek to correct a child's behavior, it is good to remind him that he has a place in God's story. Bible stories are about real people, and they show our children that others have felt the same emotions, and how God viewed their choices. 1 Corinthians 10:11 (ESV) tells us, "Now these things happened to them as an example, but they were written down for our instruction, on whom the end of the ages has come."

Is your little son covetous of a sibling's toy? Achan in the Old Testament was covetous, and lost all that he held dear as a result. Is your daughter feeling lonely and friendless in her Sunday School class? Sarah's Egyptian maid Hagar felt that way, but God saw her and spoke words of comfort and direction to her in the desert, not once, but twice! Time after time, a Bible story can instruct and comfort our children better than the more easily-isolated "do this" verses that direct us how God would have us behave.

Finally, let me encourage you to relate your child's story not only to historical and biblical contexts, but to locate it in your family's history. There's a popular saying: "What good parents give to their children are roots and wings." I think there's something to this. Children who have a knowledge of family history have an anchor in troubled seasons. There's a security that comes with knowing the names, values, and cultural backdrops of parents, grandparents, and great-grandparents.

Do you know who your forbearers were, where they lived, or any stories about them? Before the advent of electricity and modern entertainments, families passed down such things through storytelling on long, dark evenings. We call this "oral tradition." You might consider purposefully researching your family's ancestry (there are websites that make it easy) and telling your young children what you learn. With older children, you might have them help you with the research as a fun summer project! Once you learn the stories of your ancestors, the next step is to tell their stories.

You may not think of yourself as much of a storyteller. I know I don't! My husband is the one in our family who can spin a great yarn at a moment's notice, hold people's attention for hours, and never seem to be at a loss for words. But, I've found that with the right prompts, I can tell stories that my children love and that edify them because they are true. I believe that you'll find that your children are interested in what you consider to be very ordinary things!

I have found that my children (and these days, my grandchildren) really want to hear about what it was like for me growing up. They are as amazed to hear that I remember days with no Internet, home videos, or microwave ovens.

The more specific I get, the more interested they become. I tell them that their mommy or daddy was my child, in my womb, just like their coming sibling is now.

I can tell about the time that I was in school and didn't quite make it to the bathroom. How embarrassed I was as I snuck back to my classroom in wet undergarments! How my mother despaired as I had accidents because I was too wrapped up in my little projects to take time to get to the restroom. You can see them wondering if I'm really serious: *You, Nana? Really?*

It's important to tell the Bible message as a story because we can always find ourselves in that story.

Going back in time with such stories helps us to remember how it felt to be their age, and can give us more patience with their childish foolishness. Telling such tales helped my children (and now helps my grandchildren) to relate to me as a person. I was not always the slow-moving, careful and—let's face it, a bit boring—woman that I am now. (*You* used to ski down snow-covered hills in races when you were twelve years old? *You* used to row crew in high school? *You* used to spank your little brother when you were five and he was one so that he would cry, and then you would get to hug and comfort him? *Mom! Nana! Really?*)

Yes, and I was a radio DJ for a time in college, and I traveled to Europe at age fourteen to ski in the freshly-fallen powdery snow of the Austrian Alps, and I really loved my parents, but had a hard time telling them when I got myself into trouble.

And, I was a great sinner in college—a lawbreaker, in fact—and yet, I found a great Savior while there. When I had truly nothing to recommend me to God, He set His love upon me and I became His. The change in my life was so great that two of my college classmates became Christians just by watching me be significantly transformed in a short amount of time! And then one of them went to be with Him when she was hit by a bus a year after we all graduated...

At college, also, I met your Dad (or grandfather). I didn't really like him all that much when I first saw him. He didn't like me, either, because he had heard from my roommate that I was pretty awful. (I really *was* awful, children.) But he had learned from his mamma that we're all sinners in church, so he wanted to see me know God and get better. He offered to teach me the Bible (since I had never read it before) so we started to study the book of Romans together, and became friends, and then...

* * * * *

All those stories about me above are true.

It's not that hard to tell stories about being weak and young, being foolish, being silly, or being surprised by joy or love or tragedy, or by God's undeserved mercy. These are stories like the ones that are in the Bible because Bible stories happened to real people. And God's old, old story is still being told, daily, in our homes, in our communities and in our world.

The more you talk about these things with your children as you walk in the way, the more they'll make connections between Bible teachings and their own lives. And, the more rooted they will be, knowing where they have come from and where they are headed. That's how you give them both roots and wings.

So, today, tell your children *the* story, again. (Like Grandfather Spurgeon, someone else may tell the story better than you do, but they have not a better story to tell!)

And then tell them a new story that's from your own life, and weave into it those great themes of lives lived before the face of God. They'll be there if you look for them, because He is the Author of it all.

24.

To summarize the numbers (which sometimes get cited differently), learners retain approximately:

90% of what they learn when they teach someone else/use it immediately.

75% of what they learn when they practice what they learned.

50% of what they learn when engaged in a group discussion.

30% of what they learn when they see a demonstration.

20% of what they learn from audio-visual.

10% of what they learn when they've learned from reading.

5% of what they learn when they've learned from lecture.[1]

Useful Categories to Know When Considering Curricula

Having set our course by guiding stars that are this season's reasonable and specific goals (Chapters 2-3), and having learned about how pedagogical categories can

1 "How to Retain 90% of Everything You Learn," <http://www.psychotactics.com/blog <http://www.psychotactics.com/blog/art-retain-learning>. Retrieved 8 January 14.

help us to assess published curricula (Chapter 4), and having thought about how gender differences among our kids can affect the ways they learn and we teach (Chapter 20), and then having thought about the wide variety of approaches that varying our teaching modalities can bring in the last three chapters, we're now ready to wade into some technical terms and homeschooling jargon that we use to discuss various kinds of curricula.

First, let's define this word "curriculum." The word is rooted in the Latin verb meaning "to run." It has the sense of a race course that is set out for runners to use. So, a curriculum is a plan of study through which we run our students.

Technically, then, we should speak of curricula (the plural of the word) as the plans themselves, and then any materials that the plans employ as "resources." So, if a plan of study recommends certain books, or maps, or activities, or videos—these are resources (or materials) that the curriculum requires or recommends for its course of study.

When you start to explore homeschooling curricula, you'll quickly discover that (as we noted in Chapter 4) designers of learning materials have specific goals in mind for students and teachers. Thus, the curricula available to you can be categorized according to their approaches. This is good news for you as you try to organize information about your options, so that you can explore and compare them! In this chapter, we're going to focus our attention on three main categories of curricula: Textbook (and worktext) based programs, Unit Study programs, and classical education programs.

Textbook and Worktext Programs

Since many of us were schooled in traditional settings, let's start with the approach that is probably most familiar: the textbook approach, which is divided into grades by age (K-12), and into subjects of study (handwriting, phonics, math, history, and so on).

Description

In textbooks, experts in various disciplines of learning (typically called "subjects") have distilled knowledge into surveys that are relatively easy for the student to absorb—at least for the short term. Textbooks are written at age-appropriate reading levels. Each one generally centers on only one subject (like ancient history or biology), and for only one grade.

The student is meant to read the textbook independently. Many publishers include aids to reading and retention, such as bolded text for key terms, divisions of the text into short paragraphs with helpful headings, and short lists of review questions at the end of sections or chapters.

For teachers, there are typically accompanying manuals that provide teaching aids. Some manuals reprint copies of the student text with commentary, others give class plans, and still others give discussion outlines or questions that a teacher may choose to use. These programs also tend to include published tests that teachers may give (along with answer keys for efficient grading of these tests).

Also included in this category are the so-called "worktexts." These are consumable workbooks because the student writes in them. They both teach concepts and offer problems or exercises for the student to complete. Most common among these are math, grammar, and handwriting worktexts. Typically these are offered for younger students, from grades K5 to 4th, but some programs use them beyond these levels. As with textbooks, teachers' manuals and answer keys are usually provided.

Central Goals and Educational Focus

One powerful goal of the textbook-based program designers is to facilitate their use with larger groups of students led by a single teacher (as in traditional school classrooms). In such settings, students work through textbook assignments independently (often as homework) and then, during class time, teachers review the content with them, either by using questions provided in their teacher's manual or by lecturing to supplement the independent learning that the students have done.

Another goal of textbook publishers is to present, in a highly compact fashion, the essentials of the subject. Through textbooks, students can take in well-researched, cogently expressed visual presentations of a subject in an efficient, self-directed manner.

Pros for using textbooks at home

While homeschoolers don't generally have large classes of many students to teach, we can face a similar challenge because we may have multiple children on a variety of learning levels. Textbooks have appeal for busy parents for the same reasons that they remain popular in schools: they are efficient and easy for teachers and students to use.

They offer a way for students to learn independently. Another attraction (especially for parents who are not well versed in a subject) is that they offer strong support for the teacher. Also, as an introduction to a subject, or in the case where we must teach a subject that neither the student nor the teacher feel is central to our overall learning program (such as when states mandate that we cover an elective on Government, but the student is all about art for a career), textbooks can be useful tools.

Cons for using textbooks at home

The biggest downside to textbooks from an educational standpoint is undoubtably this: their information tends to lodge in most students' short-term memory with a minimum of effort, but is also difficult for many students to retain over the long term.

Furthermore, because the information is, if you will, pre-digested, the original "flavors" of the subject are blended together and become, well, as boring as baby food! Subjects (like ancient history or biology) have clearly fascinated those who have studied them deeply and widely (enough so that scholars then became expert enough to write the textbooks). But because the information is distilled, many interesting details are lost. Furthermore, as a result of the summary nature of textbooks, their prose tends to be somewhat formal and not rich in imaginative presentation, so it does not tend to arrest most students' attention.

But more problematic than the fact that students' interest in the subject may not be ignited, is the fact that there is little to no problem solving, or wrestling with ideas, in such curricula. The central goals of efficiency and independent learning produce an approach in which the student is a passive learner: he is called on merely to receive information via reading and lecture, then remember it just long enough to pass a quiz or test. In fact, students using textbooks often become focused on passing quizzes and tests, rather than learning the subject's information. As a co-op teacher, I used to allow my students to ask all questions but one: "Will this be on the test?"

Compared to other approaches, textbook learning does not seem to train our children to think. If they do retain the information, they have not made much progress towards learning how to gather, organize, compare, condense, and apply new information for themselves.

The student's mind doesn't need to do any original work. His book tells him, say, a few isolated facts about the climate, societal structure, and living conditions of ancient Egypt. Then it organizes those facts into a comparison and informs him that he would not be likely to find it a pleasant place to live if he were a slave. The author has done all this work, but the student has not.

The student is also not invited to critique the textbook's author or challenge his assertions. He doesn't tend to ask, for instance, what other facts might the book be leaving out? If a youngster knew that some slaves in Egypt were allowed to hunt hippopotami and charm snakes, he might be eager to try slavery (even if it wouldn't really be a good idea).

Interestingly enough, when very little original work is required of a student, his retention is much lower. Humans learn by grappling with a subject, organizing its elements and constructing our own summary of it. Even making mistakes is, surprisingly, a huge part of long-term learning!

How to make it work best

For some academic disciplines, textbooks make a lot of sense, and in some disciplines they can be used in ways that are not passive. Take, for instance, the math textbook: it is full of problems to do, and teachers are meant to supplement its instruction with explanations. Any problem-oriented textbook is going to help students learn because they must wrestle with the problems themselves, though the textbook's style of presenting the material may not put the joy of learning in their hearts as other approaches may!

When studying heavily informational topics (history, church history, the arts, science, government, etc.), textbooks can be useful as an introductions to, say, the Renaissance, or the human body, or American government. They do, after all, present good summaries of the important information about each of these subjects. However, if you do use textbooks, I believe you would be wise to supplement them heavily with additional in-depth reading from sources written in interesting styles—such as a fictional story in which Leonardo da Vinci (the famed Renaissance painter) is a character, for instance. You might also use audio/visual presentations, or hands-on learning, in order to give your students a well-rounded set of lessons.

In summary: there are generally two reasons why those new to homeschooling choose to use textbooks: 1) they are familiar to us as new teachers, and 2) they seem like an easy, well supported way to get our subject boxes checked off.

Also, for some heavily fact-based subjects such as maths and sciences, where there is much that must simply be memorized and relatively much less that is open for discussion or reorganization, textbooks still seem to be the best method available. Many of us start this way!

As you get into the journey, however, you'll probably feel more confident and you may want to spice things up. At that point, you may not recognize that you're actually doing a lot of extra legwork as you seek and find supplements to the textbooks. It is at this juncture that you may want to try a different route to the goal of a well-rounded education.

Unit Studies

When newer homeschoolers hear about the Unit Study approach to learning, it is common for our hearts to both leap for joy and simultaneously quake with anxiety. This is because Unit Study tends to be open-ended and messy, especially when compared with textbook learning. But, let's explore this genre of homeschooling curricula.

Description

The Unit Study approach takes a central topic and makes it a sort of "hat rack" upon which the teacher selects (or "hangs") information from a variety of traditional subjects: history, geography, literature, government, etc. It is a unit because all of these subjects are studied in an interrelated fashion for as long as the teacher decides.

To illustrate, ancient Egypt might be your central topic (your hat rack). This study would be far-ranging and open ended. You could "hang" geography, history, cultural studies, literature, arts, and sciences of ancient Egypt on this "rack." You could do it in an open-ended fashion for as long as the time you allotted.

In the homeschool setting, unit studies can break down age separation, because students of all ages can learn about a single *topic* at their learning level, provided they all have *resources* from which to learn. Such resources may vary widely, ranging across all of the modalities that we listed in Chapter 22, "Lesson Planning with Modalities in Mind."

So, to offer a typical tableau, a ten-year-old who is a fluent reader may be explaining an illustration in his six-year-old sister's picture book on Egypt to her, spicing it with comments of his own from the related story that he is reading about a boy growing up in ancient Egypt. Nearby, their twelve-year-old brother could be working on a model pyramid that he is making out of sugar cubes. Across the room, their fourteen-year-old sister may be using Mom's laptop to write a one-page report on the religious beliefs of ancient Egyptians (which she has pieced together for herself from three different books that her mom gave her to read, plus Internet research and perhaps a documentary video).

On the upcoming Saturday, Mom might have decided to take them all to the local museum to see an exhibit on Egypt, or they might be planning to watch *The Ten Commandments* as a family on Friday night.

Central Goals and Educational Focus

The central goals of a Unit Study approach to learning are:

- To make learning interesting for students (some call it "delight directed" learning).
- To cross "subject" divisions in pursuit of integrated learning. This is meant to add richness, depth, retention, and texture to knowledge.
- To make use of a variety of modalities, which again contributes to both interest and long-term retention of information learned.

So, to continue our example of learning about ancient Egypt, here follow *some* possibilities of how we could do a unit study in the home that would last about a month:

- We would want to explore Egypt's geography: the location of the culture on a map and information about climate, flora and fauna there.
- We could look at the daily activities of ancient Egyptians from all walks of life: fashions of clothing that Egyptians wore, foods that they ate, games that their kids played, what kinds of work they did, what roles women and children had in the society, etc.
- We would study the history of ancient Egypt: when did it flourish, and what stages of development did it go through? (Older students might compare this culture with other ancient ones or with our own modern lives.) We'd ask, "How did this culture interact with or affect surrounding peoples?"
- We could study the literature of ancient Eygpt. Did you know that we have poems, myths, and stories from this fascinating culture? We could read these aloud or study them on higher learning levels, again comparing them with

literature from other cultures.

- We would want to study the arts of this ancient land similarly.
- We could include looking at ancient Egypt's government.
- What about science? Did the ancient Egyptians know anything about germs or surgery, or make accurate calendars, or have any idea of the course of the stars?
- We'd explore their religious beliefs and analyze them using biblical categories. In connection with this, we would learn how and why the Egyptians built their famous pyramids and mummified their pharaohs!

In addition to taking in information, when doing unit studies, students generate product as well. Here are a few ways students can interact actively with what they're learning:

- We might have younger children write a little skit or play and act it out as part of our Unit Study.
- Or they might make a display board about how pyramids are built or how Egyptians made a variety of useful things out of the papyrus plant.
- Older students might write reports about daily life, or essays that analyze one of the above listed aspects of Egyptian culture.
- Students could make salt (or edible dough) maps of Egypt.
- They might model a working Nile River, complete with grass that grows, so better to understand why it flows "up" on maps but downhill on the globe.
- Students could make costumes and dress up as Egyptians (especially if producing that skit they wrote).
- Students might take a day to cook Egyptian dishes that the family can enjoy during one or more evenings during the unit.
- Students could make model pyramids or create dioramas of Egyptian homes or temples.

This is not a complete list. It merely gives one an idea of the variety, scope, and open-ended (read: messy and unscripted, unless we are willing to do extra work to impose order) character of this approach to learning!

Pros for using Unit Study at home

In contrast to textbook (or any strictly book-based) approaches, the Unit Study offers a dazzling array of information, presented in a variety of interconnected modalities that is highly attractive to most children. If you want to promote a love for learning, the Unit Study approach is one sure-fire way. This is especially true if your student is coming out of years in traditional schools, where his interest in learning has been dulled, or his desire to explore school subjects at his own pace was squelched.

Typically, Unit Study learning facilitates interaction with the information in both passive and active roles. Students take in information via a variety of resources—books, videos, lectures, or discussions, for instance. But they also reassemble what they take in into products of their own, as listed above.

Furthermore, because the Unit Study often includes tactile learning, students must do problem solving in order to complete projects, models, or cooking. And generally speaking, people remember what they wrestle with!

So, in summary, Unit Study is both varied and detailed enough to gain our children's interest, and it's interactive enough to promote long-term retention of what they've learned. What's not to love?

Cons for using Unit Study at home

The biggest con for the new homeschooler has to be the open-ended nature of Unit Study. Some families who are new to homeschooling are going to feel challenged because once you open the door to this "delight directed" learning of related topics in various "subjects," *where* is "the end"? When will you know *enough* about Egypt to move on? Will you need to have your husband dress up like Moses and lead you out?

If you are one of us who has trouble with worrying about doing an adequate job in teaching, the open-ended nature of unit studies can drive you batty unless you have someone who says to you, "Dear Heart, this is good. You've done enough. You can move on to the Greeks now."

Another con is that Unit Study is definitely *not* efficient. Cast your eye back over that list of possible elements in a study of ancient Egypt. Think about assembling craft materials, cooking Egyptian dishes (where can I find the ingredients, never mind the recipes?), and having five salt maps drying all over your house, waiting to be painted. And where are the ready-made questions and answer keys for discussions (because we *do* need to discuss all that we're reading, or else we'll only remember random facts, plus how we decided to mummify our recently-deceased hamster with toilet paper), the quizzes, and the unit summaries? You'll have to produce your own.

Once you have these assembled, consider the amount of time that it takes to build a model pyramid out of sugar cubes, or mummify that hampster, or assemble that display board, or make that costume? Unit studies are rich, rewarding, and promote both the retention of information and the love of learning, but they are also time consuming and require a lot from you, the teaching mom, as a planner, administrator, teacher, guide, and grader—especially if you have a houseful!

Of course, the open-endedness and inefficiency I mention are mostly a problem only if you're making up your own unit elements from scratch for yourself. Happily for you, because Unit Study is such a great approach, nowadays there are a variety of published curricula that give strong support to moms who are just starting out. They suggest what to teach, when, and in what order or combination for a given unit.

Companies who publish Unit Study guides often also sell or recommend resources that you can use to get the job done. Some authors of such programs are highly directive ("do this on Monday and that on Tuesday") for moms who want to step in another's footprints. Others are more flexible and give structure with options ("choose two activities to do this week from a list, and read three of these five books aloud") for those who want to follow another's path but with room to veer off for a moment to pick flowers or stop to admire the scenery.

Some Unit Study publishers provide maps, tests, and in-depth discussion guides with questions and answers. Some even include ideas for end-of-the-unit celebrations that tie together food, costumes, and presentations!

How to make it work best

If you are new to homeschooling and you want to try Unit Study, I suggest that you purchase a program that is somewhat directive and also lists specific resources that you can easily purchase. At the same time, since I firmly believe that any curriculum you pick will need some tailoring for *your* unique homeschool (see Chapter 26, "Choices, Choices"), I recommend you look for a program that has some flexibility and options.

For instance, if you're not into doing crafts, you might look at a program that includes lapbooks or craft kits, or other somewhat contained tactile approaches. Some programs include activity books that list specific materials needed for each hands-on project and give detailed directions that older students can follow independently.

Unit studies by nature incorporate and integrate information from a variety of subjects (history, geography, etc.). However, it is possible to limit their scope. For example, many Unit Study programs center on just literature or history. Some encompass more subjects in the humanities, but do not include math or science. If you are not up to the task of adding those elements yourself, you might limit your Unit Study subjects at the start and follow a textbook approach for math and science, for instance.

It seems that, for most of us, there is a steep learning curve to almost any approach to teaching. Unit Study is no different. It may look scarier to newcomers at first because we love to be told exactly what and how to do things when we start. But because you and your children are individuals, you will usually find that you end up tweaking whatever program you buy.

So, the word for those who are anxious about doing it "wrong" or "not doing it enough" or "never getting out of Egypt" is this: don't worry! Set some goals, make some choices, and settle in to teach. If your kids are young, you have lots of time left to make mistakes! Homeschooling, like mothering, is a guilty business in that you can *always* do more, or better, so don't aim for perfection. Work at faithfulness, and trust the God who has called you to this great work.

In summary: the delight-directed, open-ended approach to learning is, as I said, both exhilarating and terrifying. But that shouldn't stop us from taking on a few adventures as we make the homeschool journey!

Classical Education

Curriculum designers in this camp center their information delivery around both how children best learn at various stages of development, and what the content of their course of study should include. Be aware that these publishers use similar (if not the identical) terms to mean somewhat different things when they come to apply them practically. But, let's give you a broad overview before we get into those details.

Description

By definition, classical education is a method of learning that hails back to Medieval times, when universities grew up in major towns. Classes were usually conducted in the side rooms of Roman Catholic cathedrals at first.

When you think of classical education in this context, think of formal debates. Instructors were masters of subjects who were hired by students to debate a given statement (called a "thesis") such as "God exists" in front of the class. Students purchased a few resource books and read them before the classes, then discussed with one another the points that the masters had made after the debate ended.

Many instructors were monks; Martin Luther was one of these, for instance. He taught theology in the university town of Wittenberg, in what is now Germany. When Luther nailed those famous 95 theses to the door of the church in October of 1517, he was posting 95 "debate starters" for scholars and churchmen to support or attack according to the customs of his day. He had no idea that this action would spark the Protestant Reformation!

During Luther's time, the process by which children were educated was called the Trivium (meaning, from the Latin, "three way"). Simply summarized, children learned to read in Latin (grammar), then to argue in Latin (dialectic), and finally, to persuade in Latin (rhetoric). After this, they were admitted to schools of higher education, where they pursued the Quadrivium: a collection of four main subjects (arithmetic, geometry, music, and astronomy).

> *Together, the trivium and the quadrivium comprised the seven liberal arts (based on thinking skills) as opposed to the practical arts (such as medicine and architecture). ...In turn, the quadrivium was considered preparatory work for the serious studies of philosophy... and theology.*[1]

As the quotation above indicates, the goal of education in Medieval times was to create a thinking man who could quickly gather and organize information, analyze problems, and synthesize solutions or find ways to apply that information skillfully. Education was the privilege of the wealthy: the poor lacked both time and resources for study. We get our term "liberal arts" from the Latin word for free: "liber."

During the cultural shifts brought on by the Industrial Revolution and spread of democracy, education in Europe and Americas became free and public. These eras brought us age-segregated classrooms and efficiency. More and more, educational goals shifted towards both specialization (learning focused on mastery of one very

1 "Quadrivium," Wikipedia contributors. Wikipedia, The Free Encyclopedia, <http://en.wikipedia.org/w/index.php?title=Quadrivium&oldid=584484117>. Accessed 4 December 2013.

small area of study)—made necessary by the increasing complexity of the world and the exponential growth of information—and vocation (learning only what was needed in a profession).[1]

The study of the liberal arts as a means to becoming a deep-thinking, problem-solving, lifelong learner who has the necessary thinking skills to examine any new subject is no longer in vogue predominantly, at least in American institutions of higher learning. Political and cultural agendas and/or vocational pursuits now drive college curricula in a different direction.

Let's leave the history lesson on the course of education for a minute to note, also, that classical education developed not only as a method, but as a body of works to be studied. There developed what is called the Classical Canon (or the Western Canon, or the Great Books of Western Civilization), which is a list of books that any person calling himself well-educated would have read, up until about World War II. These works span the course of human history, from ancient times to the early twentieth century, and collectively express what many call the Great Conversation.

There are works of philosophy, theology, history, poetry, prose, and fiction among them. There are treatises and essays on government. There are military histories, memoirs, biographies and travel books, works of mathematics and religion and science. The Bible is on the list!

Together, these are the Great Books—the ones that have expressed how people have thought of themselves, their world, and the spiritual realms beyond. They are books that have stood the test of time, ringing true for many readers from generation to generation. They may not all express divinely revealed truths, mind you, but (especially taken as a whole) they do accurately express many human beliefs and feelings, how our race has developed in thought, and what ideas have been tried as experiments in living, and with what results.

With a few exceptions, most classical education curricula that you'll encounter deem most of the Great Books as worthy reads, though not all programs assign all the books to students in their original forms, and some programs add to the Canon when publishing for younger students.

To return now to our history lesson about the course of education, in the 1990's there was a rebirth of interest in classical education—both the method and the con-

1 I have actually noted a clear shift of emphasis in education over the span of my lifetime. When I was an adolescent applying to colleges, adults used to ask, "Where are you going to school?" Nowadays, the question they ask young adults is more likely to be, "What are you going to school for?"

tent—among some educators working with traditional schools. These persuasively argued that a new approach to Christian education was sorely needed, that Christian education should return to a focus on liberal arts in a Christian context. Among other voices, an address given at Oxford by British author Dorothy Sayers in 1947 (entitled "The Lost Tools of Learning") gave educators an excellent indicator of where to head. Sayers' article was widely republished (indeed, you can find it easily for free online by using Google) and became highly influential among homeschoolers as various publishers produced materials that incorporated her ideals and included the Great Books.

Today, the classical education genre of Christian programs is robust and growing. You'll find many programs that have adopted all, part, or just some of the essential elements of Medieval education. Not every program that calls itself "classical" is created equal, though, which is why reading Sayers and other leaders of this genre is a good idea if you plan to try this path on your journey.

Pros for using Classical Education at home

The most obvious positive argument for adopting a Christian and classical curriculum is that the approach (properly executed) manifestly produces well-rounded, problem-solving, thinking humans who have a broad understanding of the history of human thoughts and experiences.

This is what people today often call a *serious* or *rigorous* education—one that is intended to form a deep-souled, thoughtful person who is wise, skilled in enjoying beauty, able to analyze a host of different kinds of problems and synthesize solutions, and enjoys the humanities and sciences for his whole life, no matter what his vocation may become.

Because the content is a limited list of books, the classical education is not as messy as Unit Study can be. Also, though many of these books are good hard work to read and require some explanation as well as discussion, there is a fairly straightforward methodology to follow. So—at least for high school students—the road is already clearly marked!

If you have no experience with them, don't let the list of "high brow" books scare you off. As I said, owing to the popularity of this approach, there are many fine programs available for the new homeschooler. You certainly can learn as you grow if classical education is new to you. And for you free spirits, who want to choose your own book list, thank you very much, let's note that, while classical education may lack some of the free wheeling joys of Unit Study, it includes those grappling and wrestling elements of the interactive qualities that textbooks lack.

When children are young (in what is called the "grammar stage" of learning), the central focus of this approach is to give them an introduction. Young children are sponges; they soak up facts, experiences, and impressions better at this stage of their development than at any other. Sayers called this the "pole-parrot" stage because children mimic everything they see or hear. Thus, many programs that orient themselves towards classical education include a hefty amount of rote memory work. (This feature is discussed in more detail in Chapter 27: "What About Memory Work?")

As students enter the developmental stage of puberty (usually during the traditional Junior High years), they typically become argumentative as their brains are seeking to create mental pigeon holes into which they can classify and organize information that they soaked up when younger. Classicists call this the dialectic stage. The Classical method seeks to harness this natural development by giving students training in debate and formal logic, so that they may learn to support their arguments and listen to the points that others make.

This is a good stage, too, for learning the grammar of foreign languages, which develops their minds organizationally and also can teach a valuable life skill (communication, if a living language is learned). Students are also continuing to read and grow in other skills as well.

When students have passed through puberty and become young adults, they are ready to analyze complex problems and synthesize new solutions. This is known as the rhetoric stage. For these older students, the core activity of a classical education is reading the Great Books, which are challenging, but not out of the reach of most young adults who apply themselves. To this reading, one should add discussions that help the student process what's been read. Finally, students make a response, typically in the form of written product, but sometimes by giving oral presentations or in other formats.

During both discussions and responses that are a part of dialectic and rhetoric phases of study, the student uses his mental bank of facts and connections as he repeatedly practices processing arguments logically and constructing sound responses. If he is a Christian, the student shapes arguments informed and instructed by God's Holy Word. Through this process, the mind of a thinker is shaped by a Christian liberal arts education, and this is an admirable base from which almost any specialized vocation may be pursued.

Cons for using Classical Education at home

I need to tell you something from the beginning as I write this section. As you may already have guessed, I'm a fan of classical education. I was educated this way in high school, and I loved it. I used this approach with all six of my now-adult children, and they loved it.

As you have doubtless read in my bio on the back of this book, I've spent eighteen years writing and perfecting an entire program (K-Mom) integrating the humanities so that homeschooling parents can be supported in combining the best features of classical education and unit studies for the subjects of History, Literature, Church History, Philosphy, Geography, Writing, and Government. We call it *Tapestry of Grace.*

I'd like to note that our family, and many of our customers, also use traditional textbooks or outside classes for subjects such as math, science, grammar, and languages. Indeed, some of our customers use *Tapestry* by employing paid teachers in group classes!

That said, the cons for me with classical education are few and far between, but I will do my best to explain the cons that other women have shared with me as they tried it and found that it wasn't for them.

The biggest hurdle that I see for the beginning homeschooler who contemplates giving her children a classical education is her lack of familiarity with the Great Books. Because they fell out of favor in the last half-century or so, and because they take some work to understand, many of today's parents who wish to educate classically are afraid to try it, knowing that their own educations did not convey key skills and knowledge that understanding (much less teaching) the Great Books requires.

To such parents I would say that, if you can either find a program that will give you strong guidance in teaching classically, or find a group of homeschoolers that is committed to this method and can mentor you, this first objection may be overcome with some work on your part. You yourself can read the Great Books; you can learn right along with your children, especially if they are young, because earnest perusal of the Great Books doesn't begin before late junior high at the earliest, or in most cases, the high school years.

Most beginning homeschoolers have young children. Classical education is not difficult for a novice in the younger years, and there are a lot of these years to go! You can begin with young children by making those introductions and doing that memory work that are the basis of a classical education now, and seek to read the classics for your own edification in the years to come. (Remember, they are called Great Books because they really are worthy reads!) By the time that your children need you to teach them the content of these classics, you can have a working knowledge of them. You will have taught one pupil—yourself—and be ready to begin teaching your children as they come of age. But this approach may simply be either not feasible for—or not palatable to—many of you in the exhausting years of building and raising a young family.

Another stopper for some parents is that their children are highly oriented towards active or tactile approaches, or have great difficulty reading because of learning disabilities. Sitting to read, or to thoughtfully discuss ideas, can be hard for some children. Possibly they are more gifted in and drawn to sports or animals or agricultural pursuits than intellectual ones. If this describes your family, you may want to lean more towards a Unit Study approach, at least for the first few years of homeschooling.

That said, there are many ways to marry the activities of Unit Study with the content and structures of classical education (which is what my curriculum, *Tapestry of Grace*, does), so you don't have to abandon the strengths of classical education altogether in these early years. You can adjust them as your unique children require. Such is the beauty of homeschooling, and part of the real secret to enjoying the journey!

Miscellaneous Categories and a Few More Terms

In this (somewhat lengthy) chapter, I've centered your attention on the three main categories of curricula that you'll encounter as you begin to evaluate specific programs. But I don't want to leave this chapter without defining a few more commonly used terms that you'll encounter as you begin to survey the homeschooling curriculum choices before you.

What does the term "complete curriculum" mean?

Generally, this term means that the provider has included or integrated many traditional subjects into one program. The term is a loose one, and it will serve you to peruse a list of exactly what "complete" includes. For instance, a complete humanities program (history, literature, arts, and geography) for 3rd graders may or may not include composition (writing) and handwriting components. It definitely won't include math or science components. But, still, it might be listed on a homeschooling review website, or at a conference, under "complete curricula."

Also, "complete curricula" may fall into the category of textbooks (because it's complete in that the program publishers have chosen a set of textbooks for all subjects) or it may employ Unit Study or other approaches (like video-based teaching, on which we have not touched).

What is meant by the term "whole book"?

This term is used to divide programs that use summary textbooks and anthologies (which generally abridge or excerpt works) from those that ask students to read entire books.

What does it mean to say that a curriculum is "spiral"?

It means that the authors have planned to first introduce concepts and then later circle back to the same concepts several times as the child works through the program. (Think of wrapping a wire around a cone-shape. That's the kind of spiral that's meant.) In spiral approaches, a child doesn't have to master concepts the first time through, and revisiting them several times gives review and adds to long-term retention.

Conclusion

I hope that this introduction to various categories of curricula was helpful to you. It is hardly exhaustive, but it was meant to give you some pointers and, more importantly, to model the process by which you can begin to collect and organize information on the programs that are offered for your consideration.

Remember, at the end of the day, it's *your* homeschool, and God (with your husband's leadership) will help you find your initial path. Remember that seasons change, so the approach that you adopt as you begin to teach may not prove to be the only one you use on your way to your destination.

25.

To trudge: the slow, weary, depressing yet determined walk of a man who has nothing left in life except the impulse to simply soldier on.

Chaucer, in A Knight's Tale

When Trudging is Called For

If you are schooling young children, as most beginning homeschoolers are, you will soon discover that there are some basic academic practices that are necessary, but not fun. These are tried and true means to the end of a solid education, and (just like dust and aching muscles) they are a part of the journey. However, they can sap our joy. Why? Because, as Beverly Bullmore so aptly put it in a comment to her husband one morning, "The problem with life is that it's just so *daily*!"

Few things kill the love of learning and make us want to try another path more than what I'll call the "basic disciplines." These are things like memorizing math facts, tracing and re-tracing letters as we learn handwriting, and taking daily dictation.

It's bad enough that these are unexciting. Worse is that they require sustained and focused effort in order to produce good results. What I want to do in this chapter is to give you some vision for this part of your trip, for the good of your kids and to the greater glory of God.

Math Memory Work

Let's start with memorizing math facts. Most curricula start with addition, then go on to subtraction. After the child has had some practice with using these facts in triple-digit (with carrying and borrowing) and/or single-column sums, he moves to memorizing multiplication and division facts.

When you start the process, you typically have a chart of 144 squares, representing combinations up to 12 X 12. To a young student, that looks like a daunting number of facts to memorize! The good news is that the rows of 1's and 2's are quickly mastered, so the student usually has early encouragement. (What we used to demonstrate this to our youngsters was taking a highlighter and having him color in the squares representing the facts he'd mastered on the chart as he went along. That way, he would see how many he already had done from the earliest stages, and as he want along, he could see his progress.)

Most families purchase or make flash cards; they seem to be the most popular means to the end of getting these facts down cold. And that's the key: getting them down *cold* is what you are working toward. Let me tell you why by sharing a story from my own childhood.

I was firstborn, and I went to the local, suburban public schools. I have never been anything like math minded, and this showed up early. I was probably in 3rd grade, and struggling through my homework in tears, when my dad realized that I did not know my addition and subtraction facts cold. He quietly told me to put my homework away, got out some index cards from his desk, wrote on them for a few minutes, and (having created flash cards) began to drill me on my basic math facts. He did this every night for two solid weeks. At the end of these weeks, I had learned my addition and subtraction facts, and found that I could easily and happily do my assigned math homework. Knowing those facts had turned nightly math homework from drudgery to delight in just a few short weeks of applied effort.

So, why don't more kids learn math facts cold? I know of one reason: not unlike potty training, it takes a few weeks of focused and sustained effort, and many of our children don't want to do the work. Some of this resistance may come from our entertainment-oriented (and saturated) modern culture, but there was less of that when I was a child, and yet I remember not wanting to do the basic chores of schoolwork.

More useful, perhaps, is the observation that kids don't yet know of the rewards that trudging can bring later. In my case, I had a presenting problem: the math homework was beyond me and I knew I was floundering. I would have grabbed hold of almost any lifesaving ring that my dad tossed me!

Also, because I was a bit old to be learning those facts, I probably learned them quicker than many children do who start them *before* they are trying to do more advanced problems. The sudden transformation from slogging to sailing through my homework that I experienced upon learning those facts made clear to me the worth of doing the work to memorize them.

So, I have a suggestion for you: show your kids the power that memorizing their facts will give them in doing later, more complicated problems. To do this, have your child memorize the first half of the flashcard deck, say up the the 4+'s. Then give him some three-digit (or column) problems to work that involve *only* the facts that he knows cold. Finally, give him some similar advanced problems that *only* feature the digits he has *not* yet mastered: the 8's, 9's, and 11's, for instance. He should quickly grasp that it's far easier to work advanced math problems if you have these facts cemented in your mind.

Now, here's some encouragement for you. While your young child may resist the repetition and "daily-ness" of flashcard work, memorizing is not as hard for him as it is for you. Youngsters are in just the right stage of mental development for this work. (I referred to this in our last chapter, when discussing classical education and the three basic stages of learning, and I write more about this in Chapter 27.) Unless there are learning disabilities, memory work comes easily to youngsters; it's usually the lack of fun or excitement that makes it trudging, not the difficulty of getting it into their heads.

This is why there are an abundance of apps and computer games available on the market that will reinforce memory work of many kinds. You may want to purchase one or more of these, but before you do, consider whether or not some honest toil might not be good for your child's character development, as well as his math mind.

Plenty of times in adult life, it becomes necessary to trudge! If your child is not a seasoned trudger, how will he cope with those difficult times that lie ahead?

Here is where your job as teacher becomes more like that of a coach. It has been well said that a coach is someone who makes you do what you don't want to do so that you can become what you've always wanted to be. Your child is too young to know that he wants to be able to do math problems quickly and easily, but you are not! As a homeschooling parent, your job is to make sure that he gains the skills he needs to succeed later on!

Perhaps the analogy of a coach doesn't grab you. Let me give you another way of looking at it. We Christians trudge difficult roads with the aid of hope, but it is seldom fun, or easy (and often not quickly over) when we do. Synonyms for trudging are: faithfulness, steadfastness, and perseverance (especially in trials). There are many helpful passages that encourage us (and that we can share with our children) when trudging is called for. Below are two that are especially helpful in our task of requiring our children to discipline their emotions and do hard things:

> *For the moment all discipline seems painful rather than pleasant, but later it yields the peaceful fruit of righteousness to those who have been trained by it.*
>
> *Hebrews 12:11 (ESV)*

> *Count it all joy, my brothers, when you meet trials of various kinds, for you know that the testing of your faith produces steadfastness. And let steadfastness have its full effect, that you may be perfect and complete, lacking in nothing.*
>
> *James 1:2-4 (ESV)*

Handwriting Practice

Here's another discipline that most children don't enjoy. We must ask them to copy letters and numbers over and over in order to train their small muscles. Such work is hard for youngsters, because in their stage of development small muscles remain weak and uncoordinated.

In fact, this is one area where that idea of "better late than early" comes into play. If your child is a late bloomer in other ways, consider delaying a focus on handwriting and use other tools to teach lessons until his development catches up! However, if your child is able to do the work fairly easily, it is worthwhile to urge him to do it. Handwriting practice helps to strengthen these little muscles with time, and the practice with letters enables your child to write quickly and legibly in later life.

Some would argue that today's children don't need to develop a cursive hand at all, and hardly even need legible handwriting, given the digital age in which we live. I would counter that they will need to print their names on the occasional form, so I'm assuming that they'll learn to print. But, let me make the case first for developing a neat, printed script, and then also for developing a good, cursive hand.

First, let's think about having good handwriting of any kind. Though it is true that we do live in a digital age, there are still a multitude of times when writing by hand comes into play. In our personal lives, we jot down phone messages, we make shopping lists, and we leave notes for children or spouses. Professionally, we make notations on others' drafts, or write drafts of our own. Doctors must write prescriptions; lawyers make notes while hearing the client's complaints and listening to the testimony of witnesses. Pastors make notes when listening to a counselee pour out his pain and trouble. In almost any field you can name, legible handwriting is useful, appreciated, and nowadays rare!

Secondly, we want to do all things well as we image our Creator God (1 Corinthians 14:40). Good handwriting, while hardly a guarantee that your child wishes to glorify or imitate God, is one more small way that he is learning to imitate and value the orderliness and beauty that are part of God's nature.

Third, your children may someday be parents, with children to teach in their homes. Especially if your child is a girl, she must learn to have good handwriting if she is to pass down this tradition when she becomes a mother. So, this discipline can be a lasting legacy that you give your child.

Now, I'd also like to make an argument for a focus on teaching cursive handwriting. Traditionally, we teach printing first because it looks like the simplified letters that the young child is learning for phonics lessons and sees in his early readers. Well and good. The problem is that, in many homes, the child learns to print quickly and well, and the mother is uninspired to then re-teach a whole new alphabet (actually, two new ones since capital letters must be learned as well) in cursive, and so the child prints for the rest of his days. Why is this a problem? I'm so glad you asked!

Did you know that classic cursive handwriting (the kind that joins most of the letters into one flowing script) was developed as the fastest possible form of legible handwriting that was also easiest on the hand and arm muscles while allowing ink to flow freely and not blot the page? Because of the joined letters, there is not the constant raising and lowering of the pen to the paper that unjoined letters require, so it is both easier on the hand and faster to write. (And note, too, that individual printed letters themselves often require several liftings of the pen, where only a few cursive letters require more than one stroke.) So, let's agree that, once mastered, cursive handwriting is easier, faster, and better sustained, especially when writing a long missive.

But—you object—that's just it. When will my kids have to produce a lot of handwritten text? Well, how about on college exams? Even in our digital age, most colleges still require exam essays and short answers to be handwritten! Do you remember having to write two or more essays during a two-hour exam? I do! I remember shaking my hand to keep it able to continue writing into the second hour! And, all my earlier examples about how we still use and need handwriting hold true for the argument for cursive as well as printed handwriting.

I will, however, add one word of caution at this point. Obviously I have been making an enthusiastic case for cursive writing, but remember our example of how "they say" your son needs to learn from a Suzuki violin teacher? I do not want to make handwriting the last straw on your breaking back. So, I encourage you to do with my advice what I have encouraged you to do with the advice of others: take it to the Lord and to your husband, and ask whether handwriting should be a priority for your students in this season.

Now, assuming that you do have time for handwriting practice in your quiet home, and that you've become convinced that you will coach your child through handwriting practice, when will you teach him to write a cursive hand? Will it come before or after printing? I argue that you don't need to teach printing first, but not everyone agrees with me. Why do I think so?

One reason is that I don't believe that the argument that a young child needs to learn the handwriting that matches her early readers is correct. I think that the young child is more than capable of learning that the "A" in the reader is a symbol for the same sound as the cursive "*A*." To demonstrate this, think with me about the fact that children are learning to associate the "a" sounds with the lower case "**ɑ**" that they print and the lower case "a" that many readers use. These look different, and differ still more from the upper case "A," yet children can easily learn this.

Secondly, I argue that, if we are going to teach handwriting—and require hours of practice in order to perfect it—why not start out with the system that the child will use most often for her entire life? Let her learn printing later, after it's easier, so that her first, default handwriting will be cursive (which—remember—if both are thoroughly learned, will always be faster and easier to do).

Finally, the effort needed to learn any system of handwriting is going to help to perfect, while taxing initially, the small motor movements of children's hands. If the argument is made to wait, that's fine. We can meantime teach them keyboarding! The font will most closely match their readers that way, and there are wonderfully entertaining computer programs out there that will teach them this valuable skill quickly. I'm all for this option if (and only if) we don't neglect the discipline of learning a fluent cursive hand as early as is practical.

Taking Dictation

Dictation is the third major discipline that I want to discuss. It takes time for both teacher and student, and can involve serious trudging for both. So, what is its purpose? We generally use dictation exercises for teaching proper punctuation and grammar in written compositions, and because it is a very effective tool, if not glamorous.

For those who have never done (or taught) dictation, here's what it is in a nutshell. The teacher chooses, say, five sentences to dictate. The student sits with a pencil and a properly headed, lined piece of paper. The teacher says the first sentence once aloud, slowly. Then, she says it again, phrase by phrase, and the student starts to write it down. The teacher waits for each new phrase to be completed while the student writes. If the sentence is long, the teacher might repeat it one more time while the student is writing. Then, when the student is done, the teacher will say the sentence one more time while the student proofs what she has written. Then, the teacher would move on to sentence #2.

Sentences are chosen (and often concocted) by the teacher for their grammatical and/or punctuation features. The exercise can be used with any grammar curriculum that you choose, whether or not it includes direction for it.

Let's say that your student is learning about comma usage. You would often find or make sentences that have sequences (Johnny, Martha, and Sue all like potatoes, raspberries, and ice cream.) or dates (John and Martha were both born on February 14, 2000.) or places (He was born in St. Louis, MO.) that demonstrate whether the student has learned the proper punctuation rules here.

As you can see from these examples, dictation exercises are also good for checking to see if students can properly capitalize and spell difficult words. It also displays their comprehension of commonly used forms and exceptions to rules. For instance, I might give this sentence: "Mary likes summer best, but Sue likes winter because it has both Christmas and Valentine's Day in it." Seasons are not capitalized, but holidays are, and there's a comma before the conjunction in this sentence.

Once the sentences are written out, a teacher can either have the student self-correct (if she is using a published dictation manual or has taken the sentences from the grammar textbook, or even a work of fiction) or the teacher can correct the exercises. The student should then rewrite the sentences she got wrong as the final phase of the lesson.

What's the long-range benefit of this trudgery? Simply put, it is a direct and effective means to the end of teaching children to write proper English. There is a real problem in today's workforce, often lamented by employers: people do not know proper usage and punctuation! Many editors and proofers make their livelihood correcting these mistakes in many sorts of publications. Employers are always eager to find employees who know how to use English properly. Along with a cursive hand (which, by the way, is needed for doing the dictation exercises in the first place), proper usage of English enables your child to communicate effectively, whether to her boss, her co-worker, her husband, or her friends. If God blesses her with children to homeschool, she can also pass this valuable skill on to the next generation!

Conclusion

The three types of trudging that I've mentioned above are not the only types of learning that may seem lackluster and/or pointless when they are first undertaken. For older children, learning the vocabulary and grammatical forms of foreign languages, or committing scientific terms to memory involve similar fortitude.

I think that the key to trudging—or, in more biblical language, the key to steadfast perseverance—is hope. Unlike Chaucer, we have something more than "the impulse to simply soldier on." We have the hope that discipline is given by God towards a purpose—a good, loving, kind, and beautiful purpose, though we might not yet see it as such while trudging.

I believe that what I can do for my child is be *more* than a coach who makes him do what he doesn't want to do so that he can become what he's always wanted to be. I can explain to him the greater purpose behind the exercises that I'm asking him to do. I can envision him for the goal of the exercise. I can encourage him about how well he's doing and (hopefully) commend him for his perseverance with cheerfulness. And I can remind him that "for the moment all discipline seems painful rather than pleasant, but later it yields the peaceful fruit of righteousness to those who have been trained by it" (Hebrews 12:11, ESV).

Unlike Chaucer, we have something more than "the impulse to simply soldier on."

While reminding him, I can also remind myself that to him it seems painful, and show compassion even as I require diligence. Even though God has promised peaceful fruit for us if we persevere in discipline, that doesn't always make the road smooth before us!

So, I can do one more thing: I can model the same kind of steadfast perseverance with those elements of my days and weeks that amount to trudging for me! I can ask my children for prayer that I would remain faithful to the little things that I'd rather not do. For me, these were always things like cleaning the bathrooms and cleaning off my desk regularly. I also don't enjoy food shopping much. These are places where I tended to grumble and complain as I pushed myself through them and was unintentionally teaching my kids to do likewise.

Remember Chapter 5 ("You Share Who You Are")? We talked about our pursuit of personal discipleship (or lack thereof) as having the most effect of all on our children's "soul soil." In this chapter, I've been arguing that we should require our students to undertake some lackluster disciplines (the practice) because they cause them to grow through discipline and hard work for their good and God's glory (the principle). But perhaps there's an even deeper principle to be gleaned here: it is that we parents should purposefully work to model a biblical, God-focused response to our own challenges if we expect our children to grow towards God while submitting to such disciplines.

So, academic trudging becomes one of those examples of how God uses homeschooling to sanctify parents! We have a chance to grow along with our children as we learn to love the journey all the more for the fellowship of sufferings it includes, and the longing that it prompts for the coming King.

> *And let us not grow weary of doing good, for in due season we will reap, if we do not give up.*
>
> *Galatians 6:9 (ESV)*

> *If we are afflicted, it is for your comfort and salvation; and if we are comforted, it is for your comfort, which you experience when you patiently endure the same sufferings that we suffer. Our hope for you is unshaken, for we know that as you share in our sufferings, you will also share in our comfort.*
>
> *2 Corinthians 1:6-7 (ESV)*

26.

If any of you lacks wisdom, let him ask God, who gives generously to all without reproach, and it will be given him.

JAMES 1:5 (ESV)

Choices, Choices

As I mentioned in Chapter 9 ("More Isn't Always Better"), all teachers need to make choices concerning a host of things. First, as we've covered in that chapter and others, there are the choices concerning which subjects to cover with which curricula, and choices of when to schedule both lessons and life in the home. Beyond these basics, however, there is almost always a need to tweak (or tailor) the curricula you buy to properly fit your unique children because each family has unique learners, and homeschooling amounts to a tutorial approach for each child. Since many new homeschoolers feel anxious about this aspect of teaching, I thought that a brief and practical chapter on this topic might be helpful.

As a society, Americans have long embraced the concept of specialists (people who have mastered one small area of knowledge to the exclusion of many others). In the modern era, such specialization has been a natural result of the sheer volume of information and opportunities that confront us. The Jack of all trades truly can be master of none. No one can be an astronaut, a brain surgeon, and a professional farmer all at once—or even, arguably, in one lifetime. There is too much to learn, and there are too many years of practicing needed for mastery in any of these fields, not to mention the financial expense of pursuing these disciplines. So, as a society, we specialize and are comfortable with consulting the "experts" in given fields in order to get information or form our opinions.

Furthermore, if you've read my chapter (or the *Why Gender Matters* book) on male and female differences, you'll probably agree that we women are more likely to search out and rely on the expert (or, at least, experienced) opinions of others, rather than trying to reinvent the wheel or wing it on our own. Speaking generally, women tend to feel more comfortable with "how to" guides that are clear and knowledgeable. And the more important the project, the more we desire to get trusted opinions of others before venturing forth.

If this is you, I have words of comfort for you! First (in relation to the "experts") there's something that you need to know about homeschooling. From the get-go, you *are* the expert in one way at least: you know your child best! You may have never taught a single academic lesson, but you have been training your child for about four years before you ever crack open a curriculum. In this one way, you are miles ahead of anyone else (saving your husband) that you might consult when making academic choices. God Almighty has given your child(ren) to you, and you to them. He makes no mistakes.

Furthermore, as I've written before, we shape our children. Well, it's also true that our children shape us. Families (which include parent/child relationships and marriage ones) are one of the strongest influencers that God uses to sanctify His people. If you are a believer in Jesus, again I'll mention that powerful, comforting verse that you can lay hold of: Romans 8:28-29 (ESV).

> *And we know that for those who love God all things work together for good, for those who are called according to his purpose. For those whom he foreknew he also predestined to be conformed to the image of his Son, in order that he might be the firstborn among many brothers.*

Once again I remind you, this passage indicates that God Himself has ordained *everything* in your life for the glorious purpose of making even *you* into a replica of Christ. So, for both you and your child, my second word of comfort is that God is working on your behalf in a way that truly affects how you process the advice or "experts." As counter-intuitive as it may seem to you when you open those first purchased packages of five-star curricula at the start of your homeschooling career, your Lord, your husband, and you are the ones who most love and best know your child.

You are the expert in one way at least: you know your child best!

Furthermore, your husband and your Lord best know you. If you can cultivate the habit of consulting them when you are making decisions—or are confused by circumstances or the well-meaning counsel of others, or are simply discouraged by the setbacks and exhaustion of mothering and homeschooling—you will benefit tremendously as a person and teacher.

I'll say again in this context something that I've written repeatedly (because it bears repeating): it is *still* a well-kept secret that homeschooling is a tool in God's hand for the sanctification of the parents as much as for the children in the home! He is *the* active force in your homeschool, and He is working in and through you for the good of all the Christian disciples—present and future—who are part of your homeschool. So, believe me when I say that you have an important, real, and solid foundation for making important choices, even as a beginning teacher.

Here is a third important truth to soak in: learning to teach takes time and experimentation. Those who do it for a living (those "experts" or "professionals" that we beginners so want to consult and trust) were not born knowing how to teach, even though they might have been given significant giftings as teachers. It takes study, practice, and diligence to become a skillful teacher. It takes trial and error, insight into varying problems and into the complex human heart.

Just as in most vocations, every good teacher is constantly honing her abilities as she herself grows personally. While experienced teachers can and do give us good advice (and we can grow more quickly if we humbly ask those who are more experienced for their opinions), you will need to come to grips with the fact that it will take you some time and experience to come up to speed and feel like you know what you are doing. But, read on!

No matter who tells you otherwise, remember that there is no one golden, perfect, or "right" path to learning that fits all students. There may be educational standards to which we are obliged to teach, and there are certain subjects (like math and foreign languages) that must be learned sequentially (because in them one piece of information is built upon knowledge of another), but as we discussed at length in the chapters on modalities, there is no one standard way to learn.

Children are complex human beings. They typically grow in a stair-step kind of way, such that they make a big step up and then coast for a bit in that mode while gathering skills and strength for the next step up. Learning to teach to a variety of children who each learn differently and are in different stages of development is the central challenge of home teaching. This is why purchased curricula will most certainly need customizing in order to fit your unique learners.

But again: let the very thing that makes group teaching in the home challenging also comfort you, because again, you've been practicing with these learning stages and know these children best. Only your eldest child's development is truly a "cutting edge" learning curve for you. (Well, that and teaching academic lessons at all, if you're just starting.)

There's a fourth comforting fact to add here: children are resilient. Moms who are starting homeschooling are naturally concerned about doing lasting harm to their kids by inadequate teaching. Typically, I find that young homeschooling moms err on the side of being too careful (stressing themselves unnecessarily) and doing too much, rather than too little. In making choices of all kinds, new moms are often most concerned about permanently damaging their kids by leaving out crucial components of schoolwork through inexperience or a lack of knowledge about teaching. Thus do they tend to pack in too much schoolwork for the young child.

I'd like to reassure you that, especially when kids are young, you almost can't mess up in any meaningful or lasting way as a teacher—*unless* you lack the diligence and discipline needed to actually accomplish lessons. Young children are generally eager to learn and filled with wonder at most every discovery, and they thrive on having your attention. If you have done a solid job mothering (and here's where that quiet home proves its worth) your child will typically be eager to accept what can seem to *you* like fumbling first attempts at teaching.

Most curricula are designed to be "spiral." As I told you in Chapter 24 ("Useful Categories to Know When Considering Curricula"), this means that they circle back over a number of lessons (or years) to the same concepts or information, which are then retaught at more advanced levels or with greater detail. For this reason, you should learn to think in terms of a "first pass" over concepts in early years as an introduction to the given topic.

Lessons for young children in grades K-2 are so simple. Your goal is to *introduce* topics and concepts to little ones, not to require *mastery* of them. It is hard to mess up "Katrina: one button and one button is two buttons, see?" You're not teaching her higher math: that will come later. Now, it's a friendly handshake—an introduction to mathematical concepts. And if she forgets it tomorrow, or if you don't teach it perfectly the first time, there are lots of opportunities ahead to retrieve this ball!

Phonics is not rocket science (or even magic, though it seems that way when they first catch on!). Phonics means teaching small children that certain sounds are associated with a short list of abstract symbols (letters, or letters in combination). God has wired the young child's brain to embrace this concept. Some of them catch it early; some are late bloomers. But only the truly learning-disabled child won't get the hang of it if you diligently introduce it at the appropriate time.

Reading aloud to your child, talking to him, engaging him in educational play, as with stringing beads, practicing handwriting, or reciting memory work—all of these are well within the new teacher's reach from the very beginning. So, the academic content for young learners is not challenging for you to master, nor is it hard to tailor to your child's needs, really.

What you can most seriously mess up is faithfulness: you need to sit with your child and his buttons or beads or read-aloud book or alphabet and *do* the lessons, simple as they are, day in and day out, and so build concepts slowly, one upon another.

Really, truly, any major curriculum program on the homeschool market today that fits your style of teaching and your child's style of learning (modalities) will have the basic building blocks of content that you'll need to know about in order to teach your child successfully. So, what about those choices that you'll need to make?

Let's say you are faithfully delivering a solid, daily set of lessons. If, then, in tweaking your program you mistakenly leave out a few important concepts, or go a little less in depth in some topics in those early years, or cover a program more slowly than its designers intended, it will be okay. In almost all cases, you can make it up later, and for the rest, this is where the sovereignty of God's directive presence in your homeschool gives you needed peace.

As a fifth comforting thought, let's consider time lines together. You have *a lot of time* for both making errors and improving as a teacher. If you are reading this chapter, you are probably a younger mom who is just starting out with younger children. In America, humans remain children longer than in any civilization in history. If we take 18 as the age when most of our children will take significant strides out of our home (whether to college or to work), we then have their early childhood plus 12 years of grade school in which to learn to be excellent teachers. And that's for one child. If you have a ten-year spread between your eldest and youngest children, your homeschooling career is more like 22 years.

You have a lot of time for both making errors and improving as a teacher.

I'm here to say that, if you are working at it and are diligent, it takes far less time than that to feel like you understand how to wisely tailor a purchased curriculum (always assuming that you're settled into diligent homeschooling rhythms, as we thoroughly considered in Chapter 13 "Schedules and Structure").

Now, I have written all the above in order to say this: when you go to buy programs that have been designed for homeschooling, do not look for one that is perfect for you in its ready-made state. You probably won't buy any helpful programs if this is your starting criteria, and you may grow discouraged or (worse) develop Curriculum Buying Disorder, where you flit from program to program in a fruitless search for the ready-made "perfect fit."

For almost all of purchased curricula, you will need to bring creativity, tweaking, and changes. In this pursuit, you will need to make choices that are based on the goals for *your* homeschool that you and your husband identify, with prayer, as we discussed in the early chapters of this book.

In what kinds of ways will you typically change what you buy? Well, a program may be too rigorous for your child (needing you to cut some content), or too easy (needing you to find or create supplementation), or lack clear in-depth support material in the instructor's guide (leaving you to fill in the blanks as best you can), or call for resources that you can't find in your library. Additionally, there will be times when a program that you purchase may not turn out to be a good fit for a child, even though it seemed so when you purchased it (or worked well for an older sibling).

The goal of this chapter is to reassure you that you can (and should expect to) make changes to ready-bought programs for homeschooling from the first year you begin as a teacher. Doing so goes with the territory, and is highly doable. Most beginner moms can make these kinds of choices. What they most lack is the confidence, and that will be brought by experience in short order.

You have an advantage that I didn't enjoy starting as a young homeschooler (since the Internet wasn't even in existence when I began teaching), because you can easily find "expert"—or at least plentiful—advice any time of the day or night. Even so, I would still advise you to plan to figure out for yourself some of your choices. Be sure to ask your husband at home and pray through decisions so that you can gain skill and confidence as a teacher.

Because God is your strong support, and these are *your* children, you can and will make changes in published curricula that you buy. You will have to make choices, and sometimes, you may find that you need to go back and make different ones, or make up for lost opportunities. I advise you to start by settling it in your heart that though you are not perfect, God is, and He is the real Director of your journey. Being overwhelmed may be uncomfortable, but it's part of the learning curve and offers us the opportunity to rely on Him and see what He will do!

27.

Thy word have I hid in mine heart, that
I might not sin against thee.

PSALM 119: 11 (KJV)

When your children ask in time to come, 'What do those stones mean to you?' then you shall tell them that the waters of the Jordan were cut off before the ark of the covenant of the LORD. When it passed over the Jordan, the waters of the Jordan were cut off. So these stones shall be to the people of Israel a memorial forever.

JOSHUA 4:6B-7 (ESV)

What About Memory Work?

Since younger children memorize easily, many curricula (and most notably those written from a classical education perspective) have made memory work a significant element of their programs for younger students. The idea is that we should harness a natural strength of this learning stage. Some programs embed this work in fun activities: games, songs, etc. Other programs unapologetically require straightforward, unvarnished rote memorization effort. Some programs put the items to be memorized in context; others argue that context will come later. They see the items as "hooks" on which more advanced concepts—whether of language, mathematics, history, or geography—will be hung later, in upper-level learning stages.

As someone who has been around for awhile, I sense that a portion of the current (and sometimes intense) focus on memory work for its own sake and in large concentrations is somewhat inorganic. Let me say clearly that I'm not singling out any one program for critique here! As I say, while some programs major on memory work, almost all classical education programs (including *Tapestry of Grace*) have come to include a memory work component of some kind, because as I write this, a majority of parents are looking for this emphasis in assessing any curriculum offered for young children.

That said, I'd like to discuss the pros and cons—as I see them—for spending time and effort on helping our young children to memorize. First, let's look at the arguments for this activity.

It is undeniable that little children are wired to memorize; God made their little brains that way so that they could survive! Little people must learn so much in the first years of life: to speak and touch (or not to touch), to crawl, walk, and run, and to do all the small tasks of life, etc. So, it's easy to see that the talent is there, and it's easy to understand why many educators want to capitalize on this God-given ability to memorize while it's at its peak.

From an educational perspective, it is reasoned that since young children cannot easily do the organizing and processing that belong to later stages of development, why not spend the younger years cementing important facts, dates, mathematical formulae, foreign language vocabulary, Bible verses, catechisms, and famous quotations firmly in their young brains? Many educators believe that doing so will then give them a leg up, as memory elements will be already present when students come to connect them with larger and more complex concepts later. Furthermore, they won't have to do this basic memory work later on; thus, will there be more time for higher-order thinking skills.

It is also argued that rote memory work is not difficult, but delightful for young children. It's easy for them and, besides, they love to be able to spout off a list of abc's, of Presidents in order, of states with their capitals, of countries of various continents, of math facts and formulae, and of Latin vocabulary terms, even if they have no idea how these isolated facts that they're memorizing fit into a greater whole. And since it's easiest for them at this stage, and there are so many cute songs, hand signs, and fun chants that lighten the load even more, it is widely taught that we homeschooling moms should do all we can to push it forward.

So, we are advised to look for programs that include memory work as a major component, and then we embrace the need to spend significant time on much repetition of memory elements until kids have them firmly set in their minds.

One can certainly see that this argument has some good points, and it tends to ring true in our minds, because who among us has not spent some time doing memory work in our own formative years? From abc's and 123's to states and their capitals, most of us have learned some things in this way. Possibly, some of us remember doing so with delight, but I can't say that I'm among them, even though I have a pretty good memory and that kind of work came easily to me when I was young.

On the flip side, I can remember a fair amount of trudging when memorizing Latin forms and sections of Chaucer in junior high and high school. Maybe if I'd done that work earlier, in foundational years, I might have been grateful… but I'll never really know! One thing is sure: early disciplines almost always yield later fruit for which we are usually grateful (as I've discussed elsewhere in this book).

I would say from my experience as an adult, and a teacher of my own children and of others' in co-ops, that the theory behind (and value of) assigning lots of memory work to young children as I've pictured it above is partially correct, but only partially, and I think that it's helpful at this juncture to make a distinction between rote memory work and remembering things. I'll get back to this in a minute.

But first, let's agree that, while remembering *is* inarguably easier for younger children than for teens and young adults, it may not be easier to the *degree* that the argument for it might indicate. Teens and adults *can* memorize, and do! Furthermore, older students may sometimes have the added advantage that they can do memorization in orderly, systemized ways. Also, they comprehend the *point* of the memory work, i.e., the purpose for it.

For instance, take Latin vocabulary. An older student understands that vocabulary is the basic building block for language, and that the forms that he's chanting have relationships with the grammar of the language. Or, take Bible memory work. As I wrote earlier, teaching young children Bible verses through songs and by rote is certainly working with their strengths. But consider: if an older person has had life lessons that unite their *need* for God's wisdom with His Word, might not memory work done in upper grades sometimes be more meaningful and helpful, rather than less, at an older age?

Also, while memorizing comes easily to young children, I'm not sure that *lots* of *rote* memory work is either delightful or desirable to them. In fact, it might prove counter-productive to what I feel is a greater good for this age group: firing their love for learning and their imaginations for the great stories of the human race.

And here is where my caution is most acute. Let me present the counter argument to the above, for what it's worth, and then you decide what to do in your own family!

If children remember easily at younger ages, then why do parents need to concentrate on doing rote memory work in large quantities? Is it not like *making* a child eat ice cream for dessert? Ah, but let's say that we make him eat ice cream morning, noon, and night for months at a time. Will he continue to love ice cream? I don't think so. Even if they *do* still like it, a bowl of it would cease to be a treat (or luxury). This begs the question you may be asking, "What would you suggest instead?"

I think that it's helpful to make a distinction between rote memory work and remembering things.

Well, what if our goal was that they *remember*, instead of memorize. In contrast with memorizing isolated facts by rote, could not a story-driven approach—where we introduce the same items to be memorized, but in context and over time—not serve just as well, but be far more delightful and intriguing to the child?

Take, for instance, the idea of memorizing the list of names of past Presidents of the United States. Would it delight a child more to memorize them in isolation and by rote (Washington, Adams, Jefferson, Madison, Monroe...), or to read a storybook of the lives of these men, and possibly work at building a list of them that is reviewed, say, weekly, until both the list *and the context* are remembered?

I find support for this notion in the Word of God. Many of its lessons for life are embedded in stories, and very little of it is to be memorized by God's children by rote means. While we do memorize verses so that we have them available in times of temptation or trouble (a practice to which I raise no objection), the overall format that God has chosen to teach us His truths is that of a long, slowly unfolding story.

(See the two quotations at the start of this chapter as examples of the difference I am highlighting here. We do hide God's Word in our hearts; we also learn about ourselves and Him by means of an unfolding story, of which He is the Author.

Not only the books of Moses and the tales of the kings of Israel are set in story format, but Jesus used parables to communicate much of the teaching that He imparted, and His Gospels are also stories of His life and death and resurrection. He also used metaphors, which are stories in concentrated form: they connect with us at an emotional level. So, when we read that we are God's children, or Jesus' Bride, or His lambs—we find ourselves in a story, not a list.

Certainly facts like the abc's, basic math facts, seasons and months of the year and the like are typically and easily memorized. And I am all for Bible memory work as a regular discipline in order to establish habits of this fruitful employment. I'm even in favor of youngsters working at memorizing some lists (the useful ones) early and by rote. I mentioned earlier (in Chapter 22) that my children memorized Scripture verses set to simple tunes, many of them between the ages of three and five.

What I did not say earlier is that they memorized those verses in the context of a delightful set of story-tapes (called *G.T. and the Halo Express*) that gave meaning and application to each verse. The kids in those story-tapes seemed to really need to know those verses. My children learned them and Scott and I were able to help them apply these verses to their everyday lives. So, again, I have found that context—by which I mean a big enough picture so that the need for and value of the item to be memorized can be seen—is important.

What I question about today's homeschooling trends is the *amount* of time and energy being devoted to the practice of *rote* memory work, which more and more parents feel that they should require of young children (and themselves as teachers). Such a focus centers on short facts (or Bible verses) that can be learned in isolation.

I would argue that the early learning stages (K-6) are prime for introducing the wonder of discovery of the great story of our race that God has written through many episodes involving the lives of real people who have lived over millennia. If we introduce our children to the giants of His story, and in the course of that we do help them to memorize, review, and stress key dates, names, and places enough that our young children remember them well, I believe we would offer a kinder, gentler, and more lasting introduction to the topics that they can spend the rest of their lives plumbing more deeply. Such an approach would also cost less (in terms of efforts for young homeschooling mothers) than intensive rote memory work does.

One of the users of my curriculum recently wrote the following in answer to a newcomer's concerns about fitting in rote memory work. I quote it here because it so well expressed my own view of the direction I myself headed and have directed others to go. Teren wrote:

> *Wouldn't you say that your goal with memory work is not that they actually be able to recite a list but rather that they remember the events? And remember them in such a way that they bring order to history?*
>
> Tapestry *does it with stories, hands-on projects and unit celebrations. With* Tapestry *my kids have memories of those learning experiences and new bits of history are linked in their hearts as they relate to other stories that they remember. It has been delightful to watch the time lines that have individually formed in their memory.*
>
> *For my boys (now 12 and 15) every new story finds its place in relationships to wars; for my daughter (who is eight), the stories of history lodge in her memory as they relate to kings and queens and the fashions of the women.*
>
> *It has been a joy to watch God build the time lines in their hearts and to see their understanding grow of God's sovereign hand turning the course of world events throughout all time.*
>
> *In the early years I was often tempted to add time line memory work to our schedule because it seemed that was what the classical education world emphasized, but I am grateful now that I didn't do that. It has been peaceful to let the children build their own memories around the stories of history and fill their souls with the memorization of Scripture and beautiful poetry.*
>
> *May God bless you on this journey. Walk with Jesus. He is Peace.*

28.

Holmes: "You see, but you do not observe. The distinction is clear. For example, you have frequently seen the steps which lead up from the hall to this room."
Watson: "Frequently."
Holmes: "How often?"
Watson: "Well, some hundreds of times."
Holmes: "Then how many are there?"
Watson: "How many? I don't know."
Holmes "Quite so! You have not observed. And yet you have seen. That is just my point. Now, I know that there are seventeen steps, because I have both seen and observed."

FROM "A SCANDAL IN BOHEMIA," BY ARTHUR CONAN DOYLE

Why Do Crafts?

In Chapters 21 and 22, we took a long look at presenting the same lesson content from a combination of three modalities: seeing, hearing, and touching (or experiencing, or doing). This chapter focuses on tactile learning, and gives a pitch for why we should include it regularly in our homeschools, be it ever so messy.

Now, for some of you, I'm preaching to the choir. You yourself prefer touching, tasting, and handling in order to learn, and you can't wait for this aspect of home teaching. Others of us, not so much. Some of us see the value of crafts and other hands-on learning but dread the mess and work of it, and wonder how (with space at a premium) we're going to store all the precious products of our little ones' hands! And then there are those of us who really don't see the point and wish this chapter wasn't in this book. Let's see if I can make a convincing argument for you reluctant crafters to create at least a little space in your weeks for tactile activities.

The first and best reason to undertake the work of tactile learning is that it's fun. As human beings, we all get stale. Many of us teaching moms fall into comfortable ruts and, as long as the kids are compliant, the need to put a lot of creative energy into finding new approaches to lessons sifts down in our priority stack. Our mantra is "if it ain't broke, don't fix it." If things are good (by which I mean that the kids are doing schoolwork without complaining—much), our family settles into a regular schedule that works, and we busy moms are grateful!

But kids typically start to get tired of the same-old-same-old, day after day routine if it's not peppered with a little variety and some fun. What's most comfortable for us moms is not always what's most stimulating to them. So, the ongoing reality is that we periodically have to re-up our efforts if we're going to keep learning enticing (which, after all, is part of the reason why we homeschool).

The first and best reason to undertake the work of tactile learning is that it's fun.

The second great reason for undertaking crafts regularly is that, with all modeling and doing, children have to think hard. They have to pay attention to details (and these are proportionately more important the older the student), then think about how to render them, and then work out the cutting, coloring, and assembling of the model or costume or recipe ingredients. While one can read details in a book, or see them in pictures, crafts and activities generally cause children not only to see, but observe.

True confessions: I don't love crafts, and cooking makes a mess, and workbooks sure are easier for me than helping the kids to create display boards or mount plays. But, I have found that messy, time-consuming crafts cement learning, build memories, and are some of the best ways of keeping school fresh and interesting to kids.

So, it's worth it to me from a practical standpoint, because cheerful kids who want to learn will work *with* me. These sure are easier to teach than those who are disinterested and whiney when it comes to doing schoolwork day in and day out. Hands-on activities are actually a protective measure for me: they are the spoonful of sugar that gives energy and motivation for the trudging! Or, they are the icing on the cupcakes. Or the bling on the everyday outfit. And what's nice for us all is that they come in a bunch of forms. But before I get you all starry-eyed about the possible ways you can add crafts to your teaching, let's talk about what you should do with the finished projects.

Storage Solutions

For me this was always a problem. I had six kids who were all eager to do crafts and projects, and while I appreciated their value, for us (as with many single-income, child-rich homeschooling families) space was the final frontier! Of course, when children work hard on a project, they don't want you to just say, "That's beautiful! What a great job you did! Now, let's throw it out." Nope, creations are precious things. So, how do we handle this? I have found three really good answers to this question.

First, I found that I could assign each child a "display spot" in our home. Some were tops of dressers in bedrooms; others were on lower, open space on a bookshelf, etc. Second, each child was also given a "treasure box" that was stored in a closet or under his bed. These two defined (and limited) the spaces that my children could fill with as many treasures as they chose.

Now, the beauty of these approaches was that each child made the decisions of what to display (or store) and what to toss. It was his space or box; it was his choice. The only directive for him was that his stuff couldn't transgress those defined spaces. So, what happened when there were too many treasures for him to be able to choose without tears? Enter the camera and portfolio!

Homeschoolers have to keep records of their kids' academic advancement, and there are a number of good ways to do this. The way that I finally chose to organize record-keeping (after much trial and error) was to have the kids collect and keep memorabilia and photos of their projects in one file, finished writing projects in either a file or a notebook, and then a slim file of finished (and checked-off) weekly assignment charts. At the end of each nine-week unit, we generally took off a week. I would have the kids collect, organize, and put these collected elements into their portfolios (large binders with an assortment of pocket folders, page protectors, notebook and blank paper, etc.).

These portfolios became permanent records of their work and family treasures. My kids periodically pulled them out in later years and thumbed through them lovingly, sharing memories of past school days together.

Returning to our storage problem, this third solution of snapping pictures of food cooked or crafts completed was a winner. The beauties of the picture of a beloved project are how handy it is to store and how permanently beautiful the crafts look. (Crafts that are stored get dusty and aged; photographed crafts never do!)

Furthermore, as their photos were put into portfolios, I required the children to annotate them, explaining what the project was and what they learned about it (of course, at age-appropriate levels). I would help the little ones write a sentence or two, and require older ones to write good, edited, computer-printed paragraphs and mount them on portfolio pages. Thus, portfolio assembly became added review and writing exercises, but seemed like nostalgic memory munching to the kids!

Now that we've talked about storage, let me envision you with some easy ways to add some zest into your school days by adding tactile approaches to the book learning your kids are already doing.

Dioramas

One of our family's favorite hands-on approaches to learning was to have kids create dioramas, which are essentially three-dimensional cut-away scenes. Your young student can do simple ones, or older students can work a bit at a time for weeks on really complex ones, as time allows. Common applications for this tactile approach to lessons involve making models of rooms (say, a castle keep or Pharaoh's throne room), or the flora and fauna of a specific environment (like a river or lake environment, or undersea scene, or even the planets of our solar system).

Typically, we use cardboard boxes to house the dioramas. Shoeboxes are a nice size for many indoor scenes; for science-oriented scenes, you might get a larger box. The student first lines the box with appropriate background "scenery" (usually colored on normal printer paper) and then can make models from paper or clay to fill in the scene. He can mount models on the floors or walls using tape, or suspend some elements of the scene (such as fish swimming, or candelabras in a room) from the ceiling using fish line or white thread.

For little ones, keep it simple. Five fish to color and hang from the top of the box on its side is a great activity if you're doing a science unit on undersea animals. Add some blue paper on three sides and have him draw some starfish for the bottom and color it tan (for sand), and you're done.

Play with doughs

Here's an easy craft for little ones: play with dough. Whether purchased or homemade, play dough makes an easy and fun medium to use in switching up lessons for younger students. You can make play dough or salt dough with a few everyday ingredients found in the home (recipes are readily available online). Some fun doughs that exist commercially come in bright colors, and others come in white, air harden, and then can be sanded and painted.

With doughs, kids can model so many things: from simple shapes to real animals of a region, from fantastic creatures that they make up to historic scenes, from tablets filled with mock cuneiform to Egyptian fashions and hair styles, from historic buildings (like pyramids and ziggurats) to salt maps that show the topography of a region that you're introducing in geography lessons. When these crafts are done, snap a picture of the creations for the portfolios if you like, squish the dough that you don't want to keep in model shapes back in the cans, and voila! You're done!

Another note here is that some more expensive plasticine doughs come in really nice colors and, when baked in a normal oven, harden permanently. Professional artists who do miniatures for doll houses or architectural models use these doughs. They can even be painted with details after baking. These are great for older children doing more intricate models, like for dioramas or scenes from a certain culture's everyday life. For younger children, we used these polymer clays when making Mesopotamian cylinder seals or making up our own cuneiform languages, and we then baked the tablets for posterity, just like they did in the time of Abraham.

Fun with Food

Sweeten up your days with sweets! In many curricula, it's recommended that students make a new salt map as they begin to study a new region of the globe. These are good, of course, but... well... if you've done six salt maps, you've done 'em all.

How about doing your next geography lesson using cookie dough instead of salt dough, and icing in place of the ho-hum Tempera® paints to indicate features or boundaries? You could add candies like chocolate chips and thin licorice shoestrings to indicate mountains, rivers, or political boundaries. (This approach has the added benefit of being consumable. Take pictures of them for your portfolios, and then dig in! Edible maps are delicious, and there's no storage needed.)

With somewhat older children, how about cooking ethnic foods from places that you are studying? Some are delicious (honey wafers from Egypt, anyone?) and some are really awful (head cheese or fried ants, anyone else?)! Ethnic cooking can bring a lot of texture (and flavor) to lessons. We braided bread when learning about the Sabbath, we ate Greek food when mounting the ancient *Trojan Women* play, and we made trenchers for our Medieval Feasts. Each recipe was an adventure (because both ingredients and steps of production were new to us) and made for a lasting memory!

Period Costumes and Articles

Like many girls, my daughters enjoyed sewing and playing dress-up. My boys didn't mind swaggering around in the bold outfits their sisters designed for them either, and at times, I required them to help because I reasoned that boys should know how to repair a seam or sew on a button.

For each time period that we studied, the children would cut up old sheets to create costumes, string beads on wire to make jewelry, and so on. Sometimes we even bought cloth (or dramatically altered inexpensive garments from thrift stores) to bring historical eras we were studying to life.

The second great reason for doing projects is that kids have to think hard.

Often, while the girls sewed, the boys designed more masculine articles. For instance, they would spend hours turning wood or cardboard into elaborately decorated shields, swords, and suits of armor. Mike liked to create weapons. He and his older brother, Nathan, once made us some sturdy "dueling swords" out of PVC pipe, complete with padding that was secured with duct tape so that no one got injured during mock battles. The co-op kids enjoyed using these for years.

Interestingly, the basic sewing and handy skills that my children learned from these activities went on to serve them in later life as pleasures. Besides the fact that all of them learned spatial dimensions and how to engineer an article from cloth, cardboard, etc., my daughters are now good seamstresses, and are able to serve others with this skill. One loves to crochet or knit blankets in her spare time, while the other two *still* enjoy making an occasional costume, or helping friends with alterations to their clothing. Mike doesn't make weapons as much any more (he has three little daughters and no boys so far!), but he now loves to work on carpentry with his hands, and has made tables and other articles for his wife and a doll house for his girls.

Display Boards

For kids who are a bit older, how about helping them create some display boards? Independent readers and writers can almost always liven things up by turning whatever you're studying into a display board. These boards—made of large, stiff cardboard and segmented to bend into three sections so that they stand on a table—are dirt cheap. You can find them at your local art supply store. Assigning a display board will challenge your student to present what she's learning in a whole new way.

Topics are endless! They can be about inventions, events, hotly debated topics, scientific theories, literary personalities, flora and fauna of a geographic region, pyramid construction—or anything else that you are studying!

Your child should write paragraphs and mount them on her display. She must find, draw, or print graphics. She should also have something on the table in front of the display, such as a model of an invention, artifacts from a period, or unique foods from a geographic region. So, a lot of academic learning goes into them.

Then, the student should present her board (and its topic) to a visitor (who can be Dad or a neighbor). Many girls (and some boys) like to dress up in costume and present their displays "in character." With this added dimension of public speaking, you can readily see that display boards are a great means of honing many of your child's skills at design, writing, executing a longer project, and presentation. Those are a lot of benefits for an inexpensive, relatively neat, and easily stored prop!

Drama, Drama, Drama!

Don't forget the ham! Most kids thrive on drama. Whether they write and act out their own skit based on current studies, or work together to record a radio play with all the sound effects, or decide to do scenes from Shakespeare, almost all kids like to ham it up (for dads, neighbors, friends, or relations) if you give them the chance.

There's fodder for the dramatic everywhere you look: stories of famous lives, characters from literary works, and events from key scenes in history abound no matter what your curriculum. Work with your kids to dramatize what you're learning about, using stuff you have around the house for costumes, and your own supplies for makeup.

Older kids can do most of the work of simple skits: they can write, direct, and produce them. This can provide a group of siblings with endless, unifying entertainment, and dads usually get a big kick out of watching the finished productions.

I recall how two of my children (aged 14 and 12 at the time) brought to life a story from ancient Egypt about a scheming peasant and his victim. My kids really got into the spirit of the thing in our living room with a story from their history reading for a basic script, a lot of ad-libbing, a black paper "villain's moustache" (that kept falling off), and a younger sibling to play the donkey. "The Wicked Hemti" was a hit!

Later that year, these same two children were involved in our co-op's more elaborate production of a Greek tragedy called *Trojan Women*. My daughter credits her role in that play with the beginning of her love for theater and classical literature. She went on to write and direct student theater at her college, got a degree in literature, and eventually we hired her to write our literature program because of her love for the classics—all due in part to a little home drama!

Drama is also a great activity for long summer days. In fact, you can mount plays outside and have theatrical productions that involve neighbor kids, thus providing opportunities for your children to practice evangelism, or just build relationships with your neighbors. Such bridges might later support to an invitation to church!

Plants and Nature Displays

Spring into spring! Okay, so, technically, it may not be spring yet. But it can be in your home! You can grow Narcissus bulbs, sprout veggies (beans, carrots, sweet potatoes, or white potatoes that aren't treated work well), or get started with seeds that will become next year's food for your family in your outside garden. Growing things always liven up our homes, and starting a few plants going gives children a reason to get up each day and look to see how big things have gotten overnight!

You can do many science experiments using plants. Students can learn to keep scientific records using them. It is also relatively easy and cheap to create entire biospheres in small spaces. You and your child might make a terrarium (a glass-enclosed environment with plants and one or two small animals, such as a turtle or salamander) that is symbiotic (meaning the animal will breathe out carbon dioxide, which the plants need; the plants will then yield oxygen so the animal can breathe), or learn how to keep a planted aquarium with a few small fish. Such projects make great science unit-studies for an entire semester as you explore at the student's learning level the chemistry, interrelationships of plants and animals, and cycles of nature that God has created in all living things.

It's up to you!

There are so many great opportunities to do tactile learning! Yes, they are less efficient and less simple than doing book learning. But tactile approaches add fun, rich texture, and interest to learning. As homeschoolers, I would argue that the opportunity to offer this zest to our kids is one of the good reasons to homeschool. Many teachers in traditional learning environments would love to do this kind of thing but don't have the budget, space, or time in the classroom to do so!

Fitting hands-on learning into your schedule takes time and thought. If it's not natural to you to use this approach, I suggest that you start very small and work into it. From your curriculum, choose to offer one small hands-on project twice a month, at first. Then, as you get more comfortable with home teaching, and your children grow in dexterity and the ability to work independently, you can increase the number of projects they take on.

One word of warning: hands-on learning is so fun and interesting that your kids may balk at the also-necessary trudgery of book learning. I remember the day when a high-school biology teacher at our local resource center called to tell me that my daughter was in danger of failing her Biology course. I was so surprised because Charity seemed to me to be always working on posters or diagrams for Biology, and loved it. I found out that day that she had been spending all her time on the artistic, "extra credit" work while neglecting to do textbook reading and answering questions on paper that were required work.

Especially if you are craft-oriented, please do continue to require the book and pen elements of learning! It is important in homeschooling, as in all of life, to keep a balance between academic disciplines and hands-on discovery learning. I believe that, like meat and veggies, both are important to a balanced learning diet, so we must work to keep both elements in play!

SECTION FIVE

When You Lie Down and When You Rise

From where does my help come?
My help comes from the LORD, who made heaven and earth.
He will not let your foot be moved;
he who keeps you will not slumber.
Behold, he who keeps Israel will neither slumber nor sleep.
The LORD is your keeper;
the LORD is your shade on your right hand.
The sun shall not strike you by day,
nor the moon by night.
The LORD will keep you from all evil;
he will keep your life.
The LORD will keep your going out and your coming in
from this time forth and forevermore.

PSALM 121:1B-8 (ESV)

In this last section, we are returning to some "big picture" principles and practices. The section takes its title from the final line of our defining passage from Deuteronomy 6:7 (ESV):

> *You shall teach [My Words] to your children, talking of them when you are sitting in your house, and when you are walking by the way, and* ***when you lie down, and when you rise****.*

I have heard it taught that our need for sleep is one of the many ways that we can remind ourselves that we are creatures, frail and needy, and humble ourselves before our Creator, Who never sleeps.[1] And what is He doing when we sleep and He

1 "The benefits of sleep are obvious. As we sleep, strength is restored, the mind is cleared, and we're prepared to serve God another day... God could have created us without a need for sleep... Each night, as I confront my need again for sleep, I'm reminded that I'm a dependent creature. I am not self-sufficient. I am not the Creator. There is only One who 'will neither slumber no sleep' (Ps 121:4), and I am not that One" (*Humility: True Greatness*, by C.J. Mahaney).

does not? He is watching over us to keep and guide our going out and our coming in (which is a way to say "every moment of our lives") today and always (v. 8).

Homeschooling daily reminds us of our need as well. As we journey on, step by step, it can be easy to lose sight of eternal realities because they are lost in the myriad of daily tasks, needs, failures, and successes.

We can get discouraged when things go badly, mile after weary mile, or alternately proud when there are grassy fields full of beautiful poppies and plentiful, refreshing streams from which we drink. Most homeschool journeys include both of these kinds of paths, as well as ones in between.

My goal in this last section is to pull you back up to the God's-eye view of life, and to remind us of over-arching principles (and practices) that, when used, will refresh you in wilderness times and remind you to glorify God when things are easier.

29.

Commit to the Lord whatever you do,
and your plans will succeed.

Proverbs 16:3 (NIV)

It's About Commitment

As you go to bed each night, and as you arise each day, you can count on being regularly assailed by fears, doubts, exhaustion, and a sense of being overwhelmed. (The good news is that there will be good days, too, when you will go to bed or rise up praising God for the fruit of your labors!) This chapter is designed to orient you to a practice that will serve you as you fall asleep thinking about the day past and wake up to face each new day ahead. It is a key practice for us: to commit our way to the Lord. It's an essential practice if you want to love the homeschool journey!

I'd like to share my own story again. In assessing my challenges as a new homeschooler early on, I believe I placed my confidence and my concern in exactly backward positions, and, I am ashamed to admit, because of exactly backward priorities.

Because I initially felt inadequate to teach academics, and therefore anxious, I focused most of my attention and concerns there from the start of my homeschooling career. I often sought to improve myself and to labor hard over academics, rather than trust that God, who called me to this endeavor, was my only hope for success, and work joyfully to His glory in this area.

What I failed to see then, and see so clearly now, is that I should have put the most time, energy, prayer, and study into building up my faith and trust in a good God who would carry me through. Though all my children are today gloriously saved by God's mercy alone, if my teaching and priorities apart from that mercy had been our sole input, my children could have become merely educated fools because I prioritized wrongly. Furthermore, it is amazing to me that I even completed the journey at all, carrying as I did the burden of a misplaced personal responsibility for homeschooling success.

It's been well said that anxiety is a mild case of atheism. Anxiety is therefore a useful emotion because it can alert us to an unperceived reality that we are not believing a promise or command of God.

We know that Jesus told us, in John 17:3 (ESV) "this is eternal life, that they know you the only true God, and Jesus Christ whom you have sent." Of course we Christian moms want our children to experience eternal life; and we want this more than we want all earthly successes. Earthly successes at the price of faith or godliness are meaningless! We agree with Jesus when He says,

> *...Whoever would save his life will lose it, but whoever loses his life for My sake and the gospel's will save it. For what does it profit a man to gain the whole world and forfeit his life? For what can a man give in return for his life? For whoever is ashamed of me and of my words in this adulterous and sinful generation, of him will the Son of Man also be ashamed when he comes in the glory of his Father with the holy angels.*
>
> *Mark 8:35-38 (ESV)*

We know there is more to existence than earthly pleasures. We've read 2 Corinthians 4:17-18 (ESV):

> *For this slight momentary affliction is preparing for us an eternal weight of glory beyond all comparison, as we look not to the things that are seen but to the things that are unseen. For the things that are seen are transient, but the things that are unseen are eternal.*

Yet, even with all this knowledge, we can so easily get our eyes off of these eternal truths and fixed on the "practical" issues of this life. It's all very nice to say that eternal, unseen realities are paramount, but the fact is that our boys will need jobs someday, and to get jobs they need college degrees and to get those degrees—especially degrees that will make them competitive—they need to get into the college of their choice! Like Dorothy and her friends in the spooky forest, we begin to chant, "Lions and tigers and bears—oh my! Lions and tigers and bears—oh my! Lions and tigers and bears—oh my!," while running faster and faster and looking left and right for our fears to become reality any minute.

What are we afraid of? Failure. Pure and simple. But, follow me here: What must the reality be for us to fail? It would have to be that the responsibility for the ultimate success or failure of our homeschooling endeavor sits squarely on the teaching parents' shoulders. While doing the daily work of parenting and teaching diligently, we can easily come to believe that *we* are responsible for how our kids turn out: for how their lives go, and that *we* can ruin them. *We* can hurt them. *We* can really mess them up! Is this true? Is the responsibility on *us*?

Not really. Last I heard, God was still running the universe. His plans and His power are unstoppable. We are told in Ephesians 2:8-10 (NIV) that

> *"...it is by grace you have been saved, through faith—and this not from yourselves, it is the gift of God—not by works, so that no one can boast. For we are God's workmanship, created in Christ Jesus to do good works, which God prepared in advance for us to do."*

The converse of the fear question can be equally illuminating. How would we define a "successful homeschool" at the end of our days? In what areas would we like to boast to those who may now be our critics as we look back on our homeschooling journey? What great stories would we most delight to tell? What would "wild success" look like?

How about, "I found this *great* Chemistry tutor just at the last minute, so Joey didn't have to go to public school after all!" Or, "Our whole family plays various musical instruments, and now we tour the country while giving concerts." Or how about, "Susie got into Dartmouth College on a four-year full ride because she's such a good writer."

Let's look at Jeremiah 9:23-24 (NIV):

> *This is what the Lord says:*
> *"Let not the wise man boast of his wisdom*
> *or the strong man boast of his strength*
> *or the rich man boast of his riches,*
> *but let him who boasts boast about this:*
> *that he understands and knows me,*
> *that I am the Lord, who exercises kindness,*
> *justice and righteousness on earth,*
> *for in these I delight,'*
> *declares the Lord."*

The responsibility for success is not on us, and the glory and credit for success in either worldly or eternal terms won't be ours either. We can no more *make* our homeschools a success than we can *make* our children get saved, or *make* them love each other. These are all gifts of mercy from the unfathomably loving heart of our good God.

See, if we believe the lie that it's all about our works, then of course we will worry and fret about how good our performance is. A good contrasting question can be "Am I equally worried or fretful about my child's salvation as I am about my performance as a parent and teacher?" Often, we can be less anxious about salvation because we know that ultimately God is the only One who saves. This is how it was for me, and this is where I got off track.

I was clear on the biblical teaching that the salvation of my children's souls was God's responsibility (though I should, of course, pray for them and teach them to believe the Scriptures about Jesus), but I somehow came to think that everything else about their upbringing—especially the academics in our homeschool—were *my* responsibility. But the truth is, the outcomes of our teaching careers (just like the outcomes of all our good works, which He has prepared for us to do) rest ultimately on God's shoulders, not ours.

What *is* our role, then?

So, if the responsibility really is not on us parents, what is? What does God require of us?

I would respond that there are three activities in which we should regularly engage to keep us in good health and spirits as we make our homeschool journey. They are: prayer with faith, diligence, and obedience to God's Word.

We should not presume that because we are both Christians and homeschoolers, God will automatically cause the road to be smooth before us. We are not to strive to *earn* God's blessing, but rather trust that as His beloved children, we already have His love and strong support. In *response* to His love, we should do our best to be faith-filled, diligent, and obedient.

If we believe that we have heard from God that He is leading us to homeschool our children, then we need also to trust Him for the faith, love, and energy required for the task. As Paul wrote in 2 Corinthians 9:8 (ESV) "God is able to make all grace abound to you, so that having all sufficiency in all things at all times, you may abound in every good work." So let's look in a little bit of detail at these three parts we do play as we travel on our way.

Prayer with Faith

God's Word is replete with promises for those who trust him. Here are just a couple of key passages that reassure us of His pledges to be with us on the journey:

> *"Let not your heart be troubled; believe in God, believe also in Me. ...But the Helper, the Holy Spirit, whom the Father will send in My name, He will teach you all things, and bring to your remembrance all that I said to you. Peace I leave with you; My peace I give to you; not as the world gives, do I give to you. Let not your heart be troubled, nor let it be fearful."*
>
> *John 14:1, 26-27 (NASB)*

> *"I am the true vine, and My Father is the vinedresser. Every branch in Me that does not bear fruit, He takes away; and every branch that bears fruit,*

He prunes it, that it may bear more fruit. You are already clean because of the word which I have spoken to you. Abide in Me, and I in you. As the branch cannot bear fruit of itself, unless it abides in the vine, so neither can you, unless you abide in Me. I am the vine, you are the branches; he who abides in Me, and I in him, he bears much fruit; for apart from Me you can do nothing.

John 15:1-5 (NASB)

A good question to ask ourselves each night and each morning is "In what (or, better, in Whom) am I trusting for the success of our homeschool?" We forget the unseen truth so easily, because so much seems to rest on us. We ladies do the managing of our homes, our children's needs, our husband's requests and (with homeschooling) the day to day teaching of academics. We shoulder the burden in God's name and for His sake, but the danger is that we then come to own it. We thus need to remind ourselves each evening and morning that "it is God who works in you, both to will and to work for his good pleasure" (Philippians 2:13).

Here's another way to do a heart check as we lie down and rise up daily. Ask yourself, "What is my definition of success, and how am I doing in trusting God for that outcome?"

Allow yourself to be honest. Some days, it will be easy for you to say "this is all for your glory, Lord." Others, you might honestly say, "I just want Susie to learn her math facts. We've been at this for four weeks and she's just not getting it!"

Regular review of your current thoughts about what success looks like, especially as related to eternity and your Lord, will guard your heart and mind and give you needed peace. As you see little ways that you are becoming anxious or fretful, you can recommit to giving those burdens to the One who really should be carrying them: your Shepherd King.

The Lord is near. Be anxious for nothing, but in everything by prayer and supplication with thanksgiving let your requests be made known to God. And the peace of God, which surpasses all comprehension, shall guard your hearts and your minds in Christ Jesus.

Philippians 4:5b-7 (NASB)

> *You keep him in perfect peace whose mind is stayed on you, because he trusts in you. Trust in the LORD forever, for the LORD GOD is an everlasting rock.*
>
> *Isaiah 26:3-4 (ESV)*

After we are reminded of the true bearer of responsibility for our homeschool efforts, it is time to pray with faith the promises we find in God's Word and hold tight to them, not allowing fear of man, performance anxieties, or sinful comparisons to rob us of the peace, persistence, or joy that God has planned for us.

Diligence

My second suggestion for us on a homeschooling journey well traveled is that we must work at it. Just because we don't bear the responsibility for ultimate outcomes of our homeschool doesn't mean we don't work hard. As Dallas Willard has well said, "Grace is not opposed to effort, it's opposed to earning. Earning is an attitude. Effort is an action." [1]

Three helpful Scripture passages that encourage us to work diligently at the occupation that God has given us are printed below for your meditation and encouragement, and I encourage you to seek God's Word for more such nuggets and then post them where you will see them daily as you lie down and rise up!

> *In all things I have shown you that by working hard in this way we must help the weak and remember the words of the Lord Jesus, how he himself said, "It is more blessed to give than to receive."*
>
> *Acts 20:35 (ESV)*

> *But by the grace of God I am what I am, and his grace toward me was not in vain. On the contrary, I worked harder than any of them, though it was not I, but the grace of God that is with me.*
>
> *1 Corinthians 15:10 (ESV)*
>
> *In all labor there is profit,*
> *But mere talk leads only to poverty.*
>
> *Proverbs 14:23 (NASB)*

1 *The Great Omission*, by Dallas Willard. Oxford, United Kingdom: HarperOne, 2006, p. 61.

There are so many more! With the Apostle Paul, and with countless other believers down through the ages, we find that we work hard, but God gives the increase! The majority of us start to teach our kids with no training or experience. We thus start from ground zero, which gives us a learning curve that is straight up. If I had known then what I do now, I still would have wondered about how I was going to teach certain academic subjects. I would have still needed to self-educate, stay up late, get up early, and work daily at being a better teacher and mother. But I would have been less anxious.

So, if the responsibility really is not on us parents, what is?

We do need to soberly assess our strengths and weaknesses. When we are weak, we need to ask in faith for God to provide wisdom, an alternative, help, or peace about not teaching certain subjects. We need to be reasonably organized (and learn to be more so all the time) and diligent about caring for our homes.

We need to regularly teach the Word and spiritual disciplines to our children. Even more importantly, we want to be modeling diligent pursuit of these for them. If God leads us to have large families and learn new subjects so we can teach them from our position of faith-filled trust and prayer, we need to energetically work at mastering the new material. (See Romans 12:6-7 and Matthew 25.)

Obedience to God's Word

Obedience to God's Word is the third active focus that I have found helpful in my journey. As we consider what knowledge, skills, and directions our children need, the Word of God is our infallible guide. We need to be students of God's Word who renew our minds by it and do not allow worldliness, fear of man, anxiety, or sinful comparisons to besiege our hearts (or minds) as we lie down and rise up.

What kinds of teaching will best enable our children to succeed in living lives that are passionately devoted to the Lord and His eternal purposes—His Kingdom, His unstoppable plan? Will Chemistry or Algebra or Spanish 201 be useful? Well, they might get our son into college, which then will enable him to provide for a family—maybe! But how about the following classes as a homeschool curriculum: Life Skills 101, Peer Evangelism 202, Citizenship 306, and Apologetics 403? These, and others like them, should be the courses in which we should most desire our children to get a 4.0!

Obviously, we don't really teach these as courses, but we almost should! At the least, we can have a page in our teaching notebooks that regularly assesses our spiritual growth and our students'. We can also actively look for ways to connect typical American academic course contents with God's Holy Word. Below are examples:

- When we teach our children manners, hygiene, sibling relations, study skills, and the "rules of life," are we doing so with relation to the dictates of Scripture? (For instance, courtesy is respect and self-sacrificial love for others as God's creatures, made in His image, whom we are commanded to love as ourselves. Hygiene is part of caring for our bodies as His temple. We study to become skilled workers so that we can fulfill His purposes for our lives.)
- How are we doing at introducing our children to information or skills that are specifically required for and aimed at peer evangelism? Do we teach them that this is a goal for their studies?
- Do we regularly relate historical and literary studies to the issues of today, and then connect these with the Word, so that our children will learn to be wise and discerning citizens who live in light of God's will?
- As we work at giving our children thinking, writing, and verbal skills as well as important academic content, are we including a study of church history, theology, and God's Word so as to help them to become skilled at handling the Word of Truth?

Academics, as they're traditionally understood by the secular world, are merely the transfer of useful head knowledge. In the world, students are required to understand a body of factual knowledge and acquire a set of skills that will enable them to succeed in a vocation. And, again, it is the need to teach this body of knowledge and these skills that can tempt us moms to anxiety as we survey the journey ahead.

But as you lay down at night, and as you rise up each day, remind yourself that your God reigns supreme! His role is to lead and support you, taking you in paths that will shape your soul and fulfill His plans for the here and now and for eternity.

With faith-filled prayer and diligence, we must regularly "demolish arguments and every pretension that sets itself up against the knowledge of God, and ... take captive every thought to make it obedient to Christ" (2 Corinthians 10:4-5, NIV).

Galatians 6:9-10 (ESV) also helps us here.

> *And let us not grow weary of doing good, for in due season we will reap, if we do not give up. So then, as we have opportunity, let us do good to everyone, and especially to those who are of the household of faith.*

So, beginning homeschool moms, do you worry about the truant officer, the prom, the chemistry course, the work load of teaching a houseful of kids, your own inadequacies in education, or the college admissions officer? Have you lost sight of eternal goals because temporal tasks fill your horizon?

Jesus, speaking to His disciples, said not to fear the government officials of their day. He said instead, "I will warn you whom to fear: fear him who, after he has killed, has authority to cast into hell. Yes, I tell you, fear him!" (Luke 12:5, ESV).

God is faithful, and He alone bears ultimate responsibility for your homeschooling successes. I will leave you now with some sweet promises to take with you on the long trip ahead. Be of good cheer: He has overcome the world, and He stands ready to take the load of responsibility off your shoulders. Your required commitment is to trust in Him alone!

- Psalm 119:72
- Proverbs 8:11
- 1 Corinthians 3:12-17
- Proverbs 3:7
- Proverbs 5:21
- 1 Peter 1:13
- Proverbs 8:33-36

30.

A new commandment I give to you, that you love one another: just as I have loved you, you also are to love one another.

JOHN 13:34 (ESV)

Love is Patient

I have been privileged to teach about homeschooling internationally. Just before I left for a speaking engagement in Japan in November of 2010, I was sitting at a restaurant with my friend Yvonne, with whom I'd shared many miles of the homeschooling journey by then, and she asked what topics I would be teaching in Japan. Before I could answer with many specifics, she said with strong emotion, "I wish someone had told me, back when we were slogging along, that God's main purpose for me in homeschooling was to learn to love."

I knew what she meant. When you're in the thick of homeschooling, life is so filled with task triage and the urgent needs of others that it's easy to lose sight of the main thing. But Jesus highlighted that main thing for us: we are to love God with all our heart, soul, mind, and strength, and love our neighbors as ourselves (Mark 12:28-34). Of all the things that we homeschoolers teach our children (and remember, the most powerful kind of teaching is modeling), loving has to be at the top of the list.

To love one another was the one new command that Jesus gave us (John 13:34). It's the way, He said, that the world will know that we are His disciples (John 13:35). Loving is the culture of the family of God.

Love is what Jesus demonstrated for rebellious sinners when He came to earth as a baby. Out of love for us, He clothed Himself in human flesh and left the glories and fellowship of Heaven itself (Philippians 2:7). We are meant to feel God's love: to know it objectively and for certain by the display of love on the cross.[1]

But, love goes further even than that. Love is one of God's communicable attributes (which means that we are able to image Him in it). We are able to show love to others because He first loved us (1 John 4:19) and our cup runneth over to bless others. We don't love out of emptiness but out of the abundance that God has given. (This is another reason, by the way, why it is so important for us to return to the Fountainhead every day in our devotions—so that we receive fresh love and joy from Him to give away to others.) We can *only* love as God intends us to through faith in Him: His character, His sustaining grace, and His Spirit present in us to direct our thoughts and give us the courage that we need to act.

As I was taking an online counseling course through CCEF, my teacher, Dr. David Powlison, explained a model for getting to our heart attitudes that included eight questions. After a semester of study, I was assigned to do a final paper that involved public ministry. God again used Yvonne's comment to spark an idea: I felt led to write a series of blog meditations on love, as applied in the context of homeschooling, using Dr. Powlison's questions. When led to write this book, I decided to adapt and include these posts in this section of the book.

I decided to use 1 Corinthians 13:1-8a to systematically walk through characteristics of loving one another. That passage is as follows in the ESV translation:

> [1] *If I speak in the tongues of men and of angels, but have not love, I am a noisy gong or a clanging cymbal.* [2] *And if I have prophetic powers, and understand all mysteries and all knowledge, and if I have all faith, so as to re-*

1 We can also know God's love subjectively and emotionally, but these feelings can fluctuate, and we shouldn't rely on them.

move mountains, but have not love, I am nothing. [3] *If I give away all I have, and if I deliver up my body to be burned, but have not love, I gain nothing.*

[4] *Love is patient and kind; love does not envy or boast; it is not arrogant* [5] *or rude. It does not insist on its own way; it is not irritable or resentful;* [6] *it does not rejoice at wrongdoing, but rejoices with the truth.* [7] *Love bears all things, believes all things, hopes all things, endures all things.* [8] *Love never ends.*

I want to start my discussion with a re-praphrasing of Paul's introduction. I'm setting his ideas in the homeschool context.

If I tell my children all day long to love God and each other (even in the most eloquent terms), to study hard, to be diligent, and to love learning, but do not let them see a living, breathing example of love as I walk through the process of homeschooling them, then my words are so much noise in their ears. My words can never bring about the results that I desire. [2] *If I am the wisest of parents, having insight into my children's hearts at all times, and flawlessly delivering to them all instruction faithfully, day after day, but do so without love, I am nothing.* [3] *If, by dint of great effort and sacrifice, I find and manage to purchase an amazing curriculum that is the most expensive and lavish one available, and I work diligently to deliver all the lessons from it as directed, but do not do so in a loving way, I gain nothing.*

Being new to homeschooling, you still might not have caught on to the fact that the journey is not primarily about us imparting academics to our kids, or even about us training our children in skillful living. It is really about learning to love God and others. Even more specifically, it's about *us* learning to love God and others, then becoming an example of biblical love to our children. This is why we come to love the journey for its own sake: it's about so much more than arriving at our destination!

God gives all of his disciples the same limited amount of time each day, and a host of points where a choice must be made. These choice points are tests: how will you react and respond to the people and situations you encounter today in a world full of sinners? Our reactions and responses to these tests shape us and others. (The

Bible says that they also display His greatness to watching angels! (See 1 Corinthians 4:9 and 11:10.) This is the means by which God simultaneously sanctifies people and forwards His unstoppable plans.

God gives all of His people others to love each day as part of His training process. But you know what? To only a few of His children does God give homeschooling. We homeschooling moms are assigned a very limited number of people, who matter to us greatly, to love. Being imperfect, we often fail. Being our omniscient Father, God knows what He's up to. He's changing us into the image of Christ by the perfect means for each of us individually (Romans 8:28-29). If you are homeschooling because of a call of God on your life to do so, then this is the context in which you are to walk out the primary commands of God: love Him and love your neighbor as yourself.

What a privilege and joy it should be to realize that, even as we work to foster a desire for life-long learning in our kids, God has not yet graduated us from the school of life. We are to be life-long learners, too! And we are to embrace the lessons that He has for us with hope and faith, because He has begun this work in us, because He has placed us in this context, because He has promised to be in it with us, and because He will never tire of watching over us until His great purposes for us in the context of homeschooling are fulfilled.

Do you read this feeling that you have been bad at loving, or missed the main point? I have good news! God knows. He understands. He loves you with a tough love that meets you where you are and calls you higher. It's why Jesus came to die for you: so that you could be forgiven of your sins (both of omission and commission) and receive His Spirt and become like Him. It is for this reason that you can live this day in hope.

And you're not alone. Whether we choose to acknowledge it or not, no one reading this has loved perfectly. We can't love truly apart from His grace. But, because of Jesus, the grace that we *must* have is abundant, freely given, and inexhaustible. James 4:6-8a (ESV) assures us:

> *But he gives more grace. Therefore it says, "God opposes the proud, but gives grace to the humble." Submit yourselves therefore to God. Resist the devil, and he will flee from you. Draw near to God, and he will draw near to you."*

Some of us know that we are not living up to God's standards for loving Him or others, and we know that we should be more moved than we are. I hope that this chapter gives you new food for thought as to why you do not love more actively, and envisions for you ways to do better. For you who delay effort, I would say that there are strong warnings that, if heeded, can awaken you to the dangers of disobedience and complacency. Here is just one:

> *Do not be deceived: God is not mocked, for whatever one sows, that will he also reap. For the one who sows to his own flesh will from the flesh reap corruption, but the one who sows to the Spirit will from the Spirit reap eternal life.*
>
> *Galatians 6:7-8 (ESV)*

But I think that most of my readers are women who have been mothers long enough to have both tried hard and failed repeatedly at the great and real business of loving in God's name. For you, the main obstacle to moving forward is the paralysis of condemnation.

God is good. No matter where you find yourself on the scale of complacent to condemned, He is with you in your homeschooling journey and using it to sanctify you. He is up to something good! Let's explore the lessons of loving that we learn in the homeschool setting together for this and the next two chapters.

Can I ask you to bow your head and pray that, according to your specific need, God would exhort you, would speak His comfort, and would protect you from condemnation as you read on? Please! Do it before continuing!

* * * * *

So, "love is patient." We all know people whose patience is on full display. We marvel at them, but inwardly, we can think: *Wow, I am just not that kind of person. I could never be patient like s/he is!* But, here's a piece of good (and convicting) news: if we have the Spirit of God within us, we can *become* patient.

Patience is a fruit of the Spirit (Galatians 5:22). There are really no "naturally patient" people. When you see God-honoring patience in people, remember that they weren't born that way. It's not natural to them; it's supernatural in them! God has worked this fruit in their lives, whether or not they are aware of it. And the same Spirit is at work in you: He will prevail in the end (Philippians 1:6).

Let's remember, as we focus on patience, that we are really talking about love. If "love is patient," then being patient is one of the ways that we love others. We choose to lay down our lives (our wants and our needs) to prefer theirs. This is the essence of patience. We wait for others (or things) because we love; we love as we wait.

I wish someone had told me that God's main purpose for me in homeschooling was to learn to love.

But, it's not just the patience inherent in waiting that we're examining here. There are unbelievers who can learn simple patience. The man given over to thoughts of vengeance, or despair, or robbery can wait patiently for the fulfillment of his evil cravings. Unbelievers can work and save for years in order to gain worldly goals. But the patience that is so integral to godliness and to love is a self-sacrificing, God-oriented, loving patience that seeks the good of others before self. Though they may never say so aloud, those who are patiently loved sense it and are blessed, especially when—as so often happens—they know that they truly deserve the impatience of God or others.

Throughout the New Testament, loving patience is a big theme. It's often included in those lists of what godly traits are (or should be) present and increasing in the lives of disciples. (See 2 Corinthians 6:6 and 12:12, Ephesians 4:2, Colossians 3:12, 2 Timothy 2:10 for just a few examples.) So, we know that God esteems patience in the believer, and we want to please Him because we know that to do so brings us (and all who are around us) a blessing. We want to obey God and love our children and husbands, and we affirm that love is patient. Yet, patience is one of those quiet traits without a lot of instant return for the investment. We don't tend to esteem it, and we tend to quickly and blithely excuse our impatience. (Really: who *doesn't* fall down in this way?) We are thus often blind to the damage that our impatience causes!

Why is it hard to be patient, and why don't we see better how important it is? How do we grow in patience? Or, more accurately, how does God grow our ability to be lovingly patient in our context: homeschooling? And, how can we find traction in our efforts to improve?

Let's organize our tumbling thoughts by using the questions derived from Dr. Powlison's course offered by the Christian Counseling Foundation, entitled *Dynamics of Biblical Change*. I've modified them for our context. Here they are:

1. What's my challenge regarding loving patience in my homeschooling context?
2. How do I fail to respond in a loving way in these situations?
3. What do my failures to be patiently loving reveal about my wrong heart attitudes?
4. What bad fruits did I reap as my unloving behaviors created ongoing cycles of folly?
5. What does God say? How can the gospel make a difference and teach me to love better?
6. In light of what I've seen, how should I respond right now to God and others regarding my current unloving habits?
7. What does (or can or should) loving patience look like in the homeschool setting going forward?
8. What cycles of blessing can I hope for as I turn to God and grow in my ability to love?

Question #1: What's my challenge regarding loving patience in my homeschooling context?

I hardly have to paint the picture for you on this one. Patience is challenged in almost every waking moment of the homeschooling mother's life, isn't it? We are called to be patient with our children as they try and fail on every front, from chores to Algebra assignments. We also are called to be patient when they don't even try to learn, but instead resist and rebel against our best efforts to bless them. We are called to be patient when they spill, patient when they forget, and patient when they embarrass us.

But there are many more opportunities for us to be patient in our homeschooling context! How about being patient when waiting for homeschooling materials that we've ordered to show up? Or, when waiting to do the things we really want to do with our time—the yummy book that we'd love to curl up with, the crafty project that we'd love to get done, the new garden that we'd love to plan—until all the homeschooling and household chores for the day (or week, or month) are done? (This can add up to years of waiting!) What about being patient with our husbands' imperfect attempts at leadership in homeschooling or in parenting? Or how about being patient with a teen going through puberty, who thus seethes with emotions, voices many scary new thoughts, and asks hard questions?

And (finally, though not exhaustively) how about being patient with ourselves as homeschooling teachers and mothers? How often do we demand instant perfection of ourselves, and then end up overwhelmed, self pitying, or quitting a new curriculum or a new academic subject, or (gasp!) toy with the idea of quitting homeschooling altogether? Most experienced homeschoolers have had this thought at least once: *With a teacher/mom like me, they would be better off in public schools!*

Question #2: How do I typically fail to respond in a loving way in these situations?

Did you know that *it is hard to be patient*!? If we are honest, we know that this is an area where we daily fail the love test. I'll share some of my typical responses to the normal challenges in homeschooling, by way of example.

I've already shared that I'm a certified Martha. For me, it's always been important to get stuff done. I also tend to be an organized and logical person. The inabilities of children wore on me through my homeschooling years: they slowed down my agenda and tempted me to impatience. I found over time that sharp, angry demands would accomplish my will: I got what I wanted. Tasks were done, and done quickly when my tone grew sharp or loud. Children became obedient, and cheerfully so because that was one of the demands!

I also saw fit to be impatient with my husband. I criticized him frequently, used a demanding tone when displeased, and was unloving as he struggled to change sin areas in his life. We had many private conversations where I was harshly insistent that he change according to my insights. Why couldn't he see that I was trying to do him good? Why didn't he understand how urgent it was that he change? Our children were on the line, as I saw it, and he needed to change pronto! My husband, who hates confrontation, outwardly catered to my impatiently delivered dictates by altering his behaviors. Inwardly, though, he was sorely tempted to bitterness.

Nor did I respond well to others who inconvenienced me in those days. Repairmen, homeschool companies that failed to deliver my purchases on my timetable, and those who slowed me down in traffic or at shopping malls all felt the heat of my displeasure. It didn't usually make them any more eager to do my will, but it felt good to let them know that I was displeased. They had failed to measure up.

Towards myself, I was much more tolerant of all the ways that I fell short of God's standards. My blindness trapped me in these sins. However, I was often impatient with myself over them, too. We have a convicting Spirit who will not leave us in our sins, but sometimes our over-arching mindset—in this case, the need I felt to get things done in the short term—left me vaguely uneasy, and dissatisfied, when I chose unloving speech or actions in pursuit of my goals.

Things were getting done, but I was not measuring up to my own, biblically-derived but still erroneous, standard of godly homeschooling and parenting. I wanted to be perfect, above reproach, godly, and mature. I wanted the respect of family, friends, and others. When I wasn't getting those things, I would become self-pitying and often seek to flee from challenges—the new curriculum that I couldn't master would be sold, the new subject that was too hard to teach would be dropped, and (as those who know my story have heard) I nearly did quit homeschooling when my oldest two boys reached high school. At that point, my self-reliant ways couldn't handle the strain.

Loving patience is one of those traits that is not fun to acquire, and often has invisible fruits and consequences. It takes self denial. It takes waiting. It takes hope and faith in, as well as dependence on, God, which can elude us in our blindness and sinful self-dependence. It's a lot of work to be patient! And it's not like your kids will often say, "Thanks, Mom, for being so patient with me!"

Even when I managed to be purposefully patient (and knew it), I sinned. Far from recognizing God's grace to help me obey Him, I felt so good about myself. The stench of self-righteousness filled the room at these times and fueled the fires of my impatience in subsequent situations. I would think, "After all the patience that I showed him, he still didn't get the job done." Or, "Okay, I've been patient long enough. I'm going to have to raise my voice to get this family member moving!"

Those were some of my reactions and responses to the challenges that daily faced me as a wife and homeschooling mom of six. Do these confessions strike chords with you? Perhaps you are new to homeschooling, but you probably aren't not to mothering. For many of us, these challenges are universal!

I know it's ugly, but to change and become consistent in loving patience, we need to understand what is keeping us from obeying God. Invariably, when patterns of impatient, unloving speech and actions fill our days, we have issues deep down in our hearts that need addressing. We accommodate deep cravings for things other than God and His will, and we think false thoughts that need adjustments. We will never fix our horizontal relationships with people if we don't first fix our vertical relationship with God.

Are you being convicted? There's good news: if we draw near to God in humble recognition that we can't do this on our own, He promises more grace. He promises to help you in your weaknesses and change you more and more into the image of Jesus–who is always patiently loving! Let's take a good hard look at what some of those weaknesses might be so that we can get traction on changing our relationship with God.

Question #3: What do my failures to be patiently loving reveal about my wrong heart attitudes?

I'll speak again for myself; perhaps you can identify with me.

I was daily impatient (and thus unloving) when homeschooling because my heart was (and still is) self-centered and self-reliant. I wanted my kids to change in ways I thought best and on my timetable. I got tired of waiting for them to do right things. I judged that they were slow; I insisted on my agenda. My good desires for them to succeed in ways that I deemed important turned into bad demands that they do it now! Same with my husband, with my kids as teens, with homeschool supply companies, and with myself.

My impatient behavior revealed what I was truly living for. (This painful revelation was God's mercy to me, in that seeing one's heart attitudes for what they are is the first step to lasting change!) When I finally stopped long enough to ask myself a simple question, "What do I want?" I got surprising answers!

I found that I wanted my kids to obey me right away, the first time, so that things would be easier for me. I wanted them to study hard, and to like it, because teaching would be simpler for me that way, and they would become lifelong learners (my highest goal for them at that time) and validate *my* choices for their lives. I would have joy and fruit from *my* efforts. They would become what I envisioned.

I also wanted my husband to lead actively and flawlessly, so that my path would be smoother. I wanted peaceful, orderly school days and a tranquil life. I felt that I was sacrificing lavishly for God's Kingdom in even attempting to homeschool six kids, so I was owed some ease and comfort in return (though I would never have voiced it that way).

I wanted the battles of a sin-sick world to be over! My horizon was to achieve my goals and be done. I was not in it for a long-term struggle. Struggle was the problem to be solved or the pain to be avoided, not the process by which I was to glorify God and become more like Jesus. To sum up: I wanted what I wanted, and I wanted it now.

If I was honest, it all boiled down to this: I wanted to be the Queen of the World. I wasn't satisfied with God's timing, plans, purposes, or agenda. Though I would have said that God's Kingdom agenda was most important in my thoughts and daily deeds, in truth, my impatience revealed that I wanted to be God; I thought I could do a better job of running my life, and the lives of my family members, than He did.

Question #4: What bad fruits did I reap as my unloving behaviors created ongoing cycles of folly?

What's a cycle of folly? It's where you are provoked, then you choose to react in ways that provoke others, who then provoke you, and you choose to react, again, in ways that provoke others. All of this is a downward cycle that takes things from bad to worse.

Like most of us, I was unaware that I was obeying such heart cravings most of the time. I was also blind to the ways that I was hurting those I loved most, as well as actually retarding their growth in godliness. I was so often impatient, and thus unloving, with my children and others. I cringe to remember it as I honestly record this. My unloving acts not only were disobedient to God, but they initiated cycles of folly that worked against my queenly desires! Let me show you what I mean by a cycle of folly from my own life.

Because I felt justified in my self-righteous demands for my agenda to be met on my timetable, I fully believed that I was demanding right things. And, on the surface, sometimes it did get the (shortsighted) results that I was after. My cowed children did jump to obediently and immediately do that chore or get back to that schoolwork when I harshly demanded it. My nagged husband did finish the household chore that I insisted he complete. Sometimes, honking a horn in traffic got the jerk in front of me to move.

So, from my immature and limited perspective, impatience was a necessary evil of life on earth. The important thing to me at that time—my agenda—was often met because I chose to be impatient. At times, I felt a smug satisfaction. At others, I knew lingering, confused guilt. The Spirit and the Word told me that I would reap bad fruits from my disobedient choices, but I was too blind and my mind was set too much on my own earthly goals to see it clearly. Invisibly to me, though, my unloving impatience was poisoning my relationships and our family unity.

Surely, you have felt the sting of someone else's impatience? It's natural to rise to defend yourself when you are harshly rebuked or angrily judged. In many homeschooling families, years of impatient and demanding behaviors on parents' parts can produce angry and rebellious teens. When our kids are young, we have physical and emotional power to force our wills upon them. As they get older, though, and gain physical and intellectual strength, the tables turn. They've learned that displeasure should be loudly and insistently expressed. Why should they be lovingly patient with bad treatment? And, more importantly, why should they be patient with God? In what way is Christianity attractive to one who, in the name of service to God, has been consistently told that he fails to measure up, and has thus been repeatedly hassled into doing what God's Spirit has not yet enabled him to do?

Alternatively, family members can just as naturally react to unloving impatience by turning inward: becoming crushed with self-pity, quietly surly, and nursing a root of bitterness. Kids and husbands who live with our habits of impatience—which take a variety of forms from nagging to angry outbursts to cutting remarks to constant rebukes to insistent tones—can put up walls and (when possible) choose to run as far away from us (and the God we claim to serve) as they can get.

Undoubtably, the worst part of my sinful self-focus in my homeschooling years was that I consistently misrepresented God to my watching world—beginning with my kids. God is always patient with us. Always. Every time. He loves without flaw and without measure. When I was (and am) unlovingly impatient, I did not show the true character of God to the ones who were most precious to me, and whose characters I was endeavoring to shape. My impatience warped their image of Father God.

Question #5: What does God say? How can a better handle on the gospel give me hope for change?

These cycles of folly should not surprise us. God's Word warns us that we reap what we sow (Galatians 6:7). When we sow to the flesh, we reap death (Romans 8:5-

8). Which of my children ever learned a math concept quicker, or did a chore more joyously and faithfully unto the Lord, because of my impatient demands? Which of them learned to turn to Father God for help with their sinful desires after one of my impatient, harsh rebukes? Which unsaved repair person who felt my queenly ire ever went away from our household saying to himself, "There's a different Spirit alive here. I wonder what it is?"

While it might seem that I was often reaching my objectives through impatient insistence, what I was really doing was tearing down my household with my own hands, as God showed me in Proverbs 14:1: "The wisest of women builds her house, but folly with her own hands tears it down" (ESV).

Once I saw that my agenda was a root cause of my sinful patterns, the first traction that I gleaned in addressing them caused me to begin to paraphrase James 1:20 to myself. In moments of temptation, I began to remind myself: "The anger of Mom does not work the righteousness of God!"

Like most of us, I was unaware that I was obeying such heart cravings most of the time.

This clarity was the beginning of God's help for me to change. The bad fruit that I had reaped, coupled with God's amazing, convicting grace and example of loving patience towards me, woke me up and gave me a willingness to address my cravings. The first step would be repentance to God and to my family for my wrong actions. Because of the sacrifice of Christ for my sins (the gospel), I could seek and gain forgiveness, and hope for change! Only after doing this "great exchange"—His sinless life for my bankrupt one—could I look boldly and honestly at God's standard for me and how I was falling short, so that I could renew my mind and do His will.

And what exactly did God say about love, specifically patient love? It's pretty simple. He commands us to be loving. It was the one *new* command that Jesus gave us while on earth (John 13:34). Paul says that love is patient. Patience is a fruit of the Spirit and an essential aspect of godliness. If we are to please God, we simply must grow in patient submission to God in all things. This is the standard that God requires. But there's even more; we can go deeper.

Our patient love has a robust purpose that transcends duty to either God or man. We can image Christ Himself! We can woo people to the Lord through patience! We can show people the Father. We can be the hands and feet of Jesus Himself, surprising people and gaining their attention for Him.

If we are patiently loving in difficult circumstances, people will notice—and by people, here I mean our kids and husbands. They will ask themselves, "How is she doing that?" And the answer that you'll demonstrate is that God has been patient with you, so how can you fail to be patient with them? Thus can you preach the gospel without a word, and in terms much more powerful than words.

Now, knowing the power of patient love, it's a pretty miserable thing to look back and see our mountain of sins and failings in relation to what God commands and what He's done for us. It's almost as discouraging to look forward and just know that we're going to blow it again! What does God say about our sins, and how does the gospel give us hope (and a handle) for change?

God gives us reason to hope even as we look back. He says that our sins are wrong and damaging, but He also holds out gracious forgiveness for our sins through the One Who was most patient, Jesus Christ.

Question #6: In light of what I've seen, how should I respond right now to God and others regarding my current habits?

First, we repent to God, for against Him alone is our greatest transgression (Psalm 51:4). Identify your particular expressions of impatience and ask the Holy Spirit to stir up your heart with godly sorrow. Begin to see them for what they are: nails in the hands and feet of Jesus!

Then, preach the gospel to yourself: He is holy and deserves not only your trustful patience with His disposal of your life, but also your right representation of Him to others. You have failed, and failed because you wanted to snatch His glory, in that you thought you could do a better job than He does. Yet, He has died for your sins. Claim the promises that we have outlined above: 1 John 1:9 promises utter forgiveness through the grace of the Cross, and from here you can begin to change.

After repentance before God, surely the next step is to repent to those we've injured by our impatience. This is humbling, which is good medicine for anyone recovering from queenly addictions! Your open confession of sin will speed the healing process in your own heart, and it will open the hearts of those you've injured so that relational healing can also begin. So, confess fully (in simple, concrete terms, accepting responsibility without excuses or justification) and really ask those you've sinned against for their forgiveness. Do this not once, but purpose to do so daily as you encounter the choice points of life, and ask God now (and daily) for the grace to do so.

Next, it's important to realize that our goal is not to see our sin, repent, and then win the battle, thus bringing an end to it. We are not promised peaceful and comfortable lives! While we are in the flesh, we'll be battling temptations to unloving impatience daily. It's helpful to battle with weapons that will be effective, and to first and foremost renew our minds thus: *the goal is not to win the war and end it; the goal is to battle well.*

This may be a hard thing to accept: I have found it so. However, it helps me tremendously to remember that there is a good purpose in lengthy battles. God will not extend a battle unless doing so will make me more like His glorious Son. There is purpose and meaning in suffering, and the good God is using the most benign possible method of making me what I really want to be (but don't realize in the heat of living in a fallen world): I want to be like Jesus.

To help us in this long war, God gives us a number of Scriptures that use battle imagery to remind us of this truth: see Ephesians 1 (the overall context of the battle—and its only possible conclusion) and 6:10-18, as well as the following verses:

> *Since therefore Christ suffered in the flesh, arm yourselves with the same way of thinking, for whoever has suffered in the flesh has ceased from sin, so as to live for the rest of the time in the flesh no longer for human passions but for the will of God.*
>
> *1 Peter 4:1-2 (ESV)*

> *Fight the good fight of the faith. Take hold of the eternal life to which you were called and about which you made the good confession in the presence of many witnesses.*
>
> *1 Timothy 6:12 (ESV)*

> *You then, my child, be strengthened by the grace that is in Christ Jesus, ... Share in suffering as a good soldier of Christ Jesus. No soldier gets entan-*

> *gled in civilian pursuits, since his aim is to please the one who enlisted him.*
>
> *2 Timothy 2:1, 3-4 (ESV)*

Perhaps a battle metaphor doesn't grab us women? How about one of a race (or journey), then?

> *Do you not know that in a race all the runners run, but only one receives the prize? So run that you may obtain it. Every athlete exercises self-control in all things. They do it to receive a perishable wreath, but we an imperishable. So I do not run aimlessly; I do not box as one beating the air. But I discipline my body and keep it under control, lest after preaching to others I myself should be disqualified.*
>
> *1 Corinthians 9:24-27 (ESV)*

> *Therefore, since we are surrounded by so great a cloud of witnesses, let us also lay aside every weight, and sin which clings so closely, and let us run with endurance the race that is set before us, looking to Jesus, the founder and perfecter of our faith, who for the joy that was set before him endured the cross, despising the shame, and is seated at the right hand of the throne of God.*
>
> *Hebrews 12:1-2 (ESV)*

Spend some time wrapping your mind around battle or race imagery and renew your purpose to love actively and to battle temptations to act unlovingly. Paul unites both in his assessment of his life, given on the eve of his death: "I have fought the good fight, I have finished the race, I have kept the faith" (2 Timothy 4:7). May we, by God's enabling grace alone, say the same as we end our homeschooling days!

As we finish up here, let's look to see what kinds of good fruits God can grow in our hearts in response to situations that will tempt us to impatience in the future. Beyond our own sanctification, the essential concept we need to get hold of in order to fuel us for the long journey ahead is the idea that the patience that God has demonstrated *towards us* is a communicable attribute that He can use *in us* to draw others to Himself.

Question #7: What does (or can or should) loving patience look like in the homeschool setting going forward?

We will never stop battling temptations to become impatiently unloving. What will sustain us in the ongoing heat of battle? Hope is crucial for us as we seek to grow patiently loving, for remember, patience comes through practice—the practice of waiting. What is our hope, and on what is it founded?

Our hope is in the Lord, Who made heaven and earth (Psalm 146:5-6) because "behold, the eye of the Lord is on those who fear him, on those who hope in his steadfast love" (Psalms 33:18).

God, who is all-wise, has promised to be faithful to us. He cannot fail to be so. And He has placed us in our setting, with these children and this husband, as a training ground for life and godliness. We hope in His ability and promises to grow our family members into the image of Christ and give them each His calling and purposes in life. They are to fulfill His plans on His timetable. We rest hopefully and with increasing confidence in His ability to fulfill His plans!

In light of God's power to bring about what He has commanded, almost every area of homeschooling can become more joyful (and eternally fruitful) as we let go of anxieties, fretting, harsh speech, demanding tones, and urgent pushing. We can work hard to God's glory, but rest joyfully in the hope that He gives us that He is sovereignly bringing His unfailing plans to fruition in our lives. In submitting to God's sovereignty, we also cling to the hope that He has the ability to grow us to be more and more patiently loving as we seek to do our children good in our homeschool setting.

As we grow in patience, we do so not only to endure, and not only to become more sanctified ourselves, and not only to demonstrate the longsuffering character of God, but we do so with the hope that active, robust love has a purpose: to win others to Christ! It is this vision, this sense of purpose, that can strongly motivate us to keep on keeping on!

Homeschooling in light of God's helping power means that we approach each day as God's program for training us and our children in eternal things. We moms should adopt daily practices that feed our renewed relationship with God, and keep us growing.

Below are a few ideas. As you read through them, please realize that growth in these areas can take years, or even decades! (They did for me, and I am far from finished.) I counsel you to ask God which *one* of them would be a good place for you to begin during this phase of your journey.

- Carve out time for fellowship with God, where you worship Him for Who He is and humbly confess your sins so that you can receive fresh grace (1 John 1:9).
- Set an example of humility by confessing your sins to your children, then train them to do the same. When they do, extend the compassion that you have received from Christ to them, in His name.
- Purpose to look at academics from a more eternal perspective: what does the struggle with the math lesson work in you and your child? Are you growing in patience in teaching? Is your child growing in perseverance as he works? These are the important lessons. Academics may be useful in this life, but godly character is estimable for an eternity (1 Timothy 4:8-10)!
- As you go forward, look for evidences of God's grace in your husband, your children, and yourself. Share these aloud with each other for encouragement in further well doing (Hebrews 3:13)!
- All the tasks of life (and homeschooling) are means to one end: the glorification of Jesus Christ through your ongoing, incremental sanctification (Romans 8:28-30) and active loving. Ask God to make these your greatest joy.
- Finally, develop a culture of gratitude. This grace is a shield of righteousness against so many evil things. It keeps us mindful of God, humble, and gracious. Do it first, and then encourage your children to "in everything give thanks; for this is God's will for you in Christ Jesus" (1 Thessalonians 5:18).

Question #8: What cycles of blessing can I hope for as I turn to God and grow in my ability to love patiently?

Ultimately, our homeschooling journey is a walk of faith, as life is for all Christians. The task that we are about in homeschooling—raising disciples to the glory of God—is a multi-year task. The visible fruits of our daily efforts and God-glorifying actions at momentary choice points may be long in coming, and we dare not trust in our abilities alone to bring about the outcomes we desire! As we learn to trust God more than ourselves, and look to Him alone for the pace, agenda, and means of teaching our (His!) children in the small points of life, we will grow in loving patience, and we will be blessed. Our homes can be outposts of the Kingdom of God, fruitful gardens giving the fragrance of grace to a sin-sick world, where children grow in safety, love, and the knowledge of God. We don't have to love perfectly, but we do need to battle well!

Once more, let me share my story as a display of how the gospel initiates cycles of blessing. I've confessed some of the impatient acts that filled my days during my early homeschooling years. You would think that our children would never have recovered! It's worse than you think. Real change in me did not begin much before my eldest children were in high school. This meant that I had years in which to do some serious damage—and I did!

God's saving grace in our family was most manifest in my husband. Early on, God put it into his heart to daily look for opportunities to show tangibly and daily the Father God to our children. Empowered by God's Spirit, Scott sacrificially, daily, and hourly modeled loving patience and kept his eye on eternally significant goals. His spoken ambition was to see his children's children worshiping the Lord, and he seized moments too numerous for me to count to draw attention to the loving, living God Who was really ruling and reigning our home.

Things got significantly easier for Scott, and our family unity dramatically improved, as I addressed my sinful heart attitudes listed above, and truly changed. But even before I began to change, I can see that God gave my children grace by giving them a father whose far greater patience provided a different and better example than they found in their mother. I was not the only Christian who was there for them to imitate. Thank God!

Also, even before there was significant improvement in me, my children could see that I was trying, and they knew I loved Jesus. They saw in me something like we see in the Apostle Peter: a person with obvious faults, but one who delights in God and wants to be like Jesus. Also, my children knew that I loved them, and that I wanted to be a good mommy. This knowledge, in God's hands, helped them to forgive a multitude of my sins.

Today, by God's grace, all six of our adult children love God and follow hard after Him. They are all members of churches. They are building families of their own, and I love to see the loving patience with which my sons, Mike and David (in the images of their dad and Father), along with their wives, are making Scott's dream come true. The same can be well said of my daughter, Charity, with her husband, Brandon.

Our grandchildren are learning to love Father God. Though my homeschooling days are behind me, my days are still filled with advising my adult children, and a hundred choice points per day still confront me. Some of these tempt me to impatience and unbelief. But I am unutterably grateful for what the homeschooling years taught me concerning eternal goals and fruitful, active, purposeful loving.

Conclusion

I also want to remind you that such earthly blessings as I've just listed, sweet as they can be, are not all that we look to. They can't satisfy us fully. What we will ultimately see in our own hearts is worth all the effort! God, who has placed us in our homes and given us the joys and work of homeschooling will fulfill His good purposes through the battle, through the race, and on the journey.

I can testify that, by God's grace, He is much more often on the throne of my heart and helping me to be a loving and patient person for most of every day. (We are, however, still working hard on battling pride and self-reliance, and it's not like I never stumble in impatience.)

Homeschooling isn't ultimately about academic success, though we should be diligent to teach to the best of our abilities. It's not about family unity, though that is a sweet fruit that comes to many of us as we are sanctified together. No...at the end of our lives, what we'll look back on—as Yvonne and I recently have—is the certainty that God has used homeschooling to teach us, and those we interact with, how to love.

We'll love God more, we'll love grace more; we'll love the Savior more as we grow more and more like Him daily. The cycle of blessings all revolve around Him, and will forever more! So, as we lay down at night, let's thank Him for the ability that we had that day to battle well, and as we rise up, let's ask him for the grace to do even better today.

> *May you be strengthened with all power, according to his glorious might, for all endurance and patience with joy, giving thanks to the Father, who has qualified you to share in the inheritance of the saints in light. He has delivered us from the domain of darkness and transferred us to the kingdom of his beloved Son, in whom we have redemption, the forgiveness of sins.*
>
> *Colossians 1:11-14 (ESV)*

The saying is trustworthy and deserving of full acceptance, that Christ Jesus came into the world to save sinners, of whom I am the foremost. But I received mercy for this reason, that in me, as the foremost, Jesus Christ might display his perfect patience as an example to those who were to believe in him for eternal life. To the King of ages, immortal, invisible, the only God, be honor and glory forever and ever. Amen.

1 Timothy 1:15-17 (ESV)

31.

But when the goodness and loving kindness of God our Savior appeared, he saved us, not because of works done by us in righteousness, but according to his own mercy, by the washing of regeneration and renewal of the Holy Spirit, whom he poured out on us richly through Jesus Christ our Savior, so that being justified by his grace we might become heirs according to the hope of eternal life.

Titus 3:4-7 (ESV)

Love is Kind

The idea that kindness is a hallmark of Christian love seems like it's obvious at first glance, but there's much to be gleaned from these three short words of Paul: "love is kind" (1 Corinthians 13:4) as we continue to meditate on loving one another as the new command of our Lord Jesus. This chapter is structured like the last one. It's a meditation built around modified versions of Dr. Powlison's Eight Questions. Grab your favorite beverage and some quiet time, and let's dive in!

We all appreciate kindness. We feel its effects immediately when we receive it, like sweet salve on a wound. And we notice it especially keenly when we know we really don't deserve it. I once saw a plaque in a bathroom that said, "We all need love most when we are most unlovely." It stuck with me during my homeschooling days, and we can transfer its truth to all forms of loving.

We most need kindness when we have been sinning and get caught, or when we are weak because we've been brought low by accidents, illnesses, or failures, or when we have made honest mistakes and become ashamed by the consequences. We need it when we are old and sick and poor. In other words, when we are at our most unlovely (and repulsive) and least deserve it, we most need others to show us kindness.

As moms, we can love our husbands and children daily by pouring loving, undeserved kindness into the hurting hearts of our beloveds. Let's tease this topic apart some, using Powlison's modified eight questions. Here they are:

1. What's my challenge regarding loving kindness in my homeschooling context?
2. How do I fail to respond in a loving way in these situations?
3. What does my lack of love reveal about wrong heart attitudes that must be addressed?
4. What bad fruits do I reap as my unloving behaviors create ongoing cycles of folly?
5. What does God say? How can the gospel make a difference and teach me to love better?
6. In light of what I've seen, how should I respond right now to God and others regarding my current, unloving habits?
7. What does (or can or should) loving look like in the homeschool setting going forward?
8. What cycles of blessing can I hope for as I turn to God and grow in my ability to love kindly?

Question #1: What's my challenge regarding showing loving kindness in my homeschooling context?

Like patience, kindness takes effort when under stress, and many homeschooling days have plenty of stress. What kinds of temptations do we have?

Well, it's hard to be kind when family members sin in repetitive, patterned ways. It's challenging to remain kind in speech when attempting to call upstairs in a loud voice. It can be easy to be unkind when a child makes a dumb mistake, or spills the milk *again*.

How about days when our will is crossed: when our day doesn't go as we planned, or when others don't see us as charitably as we see ourselves, or when the repair man fails to show up on time?

Another temptation is the child who just doesn't understand or remember his lesson or—even harder to field kindly—when we are pretty sure that he's even not putting forth effort to learn.

We all need love most when we are most unlovely.

Our husband's reactions to our best (and worst) homeschooling efforts can tempt us to react and respond unkindly as well. Sometimes we hate others in our hearts, or jump to unkind judgments of their motives, or attribute wrong motives to their actions. And sometimes, we just let fly with accusations and kick others when they're already down.

Yep, there are plenty of temptations within the homeschooling context for us to be unkind. Let's detail how we often give in to temptations next.

Question #2: How do I typically fail to respond in a lovingly kind way in these situations?

The ways that we respond unkindly really don't look very pretty when we stop to notice them. I'll speak for myself; you see if we are at all alike.

When tempted by family members displaying patterned sins (where I think they surely should know better by now), I am usually quick to put myself into the place of God: I sinfully judge (and condemn) others. I most often express my displeasure with sharp, rapid-fire words and angry looks that let them know they're in disgrace.

The child who spills or makes dumb mistakes can get a sarcastic comment, or become the butt of a cutting joke. (This from me or, more often, one of his siblings—but if I don't correct it quickly, then I sanction the response.)

When my will is crossed and I'm not getting what I want, I often become angry and impatient, and I also choose to act unkindly. Somehow, from my most beloved family members to the repair man who is late, I feel justified in expressing my displeasure by groans, sighs, rolling of eyes, and sharp, unkind words. From body language to verbal expressions, I let them know that they are out of favor with the Queen of the Home.

Question #3: What does my lack of loving kindness reveal about wrong heart attitudes that must be addressed?

Why is it that I reduce people to stones that I kick because I'm displeased? What's going on at my heart level that lets me think that I can treat people as means to my ends? How can I come fresh from my quiet time with the Lord and immediately say unkind, impatient things to the first person I encounter?

The first, most obvious thing is that *I am at the center of my thoughts.* I want what I want when I want it (which is right away). I crave instant obedience and satisfaction for my wishes, wants, and desires. When I don't get them, I indicate this swiftly by words and other acts of unkindness. By these, I attempt to force my will on others, or punish them for their "wrong actions."

Other cravings can also rule me. I can desire to control the behavior of others by my unkind speech or actions. I can be unkind because I am striving to gain what I want from others apart from the provision of God. Fears can rule my heart. I can believe that what I don't want to happen will come to pass unless I intervene in a forceful or punishing way.

What do all these cravings have in common? In all these cravings, my will is ruling (or attempting to rule) a universe apart from God.

Question #4: What bad fruits do I reap as my unkind behaviors create ongoing cycles of folly?

We all know how it feels to be sharply rebuked when we've fallen short: not good. Our instinctive response is usually to defend ourselves—often treating others as we've just been treated. Our children are people—immature and learning fast—and they model their behaviors on our examples. They most often learn unkindness from us (but not always, and not exclusively, since they also have the seeds of unkindness in their own sin natures).

When children live with frequent expressions and displays of unkindness, they learn to shield their hearts. Understandably enough, they often become increasingly distant, sullen, angry, and embittered. This means that they will do less to please us as time goes on, and our temptations to unkind ways will increase. Eventually, the dangers of the cycle of folly are that we will lose any place of influence in our growing children's hearts altogether, and our Christian witness can be compromised.

Our husbands may be long suffering or short tempered in response to unkind treatment, but the bottom line cycle of folly when we tolerate unkind—and I'll add disrespectful, here—behaviors is a growing relational distance and a rupture of marital unity. We are supposed to picture Christ to our children and a watching world: our marriage is supposed to display the image of Christ and His Bride. We fall so far short then we tolerate unkindness in our relations with our husbands!

Unkindness can have profound effects. It stirs up strife, which eats away at our family unity and thus our Christian witness. It retards our personal growth into the likeness of Christ, and it falsifies God's very nature (as did Moses when he struck the rock in anger—see Numbers 20:10-13). Our God's nature is amazing in lovingkindness. Our proper role is to display that nature to the watching world, beginning with our children. The folly we embrace warps God's good intentions for our lives!

Question #5: What does God say? How can the gospel make a difference and teach me to love better?

Let's remember the main reason why we should endeavor to be kind, and then look at where we get the ability to be so, even when tempted sorely.

The foundation of the call to be kind is found at the heart of the gospel message, and it's neatly summed up for us in 1 John 4:10-12 (ESV):

> *In this is love, not that we have loved God but that he loved us and sent his Son to be the propitiation for our sins. Beloved, if God so loved us, we also ought to love one another. No one has ever seen God; if we love one another, God abides in us and his love is perfected in us.*

We were hostile towards God (Romans 8:7), His enemies (Romans 5:10), and without hope (Ephesians 2:12). We rebelled against the Almighty King, and grieved and disobeyed Him countless times. Yet, as with Eve in the Garden after her transgression, God came looking for us. Because He is kind, He sent His one and only Son to be crushed (Isaiah 53:10) and killed for us, His enemies. It is this truth that gives Him the right to call us higher: He commands us to be kind to others because He is kind, and we are His ambassadors (2 Corinthians 5:20).

Arguing from the greater to the lesser for a moment, consider this from Luke 6:35 (ESV):

> *But love your enemies, and do good, and lend, expecting nothing in return, and your reward will be great, and you will be sons of the Most High, for he is kind to the ungrateful and the evil.*

We have been treated with unimaginable kindness. If this is how He calls us to treat our enemies (who are our moral equals) because of His example (towards us, who were his moral inferiors), how much more should we remember and labor to be kind to our precious children and husbands? A gospel understanding of God's kindness to us as an expression of His loving nature is the wellspring of grace from which we daily draw in order to obey God and be kind.

As I wrote at the start of the previous chapter, we are learning in our homeschool contexts how to love. God is not absent; He is not unaware, and He has not left our sides! God is schooling us: He's giving us a highly motivational reason to change more and more into the image of His Son. What is it? You don't want to hurt the ones you love the most! You don't want to dishonor God in front of them! How kind of Him to give you these compelling reasons to take a long look at your reactions and responses to your circumstances, repent, and seek His help to change!

Question #6: In light of what I've seen, how should I respond right now to God and others regarding my current, unkind habits?

Why is God kind to sinners? Romans 2:4 (ESV) tells us: "God's kindness is meant to lead you to repentance." The first step in obeying His call to love kindly is to recognize how kindly God has treated you, and how much you owe it to Him to faithfully manifest His loving character to others. If you're being convicted as you read this chapter, your first step is probably to confess to God—in full, concrete, and specific terms—the depths of your sin as you now understand it.

Secondly, be sure to appropriate (take to yourself) the forgiveness that God offers you! Jesus died for this sin as well as for all others. When we confess our sins, He promises to forgive completely (1 John 1:9). God's wrath was poured out horribly on His Son; it was *all* spent on Jesus, who has been accepted as the atoning Lamb of God. You have hope for forgiveness because God's wrath is spent in Jesus, and there is no more left for you!

Next, take hope. You can change also because God has led you to read this chapter for only one reason: He wants to help you! He has long seen any instances of unkindness in your life. Now, He's lovingly and patiently drawing it to your attention so that you can change to be more like your Savior: the person He created you to be.

Another thing that you can do is to start to identify specific temptations, and the contexts in which they typically occur. Here are some examples to get you started; you can surely find others in your unique setting.

- Are you perhaps in the habit of yelling through your house for your kids to come, or answering their calls by yelling, rather than training family members to walk to find others before communicating? Yelling sounds unkind, even when we are not angry. I found this to be the case at one point in our homeschooling journey, and making a simple change to requiring everyone (even myself) to walk to find the person wanted made a big difference in our home's atmosphere. (We also purchased inexpensive intercoms that plugged into wall sockets for the furthest removed bedrooms in our large home.)
- Do you run short on blood sugar regularly? My low point daily was about 4 p.m. when I was hungry and tired, but dinner preparations still loomed, and the day was far from over. I was regularly tempted to unkind speech at this time. Our solution was to institute afternoon tea time. I would put out tea, milk, and light snacks at 4 p.m., and my children and I would take a much needed, friendly break before evening clean up and dinner chores. The daily barrage of irritated, unkind words yielded to delicious, regular fellowship and fun conversations by means of this one simple change.
- Is your schedule too tight? Are you setting yourself up for failure on an eternal plane because you are clutching too many earthly objectives too tightly? Are you tempted to unkind speech because children dawdle and there's just no time for dawdling if you're to get everything done that you have planned? Or are you often unkind because you've just got to get everyone out the door, and on to the next commitment? Homeschooling schedules get overfilled easily because we have so many good options. Take a lesson from Mary, though, and opt for only the best options, with God's leading and your husband's direction (Luke 10:41-42).
- Do you need your hope renewed? Is there a long-standing trial in your life? For instance, do you have a delayed learner, or a teen going through puberty, or long-standing sin patterns in husband or children, or an illness to combat, and so you have grown weary in doing good? It's human nature to do

> so, but not divine nature. His Spirit can help you to renew your mind and strengthen your heart so that you can renew your efforts to obey Him and be kind.

As in all things, we are not self-sufficient or alone! Turn to God in dependent prayer! The good news is that He does not call us to this high standard without helping us. He knows our frailty and our temptations (John 14:15-18). He has therefore put His Spirit into our hearts. And the fruit of His Spirit has these qualities: love, joy, peace, patience, kindness, goodness, faithfulness, gentleness, self-control (Galatians 5:22). God's Spirit teaches us to be kind, and we become more and more kind as we mature in Him. This is just one way that "He gives more grace" (James 4:6). You can and will improve if you call upon His enabling grace!

Question #7: What does (or can or should) loving kindness look like in the homeschool setting going forward?

Here's a verse that we can all put up on our refrigerators as a reminder: "She opens her mouth with wisdom, and the teaching of kindness is on her tongue" (Proverbs 31:26, ESV). The wisdom that we so desperately wish to impart to our young people is most becomingly clothed in kindness. Children may outwardly or initially spurn kindnesses (think of our first parents in the Garden of Eden), but they will generally be far more ready to receive instruction that is kindly delivered than teachings given in harsh or dictatorial fashion.

Here's a harder goal to achieve, yet with God all things are possible, and this is His Word to us:

> *Let no corrupting talk come out of your mouths, but only such as is good for building up, as fits the occasion, that it may give grace to those who hear. And do not grieve the Holy Spirit of God, by whom you were sealed for the day of redemption. Let all bitterness and wrath and anger and clamor and slander be put away from you, along with all malice. Be kind to one another, tenderhearted, forgiving one another, as God in Christ forgave you.*
>
> *Ephesians 4:29-32 (ESV)*

Our husbands and children are fellow brethren, not whipping posts, and for God's sake (even if not for their own) we show them respect and kindness. We fail as often as do they, and we have no right to demand that our expectations, timetables, and agendas are met, or to use unkindness to forward our wills. The ground truly is level at the foot of Christ's cross, so let her who is without sin feel free to hurl the first unkind word, but for the rest of us, let's walk meekly with our fellow sinners and seek to love them for the sake of Christ and because we do love them!

When we see that kind speech can transform our homeschools into places where the King is manifested in the way that we love each other, we'll put more effort into controlling our selfish passions and seeking to represent Him well to our families.

Question #8: What cycles of blessing can I hope for as I turn to God and grow in my ability to love kindly?

Kindness is contagious! If we model kindness, day in and day out, with the Lord helping us, we will teach volumes about the loving character of God by our behavior alone. (See 1 Peter 3:1.) And, guess what? When we ourselves need a little kindness back, our husbands and kids will know how to offer it to us!

We have been treated with unimaginable kindness.

Let's revisit Romans 2:4 (ESV): "God's kindness is meant to lead you to repentance." God was kind to us so that we might find our way to Him. In like manner, our kindness as wives and mothers can be one of the most powerful means of grace in our endeavor to draw our dear ones closer to Christ. Many of us homeschool so that our children will have the best possible environment in which to grow as disciples. And, as we've said before, some of the most powerful teaching that we do is modeling. Their response may not be immediate, but the timetable is not in our hands.

God is kind to sinners; He is patient. "God is love" (1 John 4:8) and thus all the qualities of love that we are exploring spring from Him. When we love by means of kindness, asking God to help us from when we rise up to when we lie down at night, because He loved us first, we show our families the true character of God, and we can thus initiate a cycle of blessing that may never have an end as our children accept the loving God for who He is and commit to serve Him all of their days.

Conclusion

Here are some last verses that give us vision for the prize that is worth running after:

> *Put on then, as God's chosen ones, holy and beloved, compassionate hearts, kindness, humility, meekness, and patience, bearing with one another and, if one has a complaint against another, forgiving each other; as the Lord has forgiven you, so you also must forgive. And above all these put on love, which binds everything together in perfect harmony.*
>
> *Colossians 3:12-14 (ESV)*

> *His divine power has granted to us everything pertaining to life and godliness, through the true knowledge of Him who called us by His own glory and excellence. For by these He has granted to us His precious and magnificent promises, so that by them you may become partakers of the divine nature, having escaped the corruption that is in the world by lust. Now for this very reason also, applying all diligence, in your faith supply moral excellence, and in your moral excellence, knowledge, and in your knowledge, self-control, and in your self-control, perseverance, and in your perseverance, godliness, and in your godliness, brotherly kindness, and in your brotherly kindness, love.*
>
> *2 Peter 1:3-7 (NASB)*

> *We put no obstacle in anyone's way, so that no fault may be found with our ministry, but as servants of God we commend ourselves in every way: by great endurance, in afflictions, hardships, calamities, beatings, imprisonments, riots, labors, sleepless nights, hunger; by purity, knowledge, patience, kindness, the Holy Spirit, genuine love; by truthful speech, and the power of God; with the weapons of righteousness for the right hand and for the left; through honor and dishonor, through slander and praise.*
>
> *2 Corinthians 6:3-8a (ESV)*

> *To sum up, all of you be harmonious, sympathetic, brotherly, kindhearted, and humble in spirit; not returning evil for evil or insult for insult, but giv-*

ing a blessing instead; for you were called for the very purpose that you might inherit a blessing.

1 Peter 3:8-9 (NASB)

32.

We love because he first loved us. If anyone says, "I love God," and hates his brother, he is a liar; for he who does not love his brother whom he has seen cannot love God whom he has not seen. And this commandment we have from him: whoever loves God must also love his brother.

1 JOHN 4:19-21 (ESV)

Love Does Not Envy

In the last of these chapters on some aspects of growth that we can embrace as we arise to each new day and retire after each one spent, we are thinking of how to be better at loving. In this chapter, we will not look at positive attributes of loving, but learn about love by considering the Apostle Paul's contrast between what is biblical love and what it is not. He writes, "Love does not envy…" (1 Corinthians 13:4).

Envy is a fuzzy concept for many of us, so I'd like to start this chapter by defining it. Envy is when you want what someone else has, be it possessions, accomplishments, or position. It is very close to covetousness. (Jealousy, by contrast, is when you feel resentful or angry that someone else has—or has gotten—something you feel that you more rightly deserve. Also, jealousy can refer to a fear that you will lose what you have.) Some dictionaries define covetousness as a jealous desire for what others have, but I think this muddies the waters. So, let's stick with a simple definition of envy: wanting what others have.

I thought about omitting this chapter from a book whose intended audience is new homeschoolers, because envy tends to rear its head more often when we are tired—pressed by life's circumstances, thorns, and snares, and have been slogging along for awhile—than it does at the start of our homeschooling journey, when there seem to be plenty of days left with no mistakes in them. Did this chapter belong here?

I decided that it did when I considered that some who are new to homeschooling may be making significant sacrifices as they start. You might be giving up freedoms, income, or relationships that you have long enjoyed in order to begin this journey. So, I kept this chapter in. I hope that, if it doesn't speak to you now, it will be a cautionary tale for you to remember after you've gotten down the road a ways.

How does envy manifest itself in our homeschooling world, and what are our common responses?

Question #1: How does my situation—being a homeschooling mom—challenge me in the area of envy?

Envy can tempt a homeschooling mother regularly. For many of us, budgets are tight and we either make do or do without. We are therefore tempted to the "what if's."

- What if I had more money for books?
- What if I had a new washing machine?
- What if we could afford a bigger house with a real school room? Then I could get organized!
- What if my house looked like all those TV ads or magazine pictures? I could be content, then.
- What if I could just afford that expensive curriculum? Then my life would be __________ (easier, better, fulfilled, successful, etc.—you fill in the blank).

Then there are the anxieties of hard times. These give rise to the "if only's."

- If only my husband hadn't been laid off, and I didn't have to think about earning income on top of all my other responsibilities.
- If only my child gets a scholarship! I don't see how else he will get a college

education.

- If only we could afford to get Johnny a tutor in math, but we can't!
- If only my mother-in-law hadn't gotten cancer just now: how can I care for her and keep school going? Isn't my life hard enough without adding *this* into the equation?

Our homeschooling friends (and their children or spouses) can provide us opportunity for unloving, envious thoughts. Common thoughts like this abound:

- It's easy for Suzy to talk about staying on track with her curriculum: she only has two kids (or her husband helps with the teaching chores, or her kids are smarter, or more obedient, or… or… or…).
- Mary is so smug. If I had her ________ (fill it in), I'd be a better mom/homeschooler, too!
- Jane is so high and mighty, just because her husband makes a good living while we're scrounging for every penny! She looks down on us because our car is so old and ragged.

Then there's just the feeling of being worn down and wishing we could give up. We begin to look with envy on the lives of our non-homeschooling friends or family. These are the "I wish" temptations.

- I wish I could just put them all into public school (or private Christian school). Then life would be better.
- I wish I didn't feel so tired all the time. All I ask is just to get a break during the day like moms who send their kids to school.
- I wish I had more time! I am always in triage.
- I wish I felt like I was giving my children a good education. Am I? I wish I knew, or that I had some objective measure of my performance.
- Wouldn"t my kids be better off with a mother who is rested and cheerful at the end of the day when they come home from school, rather than a crabby, overworked nag (like me) for a mom? I wish I could have someone else doing at least the schooling so I could be the kind of mom I always wanted to be! And, you know what? Maybe you could; but who would get the glory then? (But I'm getting ahead of myself.)

All of these kinds of scenarios and thought phrases are common to us as homeschooling moms (and if you're new to homeschooling, you've probably realized that many of these temptations are common to all women from all walks of life). I would venture to guess that, no matter what our income or situation, we've all been tempted to envy and have fallen actively into envying the possessions or situations or accomplishments or leisure or opportunities of others. The temptations to envy are real in our lives, and we often give way to them as they present attractive alternatives to the hard things in our lives.

Question #2: How do I fail to respond in a loving way in these situations?

There are a variety of ways that giving in to envious thoughts can make us both unfruitful and unloving. The most obvious of these is that we can begin to complain—first in our hearts and then aloud. And grumbling and complaining can easily become more and more common if we don't work to curb them.

Another way that we can behave is to blame others for our less-than-desirable situation. We look at our husband or children or circumstances and feel that if only they would change, we would be better off. If we entertain such envy-driven thoughts, we tend to come out with unloving comments like this:

- If only you (my husband) were more like _________. He provides for his family so that she has what she needs to do her homeschooling right!
- If only you (my child) were more like ________, respectful of your mother and eager to learn. Then we wouldn't have all this strife in our home!

We can also become hopeless as we look at what others have and we do not. We can get our eyes fixed on the good things that God has given to others and believe the lie that it is because we lack them that we are unhappy or unfulfilled.

It is a lie because our discontent comes from within us. We are blind to our own discontentedness with the lot God has given us and our rebellion against His will. And so we indulge ourselves, choosing to believe that if only we had what others have—money, time, position, ease, skills—we'd be happier, more cheerful, saner, more successful, or more diligent. We begin to believe the lie that things will never change, and then believe that our situation is beyond change and beyond hope. As long as we look around at what others have and we don't, and don't look up to God, it's easy to give in to hopelessness!

Question #3: What does my lack of love reveal about wrong heart attitudes that must be addressed?

As I considered this question, the first thing that came to my mind was that our envying most commonly reflects a heart that loves something else more than it loves God. When we give in to envious thoughts, we are in effect saying to the Lord, "I don't like how You have planned my life or the provision you've chosen for me" or "I don't believe that this is for my good," or even "I don't like to define my good as becoming more like Christ. I want to please myself, so I don't care if what you are giving me will help me to be like Him!"

Envy and love oppose one another; we can't both envy and love.

We can have a host of emotions: sadness, anger, despair, etc., as bitter fruit of envious hearts, but I believe that our primary problem is that we have put the things we want on the thrones of our hearts instead of looking to God in submission and gratitude. We tend to trust ourselves more than we do the omniscient, all-loving, all-wise King of the Universe, whom we have the privilege to call "Father." What we need to address is our pride that rears up against the Almighty, and we need to call our sin what it is: open rebellion, ingratitude, and unloving grumbling.

The opposite of envy would be love: "love does not envy..." says the Apostle Paul. So, in envy, we find both a failure to love (a sin of omission) and a choice to rebel against God, which also tends to hurt others around us (sins of commission).

Question #4: What bad fruits do I reap as my unloving behaviors create ongoing cycles of folly?

Envy and love oppose one another; we can't both envy and love. So, we miss opportunities to love, and we poison our own souls and those of others around us when we give in to envy. Here are examples:

- If we are envious of others' gifts (and we don't always see that they are gifts—more on this later), we have a hard time rejoicing with those who rejoice, loving those who have what we covet, or being encouraged by seeing that God's plans and purposes are going forward.
- When envious, we are not loving God, and so do not seek to humble our-

selves and learn our lessons (from God or others). We tend rather to become more and more ungrateful, unhappy, self-focused, covetous, rebellious, and complaining the longer we tolerate (or give in to) envious thoughts in our hearts.

- Since God has put us where we are, and we are not focused on His will being done, we "go horizontal" rather than "going verticle." We work to force a "fix" to the "problem" ourselves, rather than asking God for remedies or waiting on Him for His perfect will. Our attempts to grasp what we desire can lead to the bullying, striving, blaming, complaining, wheedling, and wielding a host of angry words that are unlovely, unloving, and destructive to our families.

Question #5: What does God say? How can the gospel make a difference, and teach me to love better and envy less?

A grumbling, ungrateful, and rebellious heart distances us from our Father and from members of our family and community. Here follow some passages that clearly demonstrate this.

Moses repeatedly points out that the Israelites who grumbled against him and other leaders while in the wilderness were really grumbling about God's determinations for their lives. See Exodus 16:8; Numbers 14:27 and 36, 16:11, and 17:5.

God is pretty severe in response: it is offensive to Him when we are ungrateful or rebellious concerning His will for our lives. In order to get the full import of this interaction between God and the Israelites, we need to recognize that it must have been *really tough* to live in the desert, constantly wandering. Think about simple daily things, like cooking, bathing, and living in tents in a hot, dry climate.

After their disobedience concerning their reactions to the spies' report, an entire generation of Israelites (save two men) lived like this, without hope for the future in any earthly sense. (See Numbers 14:27-30.) That must have been *really* hard! However, since life in this world is not about our comfort but rather God's glory, and because these Israelites did not have grateful hearts, their rebellion against God and unbelief as expressed by grumbling was not excused, but chastened.

Speaking to the Corinthians about these Israelites who wandered in the desert, and drawing a lesson for Christians in his day, Paul wrote:

> *We must not put Christ to the test, as some of them did and were destroyed by serpents, nor grumble, as some of them did and were destroyed by the Destroyer. Now these things happened to them as an example, but they were written down for our instruction, on whom the end of the ages has come.*
>
> *1 Corinthians 10:9-11 (ESV)*

The Apostle James, who was a wise pastor, is very helpful in helping us to renew our minds:

> *What causes quarrels and what causes fights among you? Is it not this, that your passions are at war within you? You desire and do not have, so you murder. You covet and cannot obtain, so you fight and quarrel. You do not have, because you do not ask. You ask and do not receive, because you ask wrongly, to spend it on your passions. You adulterous people! Do you not know that friendship with the world is enmity with God? Therefore whoever wishes to be a friend of the world makes himself an enemy of God. Or do you suppose it is to no purpose that the Scripture says, 'He yearns jealously over the spirit that he has made to dwell in us'? But he gives more grace. Therefore it says, 'God opposes the proud, but gives grace to the humble.' Submit yourselves therefore to God. Resist the devil, and he will flee from you. Draw near to God, and he will draw near to you.*
>
> *James 4:1-8a (ESV)*

God is actively sovereign over our lives. This fact gets masked by all our modern conveniences (like central heat and food stores packed with goodies), and by the secular culture in which we live that gives no honor to God, but it is the truth nonetheless. It has been well said that "There is not a square inch in the whole domain of our human existence over which Christ, who is Sovereign over all, does not cry: 'Mine!'"[1]

God numbers our days, directs our paths, and—if He has called us to Him—works all things together for our good (Romans 8:28-29). It is He who determines both our privations and our blessings. It is He who is giving to others the things that

1 Abraham Kuyper, as quoted in *Abraham Kuyper, A Centennial Reader*, (1998). James D. Bratt, editor, p. 488.

we desire; they are gifts from *His* hand, even when they seem to have been "earned." Note this passage from Deuteronomy 8:17-18 (ESV):

> *Beware lest you say in your heart, "My power and the might of my hand have gotten me this wealth." You shall remember the Lord your God, for it is he who gives you power to get wealth, that he may confirm his covenant that he swore to your fathers, as it is this day.*

Whether others have been given physical blessings, skills, or spiritual gifts, they are all *gifts* that the Father gives for His eternal purposes. The problem with envy is that it promotes ingratitude towards God for what He is doing in our lives, and covetousness after gifts that He has sovereignly chosen to give others. We distance ourselves from God and others when we envy, and grow progressively more unloving. Love does not envy.

When we see others who seem to have no worries, or who have homeschooling strengths that we wish we had, it is unloving of us to envy. When we do, we have ceased to love God first, and our neighbors second. We have ceased to rejoice in God's sovereign care of our brothers and sisters and forgotten to submit gladly to His loving and faithful will for our lives. We have ceased to be willing to learn the lessons that God is teaching us for the good of our eternal souls.

When God ordains hard circumstances for us, we may forget that He is a skilled physician who is revealing sick heart attitudes that will be cleansed in no less of a fire than the purging one He helps us to walk through (Isaiah 43:1-2). We need to remember not to despise the discipline of our Lord (Job 5:7, Proverbs 3:11-12, and Hebrews 12:3-11)! Our trials have a purpose, a good purpose, and are there to bring God glory after we have passed through by means of His sustaining grace.

No trial lasts one second longer than needed. Each one is allowed by God, and is for our good, much like chemotherapy in the hands of a trained radiologist, or the knife in the hand of a skilled surgeon who slices open our body in order to remove a life-threatening cancer. God's choices are *always* and *only* good. Any trial that we endure is assuredly the most benign possible way that we can be healed of soul-threatening sins, most of which we don't even recognize for what they are!

No evil temptation to sin is ever sent from God (James 1:13); rather, we are tempted by our own desires in response to trials. And yet, our kind and loving God always provides a means of escape from any evil scheme of the Devil.

> *No temptation has overtaken you that is not common to man. God is faithful, and he will not let you be tempted beyond your ability, but with the temptation he will also provide the way of escape, that you may be able to endure it.*
>
> *1 Corinthians 10:13 (ESV)*

Far from being a hard master who denies us good while blessing those who seem more undeserving than we are (as, in our envy, we can believe Him to be), God is a loving parent who disciplines us for our good, and helps us when we are weak under that loving discipline.

> *Consider him who endured from sinners such hostility against himself, so that you may not grow weary or fainthearted. In your struggle against sin you have not yet resisted to the point of shedding your blood. And have you forgotten the exhortation that addresses you as sons?*
>
> *"My son, do not regard lightly the discipline of the Lord, nor be weary when reproved by him. For the Lord disciplines the one he loves, and chastises every son whom he receives."*
>
> *It is for discipline that you have to endure. God is treating you as sons. For what son is there whom his father does not discipline? If you are left without discipline, in which all have participated, then you are illegitimate children and not sons. Besides this, we have had earthly fathers who disciplined us and we respected them. Shall we not much more be subject to the Father of spirits and live?*
>
> *For they disciplined us for a short time as it seemed best to them, but he disciplines us for our good, that we may share his holiness. For the moment all discipline seems painful rather than pleasant, but later it yields the peaceful fruit of righteousness to those who have been trained by it. Therefore lift your drooping hands and strengthen your weak knees, and*

> *make straight paths for your feet, so that what is lame may not be put out of joint but rather be healed.*
>
> *Hebrews 12:3-13 (ESV)*

We will never fix ourselves. We are too wicked for that. Rather, our envy reveals to us once again our need for a Savior. Apart from His grace, we cannot love aright. We need the cleansing blood of Christ in order to heed James, abandon the world, and run to God for more grace.

We are all in need of this grace; if we are God's through Christ, our trials are meant to purify, change, and sanctify us. In this, we have hope. If we look with envy on those unbelievers who have it easier than we do, let's also remember that their eternal destiny will *not* be enviable. (See all of Psalm 73.) We can only press through the temptations to envy by clinging to God and learning to better love Him and one another.

Question # 6: In light of what I've seen, how should I respond right now to God and others regarding my current, unloving habits?

We all have trigger points for envious thoughts, but they're not all the same. I've listed a few of the most common ones earlier in this chapter, but what are your most tempting moments? Do you tend to wallow in self-pity when provoked by envy? Or blame others? Or whine and complain? Or become unpleasant until you get your way? Or ___________? You fill in the blank.

Whatever your unlovely behavior, the first step is to turn to God in repentance and confess your sins. Running to God with a contrite heart is the first step to lasting change and healing.

In 1 John 1:8-9 (ESV), we read both a stern warning and one of the Bible's most precious promises: "If we say we have no sin, we deceive ourselves, and the truth is not in us. If we confess our sins, he is faithful and just to forgive us our sins and to cleanse us from all unrighteousness." We will never fix things in the horizontal dimension (with our circumstances or with our relationships) until we get right with God in the vertical dimension. Step 1, then, is reestablishing His lordship in your life.

Step 2 might be to start a gratitude journal, wherein you record each day just a few of the many blessings that you and your family enjoy. (See more on this in the next chapter.) Envy has a way of warping our view of both our own circumstances and those of our friends. Your homeschooling friend or neighbor may seem to have it all together, with perfect children and/or an ideal husband but, in our fallen world, life is seldom perfect for long. She may have secret sorrows that make your life look great by comparison. Or she may have endured fiery trials earlier in life, and this is her time of rest and recuperation.

One thing is certain: we all have trials, and no one has the ideal, perfect kids and spouse. Whereas some families may excel in certain areas, typically God gives equally profound gifts (though maybe not as flashy) to others. What we typically don't see is that our gifts are important to God's plan and to the sanctification of ourselves and our families. While we might wish that we could be sanctified through the avenues that God has chosen for our friends, what we need to confess is well expressed in Psalms 16:5-11 (ESV):

> *The Lord is my chosen portion and my cup; you hold my lot. The lines have fallen for me in pleasant places; indeed, I have a beautiful inheritance.*
>
> *I bless the Lord who gives me counsel; in the night also my heart instructs me. I have set the Lord always before me; because he is at my right hand, I shall not be shaken.*
>
> *Therefore my heart is glad, and my whole being rejoices; my flesh also dwells secure. For you will not abandon my soul to Sheol, or let your holy one see corruption.*
>
> *You make known to me the path of life; in your presence there is fullness of joy; at your right hand are pleasures forevermore.*

Step 3 would most likely be for you to share with your spouse, children, and close friends the things that the Lord is showing you through this meditation. Where appropriate, confess your sins and ask for prayer support in changing your habits. You may find that you open up unexpected doors for your dear ones to confess similar sinful tendencies, and that they ask you for prayer in kind! But, even if they don't, your example of humility and change will speak very loudly to them, and (more importantly) constitute a fragrant offering to your Father God!

Question #7: What does (or can or should) loving look like in the homeschool setting going forward?

As we become more aware of our envious thoughts and feelings, we need to repeatedly flee to our Savior for forgiveness and healing, adopt an attitude of gratitude, and humbly confess our sins to others. As we do, we can expect that our outlook on life will improve.

As we begin to express more gratitude and less envy, we will become more and more loving. We should expect that we will begin to love God more, receiving more grace and a sense of peace with Him. We can also expect that our husbands and children will be blessed as we seek to obey God.

You also may find that, as you confess that God's will for your life as revealed in your circumstances is perfect, and seek Him for sustaining grace for any trials, that your ability to focus on the daily jobs of being a wife, mother, and teacher become clearer and easier. It's always easier to work with the Spirit's direction than against Him, and His grace is sufficient for the tasks that He assigns. As with our children and their school lessons or household chores, when we accept God's assignments with a good will, our performance of them is done with cheerfulness and, yes, with love!

If our husbands and children have picked up complaining spirits from our example, or simply (like you) have a tendency to sin in complaint, we should not now quickly turn and rebuke them. God has been lovingly patient with us, and we want to extend grace, forgiveness, and mercy to them as we reflect His character. As we walk more humbly with our God, and grow in expressing gratitude and love, we can expect our children to pick up on this attitude, because He gives more grace when we humble ourselves and turn to Him (James 4:6)!

Question #8: What cycles of blessing can I hope for as I turn to God and grow in my ability to love?

The resentment and bitterness that spring from envy cause a host of unlovely behaviors that not only slime our husbands and children, but give them occasion to learn such behaviors from us. If your house has been filled with whining, complaining, and quarreling, you may find that your new tone of loving acceptance of God's will for you gradually helps others see how they can change. Your frequent confession that the Lord's will is perfect for your life, and your example of submission may birth a newly submissive attitude in your children. You (and they) may become more and more aware of the many evidences of God's grace in your lives, more concentrated on school and life lessons that God has for you, and find yourselves giving Him thanks more often. A general culture of grateful praise that glorifies the Living God, which you hardly dared imagine possible, may emerge in your household as God blesses your efforts!

Will this happen overnight? Probably not. The effects of unchecked ingratitude, grumbling, and complaining can be long-lasting. But begin each day, and end each night, by recounting the goodness of God, and praising Him for His provisions, and you will find that your heart—which is all that you can directly control—will be enlarged with love for God. Furthermore, you will know for certain that you are pleasing Him. If you have long been sinning in this area, stop to marvel at God's patience with you for all the time before, and His love in sending you this chapter to open your eyes and renew your mind so that you can have hope!

At the end of the day, if no one and nothing else around you changes, there is real joy in knowing that you are pleasing the Audience of One. Look for the grace-notes in your life that show that you are reaching His heart, and giving Him a big smile. Sowing to the Spirit is a worthy activity, and God is usually not behind times in rewarding earnest repentance and efforts to change. Here are a couple of precious passages to hang on to as you work at change:

> *Truly God is good to Israel, to those who are pure in heart. But as for me, my feet had almost stumbled, my steps had nearly slipped. For I was envious of the arrogant when I saw the prosperity of the wicked.*

* * * * *

> *Truly you set them in slippery places; you make them fall to ruin. How they are destroyed in a moment, swept away utterly by terrors!*

> *Like a dream when one awakes, O Lord, when you rouse yourself, you despise them as phantoms. When my soul was embittered, when I was pricked in heart, I was brutish and ignorant; I was like a beast toward you.*

Nevertheless, I am continually with you; you hold my right hand. You guide me with your counsel, and afterward you will receive me to glory.
Whom have I in heaven but you? And there is nothing on earth that I desire besides you. My flesh and my heart may fail, but God is the strength of my heart and my portion forever.

For behold, those who are far from you shall perish; you put an end to everyone who is unfaithful to you. But for me it is good to be near God; I have made the Lord GOD my refuge, that I may tell of all your works.

Psalm 73:1-3, 18-28 (ESV)

33.

And let the peace of Christ rule in your hearts, to which indeed you were called in one body. And be thankful.

Colossians 3:15 (ESV)

Cultivating an Attitude of Gratitude

Of all the regular practices that most enable us to love the homeschooling journey, the cultivation of gratitude in the home may be the most effective. Love is essential, and gratitude feeds it, fanning the fires of devotion to God and to our families. As we lie down at night, let us thank God for helping us through one more day. As we rise up in the morning, let us thank Him for one more chance to glorify Him on the earth. Let us thank Him that we get to work at home with those we love best, teaching them what is true and good. Throughout the day, let us look for what my senior pastor used to call "the Post-It® Notes of God's grace" on the walls of our homes.

This last chapter details some of the many wonderful ways that we can cultivate an attitude of gratitude in our homes. I have found over the years that it took daily repetitions and many instances of leading by example to counter the me-centered and man-centered influences of our own hearts and our culture at large. In order to cultivate a grateful heart, you need to be looking first up and then out, not down and in. You'll also need God's help because human beings are not naturally grateful. So, if some of these practices are new to you, be sure to ask God for His help as you begin to employ them.

Gratitude Begins with the Gospel

Do not be led away by diverse and strange teachings, for it is good for the heart to be strengthened by grace...

Hebrews 13:9 (ESV)

Blessed be the God and Father of our Lord Jesus Christ! According to his great mercy, he has caused us to be born again to a living hope through the resurrection of Jesus Christ from the dead, to an inheritance that is imperishable, undefiled, and unfading, kept in heaven for you, who by God's power are being guarded through faith for a salvation ready to be revealed in the last time.

In this you rejoice, though now for a little while, if necessary, you have been grieved by various trials, so that the tested genuineness of your faith—more precious than gold that perishes though it is tested by fire—may be found to result in praise and glory and honor at the revelation of Jesus Christ. Though you have not seen him, you love him.

Though you do not now see him, you believe in him and rejoice with joy that is inexpressible and filled with glory, obtaining the outcome of your faith, the salvation of your souls. Concerning this salvation, the prophets who prophesied about the grace that was to be yours searched and inquired carefully, inquiring what person or time the Spirit of Christ in them was indicating when he predicted the sufferings of Christ and the subsequent

> *glories. It was revealed to them that they were serving not themselves but you, in the things that have now been announced to you through those who preached the good news to you by the Holy Spirit sent from heaven, things into which angels long to look.*
>
> 1 Peter 1:3-12

What a rich treasure we modern Christians have! And yet, how hard it can be to keep the fires of devotion and the amazing nature of God's grace alive in our hearts. As C.S. Lewis aptly observed in his sermon *The Weight of Glory*,

> *If we consider the unblushing promises of reward and the staggering nature of the rewards promised in the Gospels, it would seem that Our Lord finds our desires not too strong, but too weak. We are half-hearted creatures, fooling about with drink and sex and ambition when infinite joy is offered us, like an ignorant child who wants to go on making mud pies in a slum because he cannot imagine what is meant by the offer of a holiday at the sea. We are far too easily pleased. (26)*

I believe it takes a lifetime to grow into appreciating the unsearchable riches of God's kindness and love. When I was younger, I wanted the gospel to be precious to me, but to tell the honest truth, it just wasn't. I had so many competing hopes and dreams—so much that was attractive here on earth. But, as I've become older, more settled and quiet, and with fewer earthly plans before me than behind me, it's become easier to treasure the riches of the glory of God as my future inheritance that grows closer day by day.

Much of the content of the preceding chapters has shown us our need for God's grace through Jesus' sacrifice. I'm not going to dwell any longer on this topic because, well, it just takes *time* soaking in life experiences, walking through trials and seeing the faithfulness of God in them, receiving His gifts, crying with those who weep, trudging through difficult days—all that building up of the rich "soul soil" that results in sanctification—to go deep with God and love him more.

But I do want to say this: as John Piper has so eloquently written, God *is* the gospel (the good news). He wants to give us Himself, and the best gift of the Gospel is not freedom from sin, but the fact that freedom from sin enables us to be with Him forever (1 Peter 3:18). This is where you as a disciple need to press in, first and foremost.

The point of all of life and history is God's glory, revealed in the face of Christ. Jesus died to bring us to God, so coming to Him is the central purpose of life. Though you may go two steps forward and one step back, though you may come to halts and fogs in your walk with God, though it may take years and years of simple obedience without a whole lot of obvious fruit, I counsel you to do what you can to place yourself in the path of having your love for your Savior fuel your gratitude to God and your faith in Him.

Then, let that gratitude make you freshly aware, as you lie down and as you rise up, that your Savior loves you and all is well. There are many practices that can fan the flames of devotion and duty, but there must be that divine spark, and your fire must be fed!

Gratitude Journal

One of the easiest and most fruitful means of developing a grateful heart is to record daily a set number of things for which you are truly thankful. This tool can help to develop a number of different aspects of gratitude. I'll do a thumbnail sketch of the ones I've discovered, but my list here won't be exhaustive!

Restoring Our Relationship with God

As I mentioned in our last chapter on envy, it is easy to be tempted by our own lusts to become discontented with God's choices for our lives. One of the best remedies for envy is to cultivate a grateful heart for those self-same circumstances that are rubbing us the wrong way. Let me demonstrate how by giving a few examples.

What if, instead of dwelling on all the possessions that you lack, you began to thank God for what you have. What if you made a game of it? What if you wrote down (on a piece of paper posted on your fridge) two unique things per meal for which you can honestly thank God. (You'd better write small, 'cause I guarantee, there are a lot of them!) This is especially easy for us Americans as we contrast our lots not with our affluent neighbors, but with third-world dwellers!

Or, say you are discontented with how your homeschool is going. Very well: what is going right? Can we take, say, a week to record as we lie down and as we rise up, two things for which we can thank God in each day? For instance, we are free to homeschool. We have the financial ability (at least for now) to homeschool. We have health, sanity, creative energy, gifts, talents, and time. We have children to teach! (So many couples are barren!) We have a house in which to teach them. The list goes on.

Once you get started, it is not hard to find many, many blessings that God has bestowed on us. (If you need a kick start, flip to the end of this chapter and read Psalm 103, which I have printed in its entirety for your convenience.)

Restoring Relationships Horizontally

I have found this practice of keeping a gratitude journal to be especially helpful when I, or one of my family members, was struggling interpersonally. When we are hurt by another person, or bothered by their habits, or tempted to judge them for their obvious sin patterns, it's helpful to remind ourselves of a few things. When we discover feelings like this in our hearts and sense a coolness or desire for distance developing, we need to address ourselves quite actively!

In order to cultivate a grateful heart, you need to be looking first up and then out, not down and in.

First, of course, we want to remember that we are truly no better than they are, morally speaking. Though our sins may not be as gross or obvious to us, we all sin and fall short of the glory of God. We all need a Savior. And, as I've written earlier in this book, we all need love most when we are most unlovely! So, our first task is to see how the faults or foibles of another are tempting us to sin, repent for our own sinful reactions to those imperfections, and then ask God to give us renewed love for the person with whom He has sovereignly called us to walk the earth. We do this, of course, because it is what Christ has done for us!

Secondly, we can start a gratitude journal! This doesn't have to be a book. It can be, for instance, a poster, or a series of index cards, or a piece of notebook paper. The recording format is unimportant. What matters is that you take the time to think of a set number of things that you admire, respect, or are grateful for in the person with whom you have a present struggle. Daily, determine to record two or five (choose a number) of things that you can truly thank God for in that person, and seek to pray for them after recording.

It is amazing how bitterness, envy, and strife cause us to focus on the negative aspects of a person. Abraham Lincoln is quoted as saying, "If you look for the bad in people, you will certainly find it!" When we begin to focus on those negative things, our perspective can become warped—and quickly! Pretty soon, the down sides that bug us are all we can see! This is especially true when you are living with someone. The rubbing that you do is frequent and can get pretty painful!

I have discovered that the opposite is true: because all people are created in the image of God, there is something good to find in all of them, even when they are driving us crazy! I have used this technique time and again to restore for myself a balanced perspective of my husband, my children, and my friends. I've also required my children to keep gratitude journals when they were having seasons of not getting along with their siblings or neighborhood friends, and advised it when couples were struggling in their marriages. Time and again, I've found that the combination of gratitude and prayer will do wonders in restoring relationships!

Refreshment and Relief

Gratitude journals can also be a means of refreshment for weary souls. Have I mentioned that homeschooling is so *daily*? We can grow weary in well-doing, and lose our Christian joy. Gratitude journals are a great means of restoring that joy. They remind us of all that the Giver has blessed us with. They remind us of our good reasons for trudging on! To recall that God has saved you, gifted you, given you the desire to homeschool, provided the finances (whatever they are, they are not nothing!), the creativity, and the energy—and promises to renew those daily as we wait on Him—are all means of grace to the end of refreshing our spirits as we go to bed and as we rise up.

Again, life gets tough and can beat us down. In the process of working hard, we can get focused on how tough we have it, instead of lifting our eyes to God and thanking Him for all the ways that He has blessed us. It is relieving to lift the burden of sorrow, of hopelessness, of seeing only the next task, of believing the lie that things will *never* change or *ever* get better. As my husband, Scott, says when I get down like this and start to voice my thoughts, "Can't you just smell hell's sulphur?"

Our enemy whispered to our Mother Eve, "Did God *really* say...?" He was the enemy of God, and sought to strike at Him through Eve. He is your enemy too, and when you give in to gloomy, self-defeating lies, he dances. Don't do it! Grab a piece of paper, or your notebook, and start recording all God's benefits! Again, use Psalm 103, printed at the end of this chapter as a kick-starter to help you out!

EGG Hunts

This is a humorous avenue to renewing an attitude of gratitude in which the whole family can participate, even very young children. We know that God is always at work. The Bible says of Jesus that

> *By him all things were created, in heaven and on earth, visible and invisible, whether thrones or dominions or rulers or authorities—all things were created through him and for him. And he is before all things, and in him all things hold together.*
>
> *Colossians 1:16-17 (ESV)*

Moment by moment, day by day, God is holding this sin-sick, fallen world together for His good purposes. One day, it will be made new, but until that day, it is by His grace alone that we live, and move, and have our being (Acts 17:28). It is because of His active grace in your life that you are not judged, condemned, and destroyed.

This means that every day brings fresh opportunities to thank God for his many blessings. In our family, we got to calling these hunts—**E**vidence of **G**od's **G**race (EGG) hunts! When we would sit at table, or walk in the way, or lie down at night, or rise up in the morning, we would often ask our children, "What EGGs have you found today?"

They knew what we meant, and it was often precious and sweet to see what they were noticing of the Father's work in and around our family! On Thanksgiving Day, we developed a tradition of putting up a poster on one of the walls of the house, where we and our children (and guests) recorded as many EGGs as we could. Those posters were often quickly and completely filled, and we always left them up for a week or two afterwards as a reminder to the children of all the grace that God had given us.

What Was the Best Moment of Your Day?

This is one of my husband's habits. Whenever he came home for supper, and we sat to eat, he would look around the table and see how we were all doing (and by "we" I really mean how I, his wife, was doing). Sometimes for no good reason, and other times because I looked a bit strung out or sad, he would ask one of the children, "Nathan, what was the best moment of your day?"

Though children have days that include plenty of sad or troubling moments (their skinned knees, spankings, and spats with siblings), they typically also have at least one or two exuberant moments in a normal day that they can remember, unlike we adults, who can feel like we never got out from under that little black rain cloud that's been hanging over us. As Scott would go around the table and ask the children, I'd know that the question was coming to me pretty soon. I also knew that I needed to set an example of following my husband's lead and of being thankful and cheerful.

This quiet, simple question in Scott's skilled hands has helped me out of more than one self-pity party at the end of the day! We wives can return the favor when our husbands have had a hard day out in the workplace and come home tired and burdened. Usually, if you ask, almost everyone had something in their day that went right. They just need to remember it! Also, listening to the children's answers often encouraged me that they were, in fact, loving the journey and making new discoveries along the way.

Saying Grace at Mealtimes

Whether it's leftovers, Cheerios, or steak for dinner, food is a gift from God! Did you ever stop to think that the habit you have fostered of stopping to give God thanks for the meal set before you is an act of humility, submission, and gratitude? Saying a blessing over the meal reminds our children and ourselves that food isn't a right, but a gift from Father God.

Every day, three times a day, we have the opportunity to renew the knowledge that a good, kind God is providing for our needs and keeping us alive. We should be grateful, and remember to return thanks! Many of us were not trained in this simple practice. It's a good one! It is simple, straightforward, and powerful when done with true reverence and thought towards God.

A Sacrifice of Praise

But, what if I don't really *feel* grateful? I have good news! As we used to say to our kids about their unwanted veggies on their plates, "You don't have to like it, you just have to eat it." Whether or not you *feel* grateful, God is due your thanks. He is your Creator, and He alone sustains your life. Thanking Him is what is owed by the creature to the Creator, especially when we realize that we only take our next breaths because of His mercy (Colossians 1:15-17).

You don't need to wait for a miracle to happen, or amazingly good fortune to suddenly come to you, before you give thanks to God. In fact, if you don't get into the habit of thanking Him for basic mercies (your salvation and eternal hope, and daily bread, for instance) you might forget when those more dramatic things do occur. Take for instance, the story of the nine Jewish lepers. Jesus was astounded when, having healed ten men, only one came back to thank Him—and he was a Samaritan! After he had done so, we read:

> *Then Jesus answered, "Were not ten cleansed? Where are the nine? Was no one found to return and give praise to God except this foreigner?"*
>
> *Luke 17:17-18 (ESV)*

What a sad indictment on these Jews who should have known much better! We Christians are also in the know. We know where our origins are and Who rules the universe. When we grumble and complain, or allow our hearts to be sad and gloomy, we dishonor God. Whether we feel like it or not, we owe Him all thanks and praise. The Bible calls this a "sacrifice of praise." As Christians, we have access to the throne of grace because Jesus has paid the price. "Through him then let us continually offer up a sacrifice of praise to God, that is, the fruit of lips that acknowledge his name" (Hebrews 13:15, ESV).

Privileged to Serve

Which is more characteristic of your attitude as you rise up each morning and think about the day ahead: do you "get to" or have you "got to"? That one vowel change can make all the difference in seeing that our daily tasks are a privilege.

So many of our fellow human creatures struggle, toil, and suffer without any idea of the meaning of it all, and without any real hope, joy, or purpose. If you are a mother and a homeschooler, your life has tremendous purpose. In response to the perennial question asked of women at cocktail parties during the 80's and 90's, "What do *you* do?" I used to love to respond with enthusiasm: "I am engaged in the great and real business of socializing young *homo sapiens* to become world changers through the ethical teachings of Jesus Christ! What do you do?"

It's true, you know. Your greatest contribution to the world is probably what you're doing during this phase of your life. Is it exhausting? Yes! Is it full of mundane (and some truly yucky) tasks? You bet! Will you look back someday and realize that these were the most meaningful days of your life? I'm betting so. It's been that way for me.

When I finished homeschooling, and my children were all well launched into adulthood, I went through a season of feeling new freedoms that brought new temptations. What should I do with all this free time? Should I take up a musical instrument, or collect stamps, or travel and see the world, or start a new career? Well, I could.

If you are a mother and a homeschooler, your life has tremendous purpose.

But, after all those years, I finally saw a few things. I saw how productive I'd been, day in and day out, for 22 years. I saw how being hemmed in behind and before by the chores and responsibilities of teaching and mothering six children had kept me from growing selfish, frivolous, and wasteful of the time on earth that God has given me. I realized that it was a privilege to serve, and (after a bit of rest) I looked around for new avenues of service, because I missed the blessing of feeling useful to God's people.

Today, I'm working pretty hard. I'm writing, teaching other moms how to homeschool, and serving my kids as they are raising the next generation. Because I'm older, I tire more easily. But there's a difference in how I feel about my tasks: more days than not, I've seen that I *get to* serve, and I give thanks.

Do We Celebrate Enough?

This last way to express gratitude is another gift from my husband. He always said that God was a happy God, and we should look for ways to celebrate His goodness and give thanks.

Whenever some landmark, small or large, was reached, he would get a gleam in his eye and I would know what was coming. He would raise his voice and call out loudly to all the children, "Do we *celebrate* enough!!!?" And the right answer was, "No!"

Then, we would do something special. We'd break out the ice cream, or go out to dinner, or do a joyful line dance through the house. *What* we did didn't matter half so much as the attitude with which we did it. What Scott was leading us in, time and again, was a recognition of the fact that God has been good, and that we should respond by giving thanks. So, not every time but often enough, landmarks large and small were marked by this wonderful mantra.

Scott didn't make this up. All through the Bible, we see God inviting and commanding His people to celebrate His goodness. In the Old Testament, we read about God instituting yearly feasts throughout the yearly calendar. Sabbaths were weekly opportunities to rest, give thanks, and celebrate God's goodness. When Israel won battles, or received deliverances, they celebrated before the Lord. When individuals received healing, or children, or wealth, they celebrated.

When David moved the ark to Jerusalem, he was so exuberant in his celebrating that his wife rebuked him for being undignified. She was the daughter of a king (Saul). Here's what David had to say in return:

> *And David returned to bless his household. But Michal the daughter of Saul came out to meet David and said, "How the king of Israel honored himself today, uncovering himself today before the eyes of his servants' female servants, as one of the vulgar fellows shamelessly uncovers himself!"*
>
> *And David said to Michal, "It was before the LORD, who chose me above your father and above all his house, to appoint me as prince over Israel, the people of the LORD—and I will make merry before the LORD. I will make myself yet more contemptible than this, and I will be abased in your eyes. But by the female servants of whom you have spoken, by them I shall be held in honor."*
>
> *2 Samuel 6:20-22 (ESV)*

David hadn't forgotten Who had raised him up to power, and to Whom he owed thanks and praise, and celebration.

Zacchaeus—a despised tax collector and man puny of spirit and body—had a big reaction when Jesus came to preach at his house one day.

> *And Zacchaeus stood and said to the Lord, "Behold, Lord, the half of my goods I give to the poor. And if I have defrauded anyone of anything, I restore it fourfold."*
>
> *Luke 19:8-10 (ESV)*

Zacchaeus knew how to celebrate! Let me ask you: how are you at identifying the small and large moves of God in your life and celebrating in joyful thanksgiving to a good God who loves you? I think that Heaven is going to be one big party! We probably should practice here on earth, don't you think?

Sing a Song!

David knew how to celebrate, and he also had the soul of a poet and a musical gift. He left us many precious psalms that are honest, Godward, and precious. I'm ending this book with a copy of this one because it so wonderfully displays David's grateful heart, and it can show us how to live each day a bit more aware of all the benefits we enjoy!

Read it slowly; savor each poetic expression, and review your own life in gratitude for all the Savior has accomplished in and through you, as you look to Him in faith for loving the journey more and more.

Bless the LORD, O my soul,
and all that is within me, bless his holy name!
Bless the LORD, O my soul,
and forget not all his benefits,
who forgives all your iniquity, who heals all your diseases,
who redeems your life from the pit,
who crowns you with steadfast love and mercy,
who satisfies you with good so that your youth is renewed
like the eagle's.

The LORD works righteousness and justice
for all who are oppressed.
He made known his ways to Moses,
his acts to the people of Israel.

The LORD is merciful and gracious,
slow to anger and abounding in steadfast love.
He will not always chide, nor will he keep his anger forever.
He does not deal with us according to our sins,
nor repay us according to our iniquities.
For as high as the heavens are above the earth,
so great is his steadfast love toward those who fear him;
as far as the east is from the west,
so far does he remove our transgressions from us.

As a father shows compassion to his children,
so the LORD shows compassion to those who fear him.
For he knows our frame; he remembers that we are dust.
As for man, his days are like grass;
he flourishes like a flower of the field;
for the wind passes over it, and it is gone,
and its place knows it no more.
But the steadfast love of the LORD
is from everlasting to everlasting on those who fear him,
and his righteousness to children's children,
to those who keep his covenant and remember
to do his commandments.

The LORD has established his throne in the heavens,
and his kingdom rules over all.
Bless the LORD, O you his angels,
you mighty ones who do his word,
obeying the voice of his word!
Bless the LORD, all his hosts, his ministers, who do his will! Bless the LORD, all his works, in all places of his dominion. Bless the LORD, O my soul!

Psalm 103 (ESV)

Index

A

B

C

F

G

H

I

J

K

L

M

R

S

T

U

V

W

Scripture Index

CPSIA information can be obtained at www.ICGtesting.com
Printed in the USA
LVOW03s1222170314

377556LV00001BB/1/P

9 780991 571802